Law and
Science in
Collaboration

Law and Public Affairs Publications

THE NATIONAL CENTER
FOR ADMINISTRATIVE JUSTICE

Washington, D.C.

The Welfare Family and Mass Administrative Justice
  Daniel J. Baum
Administrative Process Alternatives to the Criminal Process
  Norman Abrams
Social Security Hearings and Appeals
  Jerry L. Mashaw, Charles J. Goetz,
  Frank I. Goodman, Warren F. Schwartz,
  Paul R. Verkuil, and Milton M. Carrow
Conflict-of-Interest Regulation in the Federal Executive Branch
  Robert G. Vaughn
Law and Science in Collaboration
  J.D. Nyhart and Milton M. Carrow, eds.

Law and Science in Collaboration

Resolving Regulatory Issues of Science and Technology

Edited by
J.D. Nyhart
Massachusetts Institute of
Technology

Milton M. Carrow
National Center for
Administrative Justice

LexingtonBooks
D.C. Heath and Company
Lexington, Massachusetts
Toronto

Library of Congress Cataloging in Publication Data

Main entry under title:

Law and science in collaboration.

Based on the proceedings of an April 1981 conference conducted by the National Center for Administrative Justice, held at the Frances Lewis Law Center, Washington and Lee University.
    Includes index.
    Contents: Introduction/Milton M. Carrow and J.D. Nyhart—Changing frameworks: An overview; two models of regulatory decision making/Jerry L. Mashaw. Components of an adequate record/Wm. Warfield Ross. Some thoughts on science and scientists in the 1980s/J. William Haun—[etc.]
    1. Science and law—Congresses.   2. Technology and law—Congresses.
    3. Trade regulation—United States—Congresses.   I. Nyhart, J.D. (J. Daniel)   II. Carrow, Milton M. (Milton Michael), 1913-   .   III. National Center for Administrative Justice (U.S.)
KF4270.A75L38   1983   344.73′095   81-47783
ISBN 0-669-04907-7   347.30495

International Standard Book Number: 0-669-04907-7

Library of Congress Catalog Card Number: 81-47783

Contents

Contents

The National Center for Administrative Justice seeks to advance administrative justice in society. It conducts research and education programs in law and public affairs and training courses for the improvement of skills related to administrative and regulatory processes.

The center's research projects are normally interdisciplinary in character. Their focus is to develop due-process models suited to the unique problems arising in particular substantive areas. They have dealt with a variety of subjects involving regulatory and income security programs. The results of these works are published.

The center's education and training programs are designed to improve the skills and understanding of lawyers engaged in administrative and regulatory proceedings. Programs are conducted for government agencies and corporate legal staffs, as well as in open-enrollment courses. The center also assists professionals and technicians from other disciplines to understand administrative and regulatory processes and thus enable them to work effectively with legal staffs.

The center was established by the American Bar Association in 1972 and was initially funded by the American Bar Endowment. In 1977 it became a division of the Consortium of Universities of the Washington Metropolitan Area, and in 1979 it was incorporated as an independent, nonprofit, tax-exempt organization. It retains ties with the American Bar Association and the consortium. The board of directors is responsible for general oversight. The direction of the policies, programs, and staff is under the president, assisted by advisory groups, consultants and staff. The members of the board, including advisory members, are as follows: Beverly C. Moore, chairman; Charles A. Horsky, vice-chairman; Milton M. Carrow, president; Mitchell Rogovin, secretary-treasurer; Clark Byse; Jameson W. Doig; Carroll L. Gilliam; E. Nobles Lowe; James E. Murray; Chesterfield Smith; Harold R. Tyler; Louis H. Mayo, ex officio member; and Antonin Scalia, ex officio member.

The center conducts its work without bias, ensuring the intellectual freedom of the staff and consultants. Interpretations and conclusions in any of its works or programs should not be attributed to the board of directors or its members.

Preface and Acknowledgments

The material in this book is designed to provide a framework for regulatory and judicial decision making involving science and technology. We selected five case studies representing a cross section of present processes for fact finding, evaluation, and decision making, and then arranged for the chapters to be written on them by scientists and lawyers. These were, in turn, critiqued in written comments by persons trained in disciplines other than the authors'. In addition, one chapter was prepared to provide a conceptual overview of the subject and another to analyze the different cognitive styles of lawyers and scientists. The chapters and comments were intensively discussed at a three-day conference attended by a group of lawyers, scientists, regulators, and other professionals and then revised for this book. A transcript of the presentations and discussions at the conference is available for examination at the offices of the National Center for Administrative Justice.

Prior to the preparation of the chapters, we furnished the contributing authors and commentators with a detailed plan of the project and continued a dialogue with each of them throughout the preparation period. After the conclusion of the conference, we wrote the introductory and concluding chapters to synthesize the salient aspects of the chapters and proceedings and also, on the basis of the critiques and suggestions, to design a distinctive model for regulatory and judicial decision making involving science and technology.

This formidable undertaking was accomplished with the valuable assistance and cooperation of a number of people and institutions. Most noteworthy was that of Frederick L. Kirgis, Jr., the director of the Frances Lewis Law Center at Washington and Lee University, Lexington, Virginia. From the start, he helped and encouraged us in the design of the project and in each stage of its development. We are also grateful to the president of Washington and Lee University, Robert E.R. Huntley; Dean Roy L. Steinheimer, Jr.; and other members of the law-school faculty and staff of Washington and Lee University for the opportunity to use their splendid facilities, for their gracious hospitality to all the participants, and, particularly, for the financial contribution to the project by the Frances Lewis Law Center.

Participants in the conference gave generously of their experience and of that even more precious commodity, their time. In addition to the authors and commentators, we would like to thank for their insightful participation Mark H. Gruenwald, Washington and Lee University School of Law; Arthur F. Konopka, National Science Foundation; E. Nobles Lowe, Lowe & Knapp; James A. Martin, University of Michigan Law School; Louis H. Mayo, George Washington University; Allan C. Mazur, Syracuse

University; Francis E. McGovern II, Cumberland School of Law; Sanford A. Miller, U.S. Food and Drug Administration; Beverly C. Moore, Smith, Moore, Smith, Schell & Hunter; David M. Pritzker, Administrative Conference of the United States; Roy L. Steinheimer, Jr., Washington and Lee University School of Law; William A. Thomas, American Bar Association; and John H. Young, Office of Technology Assessment, U.S. Congress.

We also extend our gratitude to the Ford Foundation and the Administrative Conference of the United States for much-needed funding assistance to complete this project.

Finally, for conscientiously performing the arduous administrative tasks of overseeing the preparation, dissemination, transcription, review, and collation of the materials in this book, we thank Mark R. Voss, Elizabeth B. Frazier, and Nina J. Bonnelycke of the National Center staff. We owe our appreciation, too, to Gail Hogg, who flawlessly transcribed three days' discussion, and to Karuna Mohindra and Jean Pratt, for typing the final chapter.

Law and
Science in
Collaboration

1 Introduction

Milton M. Carrow and
J.D. Nyhart

One of the more elusive problems of our times is the development of effective decision-making processes of regulatory agencies and courts where science and technology issues must be resolved. Proceedings involving hazardous substances that are introduced and released in the environment, in the work place, and in the production of energy, food, and equipment are familiar examples. In recent years, the issues in such proceedings have concerned cancer-causing and other harmful chemicals, nuclear power, and the disposal of nuclear waste.

The difficulties in arriving at satisfactory decisions when science and technology issues are present arise out of the differences in data-gathering and data-analysis systems of science and law and also from the need to accommodate multiple interests. Decision making is further complicated by lack of clarity as to who has the responsibility and who in fact acts to establish policy and apply value standards.

This book examines the problem with a view toward providing a basis for improving the decision-making process. The chapters in part I provide insightful perspectives on how current problems in the regulatory sector relate to issues involving science and technology. Chapter 2 examines two theoretically contrasting models of regulatory decision making that served as a focal point for discussion by the conference participants. Chapter 3 reviews the legal requirements of evidentiary records on which regulatory decisions are made. And chapter 4 presents two brief statements of different perspectives of the science enterprise as it may affect policymaking today.

Five case studies of institutional processes dealing with science and technology comprise part II. Four of these are in the regulatory sector (chapters 5, 6, 8, and 9) and the fifth deals with medical-science processes (chapter 7). The essay in part III examines the problem of communication difficulties between lawyers and scientists arising from differences in their cognitive styles (chapter 10).

Finally, in part IV, we analyze the preceding chapters and the essence of the discussion of the work presented in this book by the scientists, lawyers, administrators, and other professionals who participated in the proceedings.

References in this chapter and the final chapter are either to the following chapters and comments or to the transcript of the oral presentations and discussions at the April 1981 conference conducted by the National Center for Administrative Justice at the Frances Lewis Law Center, Washington and Lee University. Transcript references are identified by the symbol, "tr.," followed by a page number. The transcript is on file with the editors.

Here we also describe the essential components of a model process that we believe is capable of significantly improving the quality of decision making involving science and technology.

Models for Regulatory Decision Making
Concerning Science and Technology

In writing this introduction, we have had the benefit of hindsight and have been able to select significant perceptions from the work leading to this book. Several points seem important. Many of the contributing authors to this book speak in terms of models; others present them without so naming them. To the extent that a model is a way of speaking from experience to a level of greater generality or applicability, their use seems to be a practical way to convey and test ideas. A review of the many different models explicitly or implicitly offered by the authors suggests a need to develop a new conceptual construct explicitly for decision making involving science and technology in legal processes.

In order to focus on this objective, we have found it helpful to portray a larger framework within which such an institutional design falls. Thus, this section identifies a universe of decision-making models, including our own.

We believe there are three basic structures for decision making involving science and technology: the adversary, consensus, and collaborative models. The five case studies in this book, representative of current agency practices, appear to fit into one or another of these basic models.

The Adversary Model

In recent years the traditional adversary model, which is based on the structure and process of the judicial system, has been examined and reexamined, praised and maligned, modified in some instances, and its use sought to be limited. The present chief justice of the Supreme Court of the United States, for example, has been urging that a variety of proceedings, such as divorce, adoptions, and landlord and tenant matters, be handled by some other dispute-resolution mechanism. Judge David L. Bazelon has suggested that the courts have no competence to decide scientific matters and that appellate courts should limit the scope of their review to the fairness of the proceedings. Some scientists, on the other hand, have sought to establish a so-called science court, which would employ the techniques of the adversary system in a forum of scientists by addressing questions of scientific controversy to a panel of scientists charged with preparation of a consensus statement of the current state of knowledge about the science involved, leaving aside the policy—and hopefully the value—issues.

The main characteristics of adversary proceedings involve opposing antagonistic parties or interests, one party with witnesses striving to prove facts essential to her or his case and the other party striving to disprove those facts. ("The advocate's prime loyalty is to his client, not the truth as such.")[1] Decisions are made by one or more impartial adjudicators. There are additional elements of a due-process nature, such as the right of cross-examination and argument, the need for an adequate record, and the rendering of a reasoned decision.

As a decision-making process for science and technology issues, the adversary model was sharply criticized in the discussion. The most-significant challenge to its utility was that in adversary proceedings, the evidence of technical experts is manipulated to fit the needs of the parties striving to prove or disprove facts. Ashford maintains that parties to a controversy "want to keep the experts free of values, so they can manipulate their testimony . . . in ways which they feel secure about." (tr. p. 248) Wessel asserts that "prostitution of the scientist is an all-too-common feature of socioscientific litigation and its 'battle of experts,' " citing as an illustrative example the well-known case of *Berkey Photo, Inc.* v. *Eastman Kodak Co.*[2] If this is true, and our perception is that it is, "good" science is skewed in the adversary model.

The conventional adversary proceeding is completely under the control of lawyers and judges. This circumstance creates additional problems for scientists. According to Keen, reasonably well-supported data indicate that a substantial gap exists between lawyers and judges, which creates two separate cultures. He also finds that the legal profession may be "intolerant of and impede the academic researchers' less-decisive, more-adaptive mode of work, and, hence, of expertise." (p. 235)

The adversary model does not fit readily into the regulatory process, particularly where policymaking is involved. This is well illustrated in chapter 2. There, Mashaw describes the attributes of two competing models of regulatory decision making, which are laid at a fairly high level of abstraction. One he calls the model of bureaucratic rationality (B/R model), and the other, "the model of micropolitical accommodation" (M/A model). According to Mashaw, the B/R model:

1. Is designed to collect and process data in ways that will promote effective implementation of a specific program.
2. Assumes that values have already been determined.
3. Has a hierarchical structure in which lower-level decisions get reviewed by other managerial or supervisory levels, with the buck clearly stopping somewhere.
4. Attempts to conserve decisional resources and to be efficient. (pp. 13-15)

The M/A model contrasts in several ways:

1.   Its goal is harmony.
2.   Its structure is informal as in a network where there are "a series of
     connections among people that are related both to issues and to per-
     sonalities" and in which people might play any role and shift roles over
     time.
3.   Its cognitive style is to make distributive judgments, to decide who gets
     how much of what.
4.   It seeks consensus through a process that may include virtually any sort
     of strategic behavior—negotiation, waiting each other out, strok-
     ing—whatever is within the broad constraints of fairness in politics.
     (pp. 15-16)

Lawyers are more familiar with the B/R model, partly because it has some
of the attributes of the adversary model. Both of Mashaw's models,
however, show that regulatory decision-making proceedings have institutional and hierarchical dimensions not present in the conventional adversary process in the judicial system.

The Consensus Model

Instead of the win-lose nature of the adversary model, the characteristic at-
tribute of the consensus model is the negotiation of differences until all the
parties are willing to agree. This institutional design is widely used in labor
relations, as in the mediation of labor disputes and in collective bargaining.
It is also used to resolve parts of controversies in the judicial process, as in
pretrial proceedings to determine issues on which there is agreement, as well
as to settle issues. It is also the way in which a jury is expected to operate.
     Some of the attributes of Mashaw's M/A model appear in consensus
structures, such as its objective "to produce a harmonious accommodation
of the interests that surround the issue." The methods of the consensus
model include compromise, a search for solutions that bring some degree of
satisfaction to conflicting parties; smoothing or "stroking" (Mashaw),
which emphasizes areas of agreement and deemphasizes areas of difference;
and accommodation, which seeks to achieve harmony by acceptance of less
than desired.[3]
     The consensus-development program of the National Institutes of
Health (NIH), described by Lowe in chapter 7, represents an effort to apply
the consensus model where science and technology issues are involved. It is
a carefully structured process that seeks to find consensus on medical procedures. Examples involve methods of treating breast cancer and the utility

of tonsillectomies. Its findings, however, have no legal effect, or, as Lowe points out, NIH does not "regulate." Instead, the findings are widely circulated in the medical profession with the expectation that they will be used.

Although the program is not a legally enforceable mechanism, several of its aspects may be usefully applied to a decision-making process. Of particular interest is the formulation of technical questions and the composition of the consensus panel.

Under the consensus-development program, the technology to be reviewed is selected by one of the twelve institutions of the NIH. The selecting institute "identifies critical questions concerning the scientific validity of the technology." (p. 146) Lowe points out that the questions frame the conference in which the issues are debated and that they "must be answerable on the basis of science, not anecdote, not supposition." (tr. p. B56) This is an important factor. It is a subject that is persistently raised in the chapters regarding the shortcomings of present decision-making mechanisms and will be more fully discussed in the collaborative model.

After the technology is selected, a consensus panel is organized which is responsible for the answers to the questions. Lowe says it is a panel consisting of "scientists, clinical specialists and generalists, interested nonmedical professions, and representatives of consumer and special-interest health groups." (p. 147) He also points out that panels can achieve consensus around a question or say there is no consensus. If they do the latter, they must identify the information needed to permit a consensus, in which event its acquisition and evaluation become a research agenda. The diversity of interests represented on the panel is another element that should be and will be considered in discussing the collaborative model.

Another major component of the NIH consensus construct is the assemblage of a large audience in a public forum to which the consensus panel reports its findings and listens to comments and criticisms before preparing its final findings for dissemination.

The Collaborative Model

The collaborative model incorporates several ideas suggested in this book that are designed to remedy the flaws found in the five case studies.

We believe that the concept of collaboration is uniquely appropriate for decision making involving science and technology issues. It connotes an effort among equals to solve a problem or perform a task. It is not one dominated by legal process to which all else must be subservient. It recognizes that there are different areas of expertise and different approaches to problem solving in each area. It seeks to provide a means whereby the gaps and differences in the findings of different disciplines can be bridged or reconciled.

These elements are touched upon in many of the chapters. Keen, in his analysis of the cognitive style of lawyers and scientists, says that the system must allow scientists "room to breathe, to allow them to make their explanation in their own terms and at their own pace." (p. 214) Wessel adds, "we've got to let the scientists be scientists, and we've got to let the lawyers and judges be lawyers and judges, and then fashion a framework to arrive at a resolution of whatever the differences may be that require a public policy decision." (tr. p. 212) Grobstein states that "many scientists feel that the only role that scientists play in relation . . . to the regulatory issues, is to state what is known, and to assume that the regulator is not going to take a position that will be inconsistent with what is known." (tr. p. 128)

The principles of the collaborative model combine these and other ideas essential to a decision-making process. They include the following.

1. Functions of lawyers, scientists, and decision makers should be clearly identified and related to their respective capabilities and authority. Who is in charge of particular functions needs to be established in a collaborative rather than a competitive manner. Value judgments should be related to the functions and be explicit. Ideally, the decision maker should be capable of evaluating the scientific, legal, and policy issues.

2. Questions addressed to the scientists and technologists should be framed so that the specialists can respond in a way that is consistent with their functions. In particular, value-laden questions should be minimized.

3. Communication among the scientists and technologists, lawyers, and decision makers requires a specific effort to establish trust and understanding across discipline lines. This requirement may involve translation of the scientific and technological information into the legal and policy framework in which the decision maker must operate. A lawyer or a scientist may undertake this translation function.

4. Scientists and technologists should have room to breathe in carrying out their agreed functions. That is, scientific or technical data should be gathered, developed, evaluated, and presented in a form and manner acceptable to the presenter and his or her peers.

5. Since scientific data, their evaluation and presentation, will be used in a legal process involving legal rights and powers, care must be taken to ensure that the scientific information can be satisfactorily folded into the legal process. Specifically, due-process and fairness standards appropriate to the nature of the legal process must be met; multiple interests affected, public and private, should have an opportunity to be heard and their views considered; and a record must adequately reflect the scientific and legal processes at work.

6. There should be a sufficiently equitable distribution of the scientific and technological expertise among the parties in interest so that they will accord both credibility and acceptance of the process by which the scientific work is done.

The constitution of the decision-making body in regulatory proceedings will vary with the nature of the proceedings and the nature of the agency. Since the collaborative model provides for the introduction of scientific and technological data in a technically acceptable form, the decision-making body should include appropriate experts. This is particularly important in the model because of the limitation placed on value-laden questions in the evidentiary presentation. It is also desirable to have trained judges on the body to ensure conformance with due-process and fairness standards. In addition, pertinent lay interests should be represented, depending upon the type of agency and proceeding. For example, in product-safety proceedings, consumer-group representation may be desirable, as it would be also in proceedings involving food additives. In this regard the experience with advisory committees and the NIH consensus-development program may be helpful.

In the presentation of scientific and technological evidence in the regulatory decision-making process, there are problems with regard to the validity of the data, as well as their interpretation. The data are often couched in probabilistic terms not readily translatable into a decision. This circumstance requires the development of examination techniques that are especially attuned to the knowledge and capabilities of the experts.

The way this can be done is by asking the right questions. Mashaw's discussion of this necessity is most instructive. (p. 17) He points out that to demand from the scientist a yes or no answer to the question whether "X causes cancer" frames the question in the wrong way from a scientific perspective. He then proceeds to develop questions couched in the probabilistic terms that scientists understand, which could ultimately elicit accurate responses from the scientist for the consideration of the decision maker.

Adding to the problem of uncertainty of scientific and technological findings are differences in the perspectives among experts. Brannigan, in his discussion of the Food and Drug Administration's public board of inquiry, points out that "there are distinct schools of thought in science—systems of belief which are incompatible with other schools of thought which exist among scientists. And when you choose a scientist from a school of thought, you collect, with him, the entire baggage of the perspective that he has." (tr. p. A9)

Probably the most-significant aspect of the collaborative model, and the main reason it has been given that name, is in the presentation of scientific and technological information in its technically acceptable form. The expert presents the needed data in the fashion found appropriate by his or her discipline, thus providing the room to breathe suggested by Keen and others. The uncertainty of scientific findings and the reluctance of scientists to engage in policy and value judgments must be recognized in the decision-making process. The scientific facts are not tailored to fit an advocate's cause. According to Grobstein, that is the way the National Academy of Sciences and its National Research Council prefer to perform their advisory role in government regulation. He said that it "is an organization which is operating on its own turf. . . . There are activities performed by scientists in what they regard as science's advisory role to the federal government carried out in a scientific institution. They need not be, if they choose not to be, in any way trammeled by other perspectives, or other points of view. They can behave entirely in a scientific and technical way, in terms of their own lights, as they see it." (tr. p. B18-19)

To bridge the communication gap between scientists and decision makers, Keen suggests that the lawyer must act as a translator between the scientist and the judge. Since scientists and judges function in separate cultures, he says, "A formal translator is essential, one who understands both the legal and scientific mind without being an expert in both fields." (p. 214) Meeting this need may present a dilemma because the lawyer's role in representing a client or a special interest is to advocate the client's cause, which may differ from a dispassionate presentation of the evidence. Since, however, all of the affected interests are represented in the proceeding, the decision maker may be confronted with several translations and have to choose among them. Moreover, the translator need not be a lawyer; some scientists are well able to fill the role.

The situation is more complicated in the case of advisory committees constituted by statute to serve an agency or employed on an ad hoc basis. Ashford indicates that in addition to furnishing scientific and technological expertise to the agency decision-making process, advisory committees also may provide a means for reaching a consensus on difficult-to-resolve scientific or technological issues, policy guidance when factual resolution of scientific or technological issues is not possible in the traditional sense, and a means of expanding the participation of interested parties in the regulatory decision-making process. (p. 166) Miller questioned the utility of the advisory committee as an improvement over a well-constituted decision-making body in the making of policy as concerns providing an opportunity for participation by affected interests. He points out that there is a "big danger" in agencies' being captured by advisory committees. (tr. p. A88)

Whatever the case may be insofar as the collaborative model is concerned, the National Academy of Sciences and the advisory committees provide examples whereby the scientist is a collaborator in the decision-making process rather than a hired consultant to promote a particular cause.

The due-process and fairness aspects may be obvious to lawyers but are probably less so to others. In the past decade, the courts have approved a wide range of due-process models in adjudicatory and regulatory proceedings. For example, they look to the nature of the proceeding under review to determine whether due-process standards are met rather than impose a rigid set of formal requirements based on criminal procedures. Thus, in social-security disability-claims cases, written medical reports are acceptable as evidence without personal cross-examination of the physician.[4] In school-discipline cases, an informal meeting, which includes the student, the responsible administrator, the teacher, and the student representative, has also been held to meet the due-process requirements.[5] The courts have also recognized that praticiation in administrative adjudication proceedings should be open to some categories of persons who have a general interest in the outcome in addition to those specifically affected.[6]

To the scientists and to other professionals unfamiliar with the legal process, these may seem to be cumbersome and frustrating practices, but scientists on reflection recognize that the effectiveness of a decision depends as much on acceptance and a sense of fairness on the part of those interested as it is on the power of the government to enforce.

Another viewpoint regarding the right to participate, or standing in administrative proceedings, is the recognition that in matters involving science and technology, multiple interests are affected. The regulation of a cancer-causing chemical in a food product involves the producer, the government regulatory agency, the purchaser, possible contending technologies, and general consumer interests. How their views are presented, their access to the data, and their ability to produce appropriate data affects not only the effectiveness of their participation but also the structure and processes by which participation can be provided.

A special aspect of the decision-making process is judicial review of agency action that involves science and technology issues. What goes into the record, and what is the scope of review of the issues? The record in the collaborative model will contain the science and technology evidence in their technically acceptable form, as well as the translations for the decision makers. As Breyer points out, at the appellate level there is only the record of the prior proceedings, with no opportunity to call upon an expert. He says that the reviewing court has before it a record that it can say has been developed in a fair proceeding, but it cannot say that the record is accurate. (p. 43)

Ross suggests that appellate judges obtain training to provide them with "a rudimentary understanding of basic scientific methodologies such as controlled testing, statistical measurement, probability assessment, and modeling." (p. 31) Another approach is being tested in an experiment in the Alabama Supreme Court, in which technical expert advisers are made available to the court.[7]

With regard to the scope of review, Ross indicates that there are two points of view. Judge David Bazelon, he says, believes that a reviewing court should primarily seek to enforce the use of fair and efficient procedures as a means of ensuring reasoned decision making. The late Judge Harold Leventhal, however, believed that judges should take a hard look at the substantive issues and that in reviewing administrative action, judges should acquire "whatever technical knowledge is necessary as a background for decisions of the legal questions." (p. 29) The debate has not been fully resolved.

Conclusion

In this introduction and more extensively in the concluding chapter, we have sought to pull together the many significant observations made by the participants in this examination of decision making involving science and technology. The diversity of disciplines represented, with their widely differing approaches, provided a challenge that we hope we have been able to meet, at least partially.

The chapters and comments that follow contain richly rewarding insights. We have drawn upon them, as well as the discussions surrounding them, to assemble the components of a decision-making model for regulatory issues involving science and technology. These are more fully developed in the final chapter of this book.

Notes

1. Frankel, *The Search for Truth: An Umpireal View,* 123 U. Penn. L. Rev. 1031, 1035 (1975). Judge Frankel, in this article, makes a penetrating analysis of the adversary system. For a comprehensive list of elements, see Friendly, *Some Kind of Hearing,* 123 U. Penn. L. Rev. 1267, 1279 *et seq.* (1975). See also Webster's Third International Dictionary.

2. Berkey Photo, Inc. v. Eastman Kodak Co., 603 F.2d 263 (2d Cir. 1979), *cert. denied,* 444 U.S. 1093 (1980).

3. Several of these ideas come from an unpublished paper, "Managing Conflict in Today's Organizations" by Gordon L. Lippitt, School of Government and Business Administration, the George Washington University, on file at the office of the National Center for Administrative Justice.

4. Matthews v. Eldridge, 424 U.S. 319 (1976).

5. Goss v. Lopez, 419 U.S. 565 (1975).

6. Stewart, *The Reformation of American Administrative Law,* 88 Harv. L. Rev. 1669, 1760 et seq. (1975).

7. Implementation and Study of the Use of Experts who Provide Scientific or Technical Input to the Alabama Supreme Court. NSF grant DAR 8016122.

**Part I
Changing Frameworks**

2 An Overview: Two Models of Regulatory Decision Making

Jerry L. Mashaw

A Normative Perspective: Models as Legitimating Ideals

It has been suggested that an overall theme of the case studies in this book should be "what works." That is an excellent theme. The past ten years' talk about regulatory processes has been largely criticism: We are all now familiar with not only why markets fail but also with why regulations and bureaucracies fail, so it seems admirable to take as a topic, "what works."

What is the set of criteria by which one can tell whether any particular regulatory decision process works? In analyzing that question, it is not clear whether there is anything distinctive about issues involving science and technology, as distinguished from other collective decision-making problems in which one is importantly concerned with some sort of bureaucratic structure for decision making. But let us leave that issue aside for the moment.

In thinking about the question of what works and what would be acceptable criteria for determining what works, two competing models of decision making might usefully structure the inquiry. The two competing models are the model of bureaucratic rationality (B/R) and the model of micropolitical accommodation (M/A). Neither is perfectly represented in any decision process, but each tells us something about how people want decisions to be made. The fact that each is attractive, while inconsistent with the other, tells us something about why criticism of regulatory processes is so easy and so prevalent. In many ways, the specific proposals in the chapters in this book, or the specific decision processes with which we are more or less familiar for the decision of scientific and technological issues (and others), are in fact some mediation or working out of the inconsistent desire to realize both of these models simultaneously. There are a number of different dimensions to the models, but this chapter focuses on four (see figure 2-1).

The goal of the B/R system is to implement. This is bureaucratic rationality in essentially the Weberian ideal type; that is, it is the exercise of power on the basis of knowledge. The B/R model of decision making implies that values have been determined, and there is a program to be implemented. The task, or goal, is to collect and process data in ways that will promote effective implementation of the program.

Dimension / Model	Goal	Cognitive Style	Decision Structure	Legitimating Values
Bureaucratic rationality	Program implementation	Fact oriented	Formal, hierarchical	Accuracy and efficiency
Micropolitical accommodation	Harmonious allocation	Value oriented	Informal, fluid	Consent (and participation)

Figure 2-1. Dimensions of the B/R and M/A Models

The implementation goal may suggest something else about the model. It is likely to have a characteristic bureaucratic, or formal hierarchical, structure. One knows who has jurisdiction over what. Rules have been laid down somewhere about what the questions are for decision and who has the power to decide them. The system is hierarchical in the sense that lower-level decisions get reviewed by other managerial or supervisory levels, and the buck stops somewhere. At that level, somebody takes responsibility for the decision that has been made.

This model has a peculiar cognitive style. It is a form of decision making that is intensely oriented toward the pursuit of facts. Bureaucratic rationality, as a variant of instrumental rationality, is not value oriented. The agent presumes that the goal has been specified. The decision process is designed to implement that goal.

Finally, there is a special structure to the arguments for the legitimacy or acceptability of decision making in this mode. A bureaucratically rational structure must be able to find facts accurately; otherwise, implementation will fail (or more correctly, will only succeed by chance). Furthermore, it is supposed to make decisions in a fashion that is fact seeking and accurate without forgetting that we all have other goals in life than making whatever this decision is. Bureaucratic rationality recognizes scarcity, particularly the scarcity of decision-making resources. It attempts to conserve decisional resources and to trade off the direct costs of decision making against the costs of potential errors.

This model is a recognizable and attractive form of decision making. It is the ideal of administrative governance in a constitutional democracy. Legislation divorces the bureaucracy from value judgments; sets it in place to implement, through structures that ensure accountability and responsibility; orients it toward the pursuit of facts, the development of useful knowledge; and ultimately, bureaucratic activity is evaluated in terms of its capacity to be accurate and efficient.

In some ways, the M/A model is the polar opposite of the B/R model. I call this model micropolitical because the subject here is administrative structures, not macropolitical judgment, at the legislative, or the electoral, level. These are judgments that fall under the aegis of some administrative machinery.

In the M/A model, the goal is harmony. Maintaining the possibility for continuing individual and collective action, through cooperative enterprise, is always at the forefront in this model. The idea is not necessarily to implement some particular program but to produce a harmonious accommodation of the interests that surround an issue or a decision on the agency agenda.

Structures for micropolitical accommodation have to be informal. From a sociologist's perspective, these structures might be called a network, a series of connections among people that are related both to issues and to personalities—to who they are, what their interests are, what their histories are, and how they have previously related to each other. This model is quite different from a hierarchical bureaucratic structure having formal definitions of jurisdiction and role. In this informal structure, people might play any role and shift roles over time.

In a structure based on micropolitical accommodation, the goal is to order values, to make distributive judgments, to decide who gets how much of what. People are there, with particular positions, interests, needs, and desires. They are operating in a structure that will allocate resources to some or all of them. Almost any sort of argument may count with respect to the acceptability of the ultimate distribution achieved through micropolitical accommodation. Statutory and other legal language to some degree constrains the bargaining space, but the process of accommodation itself will ultimately give meaning to the statute. Values, status, and power are as much at issue as facts.

The legitimating value of this accommodatory sort of structure is consent. Through some process the participants are arriving at a consensus ordering of the values that are available to them for distribution. That process may include virtually any sort of strategic behavior—negotiation, waiting each other out, stroking—whatever is within the broad constraints of fairness in politics.

This M/A model may be conceptually less familiar to lawyers than is the B/R model, but micropolitics is familiar in some ways. In an insider's mode, lawyers often describe the process of how things actually get done as a process of politics, of political accommodation. In that process, informal contacts are extremely important; everybody understands that there are sharp conflicts of interest and sharp value disputes surrounding those conflicts of interest. Quite often they can make the necessary trade-offs and stop the fighting. Indeed, the value of accommodation is suggested by some of the chapters in this book that are searching for a structure that would move us away from adversary types of conduct.

Both models are attractive. Both have attributes that are familiar and recognizable. They also respond to very strong strains in our views of what makes decision structures good or legitimate—that is, either they produce decisions accurately and efficiently, or we consented to the allocations or the judgments that were made. Both of those are good arguments for acceptability.

A Critical Perspective: Problems of Implementation and the Compromise of Ideals

In the real world these ideals have been elaborated into a set of compromise structures. We cannot simultaneously realize the B/R structure and the

M/A structure in the same agency. Moreover, neither model in its ideal form can be implemented. Whenever we get down to the real business of constructing an agency, we compromise between these models while perhaps adding bits and pieces of other models, yet we are never quite satisfied with the mediation of the conflict. There is a constant tension between the aspirations reflected in these two models that we cannot resolve.

The current debate about how to resolve the uncertainties that beset regulatory decision making involving science and technology exemplifies this tension or conflict, for there clusters around the problem of dealing with uncertainty a series of proposals and practices—use of advisory committees, NAS-NRC (National Academy of Sciences-National Research Council) advice, science advisory boards, the science court, citizen committees—that signal our alternating desires to increase fact finding or to restructure micropolitics. We are not certain whether we want structures that provide the best-available scientific fix on the facts or the most-acceptable accommodation of competing values.

To a considerable degree, this predicament has arisen because the Congress has refused to resolve the value questions in its statutes but has demanded that regulation be based on a factual predicate in a way that makes the fact questions seem answerable. Statutes often give agencies criteria for action that make their job look as if it requires only the resolution of factual uncertainty. Health and safety agencies, for example, are given the task of protecting us from health risks, including the risk of cancer. When deciding whether or how to regulate a particular compound, the agency is invited to ask, "Does X cause cancer?" as if it were finding a critical fact that would lead unerringly to a correct conclusion. Certainly there are substances about which we can say that, at given exposures, they almost certainly cause cancer. But there are also substances about which we can say that we do not know. There are substances of which we are suspicious, and there may even be a few about which we can say we know that they do not.

To demand yes or no answers is to frame the question in the wrong way from a scientific perspective. If the statute were to ask not the common-sense question, Does it cause cancer? but some refined, pseudoscientific question, such as, "What is the probability that X causes cancer?" then the scientific persons can begin to respond more cheerfully. They can come forward with some estimates of the probability that X causes cancer.

That is not to say that the question becomes easy. There will be at least a first-order metascientific question of the form, "How reliable is that estimate?" We then get into the methodology of determining the probabilities and the disputes surrounding those methodologies. But again that question can be translated into an answerable form: What is the average of the probabilities that the methodologies put forward?

However penetrating the inquiry, though, there are ways to structure questions such that scientific people can give an answer that is responsive and is not irresponsible from a scientific perspective. That structuring or restructuring of the questions translates factual inquiries into probabilistic terms. Therein lies the difficulty. The statute often tells the agency what to decide in the face of the facts, not what to do with probability estimates. In order to do that, the agency must make a value choice concerning risks. When it does, it cannot be operating in the B/R mode, a mode that requires previously specified goals. Thus, we see agencies continuously finding facts in ways that reveal the breakdown of bureaucratic rationality and the emergence of administrative value choice.

Let me be more specific about the meaning of value choice in this context. If the question is, "Does X cause cancer?" and that question in that form cannot be answered, then the value question for the agency is of the form, "If you turn out to be wrong, in which direction would you prefer to be wrong? Do you want to be wrong by falsely finding that something that does not cause cancer does cause it; or would you prefer to be wrong by finding that something that does cause cancer does not cause it? What is the error skew that you want in this distribution of decisions?"

The value-specification problem is potentially soluble in a number of different ways. Statutes can answer this question and let agencies get on with the job of finding the facts. They might say, "When in doubt, decide in favor of preventing cancer," or "When in doubt, act so as to maximize the predicted net benefits of your decision." This is the way that our constitutional mythology says that we prefer to solve it—by legislative judgment. The judgment about what the society's values are ought to be made in a macropolitical, democratic way. But specific statutory guidance may not be essential to democratic control. Over time, there seem to be complex interactions through which agencies get a specification of appropriate values, even if the legislation left them very much at large initially. They get it in their relationships with the courts and with Congress. All of the questions are never fully answered, but closer and closer approximations over time provide a sense of stability and comprehensibility.

Many of the issues addressed in these chapters—contentious issues of regulatory policy involving science and technology—are precisely those issues in which the complex means of redefining questions so that they can be answered is so obviously in flux. Agencies have been charged with deciding on the basis of facts that they cannot find, so they must specify values while seeming to find facts, thereby exacerbating the contentiousness of fact finding and making the scientists behave like policymakers in the process.

One lesson to be drawn from this discussion is that the B/R model is always potentially workable. It merely requires a political resolution of the relevant value questions. We can thus see reform of administrative decision processes as a constant striving toward the feasibility of B/R, which may itself suggest some things about the administrative procedures that we would prefer in the meantime. We may, for example, want to have procedures that are transparent so that the issues can more easily bubble up to the level of macropolitical action that we want to be decisive. We may want to force the agency,even though it is engaged, presumably, in bureaucratically rational conduct, to specify carefully its value assumptions and to separate them from its factual assumptions. Even though value specification suggests that the bureaucracy is overstepping the bounds of its mission, it nevertheless shows us clearly what the value choices are. One could view a large part of contemporary judicial review, as well as other nonjudicial administrative-law reform activities, as an attempt to get a formal separation of fact and value in agency judgments, so that the political process will have an opportunity to operate on the critical value questions.

In some cases we might even want remands to the legislature on the ground that the value matrix is underspecified. By and large, we have abandoned that nondelegation approach to the actions of administrative agencies; that is, we have come to accept an accommodation of rationality and politics in agency structures. We assume that with appropriate procedures and structures, stability within a complex framework of democratic governance will be achieved.

The failure to specify values at the macropolitical level, however, tells us more than that the conditions for successfully operating in the B/R mode are absent; it tells us in addition that we are in the land of micropolitics, and we know that ideally micropolitics cannot be very structured, or it will also fail. There are no neutral decision processes. Procedures empower proponents, opponents, and kibitzers. Transparency and attempts at instrumental rationality thus may interfere dramatically with harmonious accommodation of the interests surrounding an issue of regulatory policy. Even a clear decision may inhibit future accommodations as circumstances change and interests shift.

From the micropolitical perspective, we can thus challenge our previous account of administrative law reform featuring the desirability of progressive movement toward instrumental rationality. The micropolitical view would emphasize the low probability that a stable ranking of important values will ever take place at the macropolitical level. Regulatory statutes should be viewed as merely a recognition of social and economic problems combined with a desire to move the forum for discussion from the macropolitical to the micropolitical level. The quest for instrumental rationality will only suppress or distort value struggles and introduce regidities that inhibit harmonious accommodations.

This is also a plausible position, for it is certainly true that the Congress establishes programs having regulatory criteria that are vague, ambiguous, and in hopeless conflict. Could instrumental rationality be its purpose? Even if there is some movement over time toward clear rules and formal structures and procedures for implementation, that movement may be legislatively deplored rather than applauded. Such a movement seems to involve not only a misstatement of what is at issue in regulatory decision making but also an unjustified transfer of political power to technical and scientific communities. We would do better to confront directly the appropriate structure of micropolitics.

Yet however telling the arguments of the defender of micropolitics, we are no more completely satisfied with the ideal micropolitical structure than with the ideal structure for bureaucratic rationality. As the progressive formalization of informal rule making under the Administrative Procedure Act (APA) suggests, we constantly seem to introduce modifications to micropolitics that move administration back toward the rationality mode. There are several plausible reasons for unease about micropolitical accommodation. A prominent ground for suspicion of micropolitical structure is what I sometimes call the pigeon syndrome. Let me illustrate with a gambling analogy.

There are poker tables in Las Vegas where you will see five people sitting around playing cards. They appear to be playing against each other. They are not. Four of them are playing against one of them. That one of them is the pigeon. He is not really in the game; they are just dividing up his money. And they will divide up his money with great efficiency over the course of the afternoon because those four others are actually professionals, who spend their days plucking pigeons. They work in league with each other and with the casino.

We may often imagine that in any sort of informal, accommodative decision structure, in which people are ultimately to come to an agreement, somebody is likely to get plucked. The pigeon may not only not be there in the figurative sense; they may literally not be there. They were not invited to the party. Indeed, some interests are extremely difficult to invite. They are not only hard to organize; they are quite disembodied.

We may believe, for example, that the appropriate rate of intergenerational savings is zero. From a moral perspective, we have a duty to leave the next generation with exactly what we had. We have no moral obligation to give more, but we certainly should not give less. We may want to structure decision processes to reflect this view. Nevertheless, inviting somebody to represent that position, given that they look suspiciously like they are in this generation, may cause us to feel that the next generation was not adequately represented,. We may thus want to have some stronger structure of accountability and responsibility, to oversee the participation of that party who claims to represent the next generation—or any other interest that makes up what we sometimes loosely call the public interest. That is, we may be suspicious about micropolitical structures because we feel that they are highly oriented toward carving up whatever pie is available as among the participants who happen to be involved in the bargaining. In order to avoid pigeon plucking, we may flee back toward some more-structured process in which goals are better specified and procedures are more formal.

Moreover the goal of this model seems less determinable than the goal of the B/R model. The micropolitical process is supposed to produce harmony. But what is the empirical evidence of harmony? That people are not in the streets? That they are in the streets only with stones and not with guns? That there is a low level of complaint in the *New York Times*? What is the harmony question really about?

Whether an agency has crafted a regulatory policy that has produced harmony is an extremely difficult question. This evaluative difficulty combined with our suspicions of the model may cause us to applaud reforms by the District of Columbia Court of Appeals that have attempted to restructure the informality of network accommodation that might go on within informal rule making. Or it might cause us to propose a plethora of subsidiary devices—some of which are discussed in this book—to support either broader participation or a closer approximation of the rational bureaucratic mode of operation.

But we should not forget as we applaud or propose that these improvements in micropolitics require a belief either that regulatory values have been well specified at the legislative level or that we know what a good or fair political process looks like. Indeed, it may only be by addressing these fundamental questions that we can come to understand what specific reforms, however plausible and attractive, are really about.

Summary

We are engaged in an attempt to work out the ways in which we are prepared to live with the compromises between rationality and politics that current regulatory systems represent. And whether we are discussing advisory committees, science courts, citizen review panels, or restructuring the insides of agencies, in most cases the attempt is to put these models together in ways that both better accommodate our impossible dream of having both models simultaneously and deal with the well-recognized failures of each.

3 Components of an Adequate Record

William Warfield Ross

The concern of the chapters in this book is the methodology employed by governmental bodies to decide policy questions that are related in a variety of ways to scientific and technical issues. Such bodies do not operate in a power vacuum, and the procedures they employ and the rules they issue are influenced by outside forces. Any inquiry into this subject must take account of such forces, particularly Congress and reviewing courts, if it is to deal with reality.

Current law requires that rules embodying explicit or implicit judgments about scientific and technical issues be based on a record, which is a collection of writing supporting and explaining the factual, legal, and policy bases for the rule. Reviewing courts, rather than Congress, have been the primary shapers of these records, after the agencies themselves.

The role of the courts must be understood if we are to evaluate and improve existing rule-making processes growing out of scientific and technological knowledge.

The development of public policy resting on scientific and technical subject matter is bedeviled by a chronic confusion of fact, policy inference, and value choice. In areas of high political controversy, such as nuclear power, it is virtually impossible to hold a public debate that separates what is known, what is factually uncertain but possibly resolvable through investigation, and what are value choices. Even in less-controversial areas, agencies have great difficulty in making this separation in developing public policy. Congressional standards, as in *Benzene* (100 S.Ct. 2844, 1980), may blur the fact-policy distinction, and the agency can be under strong pressure to claim a factual base for a rule that in actuality is supported only by a policy-loaded inference from limited scientific data.

Judicial review could play a useful role in requiring an agency to separate and consider separately the factual and policy support for a rule. This would require the court to get its mind dirty with the scientific and technical evidence and impose a considerable burden on the agency of clear and explicit thinking. The result could only be an improvement in the quality of rules, in my opinion. (The resulting records, paradoxically, could make agencies more vulnerable to attack politically by exposing the limited factual basis for many rules, including in particular those in health, safety, and environmental regulation.) If courts also begin to apply a stricter nondelegation standard, as suggested in *Benzene*, Congress could be forced to be more specific in setting standards, which in turn could ease the agencies' burden.

An Adequate Record—From Whose Standpoint?

There are four possible perspectives from which to evaluate the adequacy of an administrative record:

1. The agency.
2. The reviewing court.
3. The legislature.
4. Any interested parties or organizations.

The perspectives of these groups inevitably will be quite different. The self-interested viewpoint of a private party will usually differ from the viewpoint of a legislature charged with representation of a larger political unit, although not necessarily from that of a congressional committee. A court that does not review de novo and sees only isolated cases will necessarily view an issue differently than an agency.

This chapter focuses on the contrasting views of the agency and the court, in part because courts have done more to shape the nature of administrative records than any other outside force and because courts are the most articulate of the various players.[1]

From a parochial agency standpoint, an adequate record is one that permits a workable, timely, and efficient decision; is reasonably calculated to further the agency's purposes, as it sees them; and is reasonably calculated to withstand judicial or political review. A record satisfactory from the agency's standpoint may not stand muster, however, on judicial review. A court may disagree with the timing of agency action; may read the agency's purpose or statute differently; may find the agency's data base of policy explanation inadequate; and may be indifferent to, or affirmatively disapprove of, an agency's need to take account of political pressure from the legislature or private interests. In sum, the court may view the adequacy of the record differently for institutional reasons. It can be expected that over time the effect of judicial review will be production of records that differ in significant degree from those that would have evolved in its absence, particularly in proceedings that Lon Fuller has characterized as polycentric.[2]

Standards Governing Judicial Review
of Agency Proceedings

A variety of statutory procedures govern judicial review of agency action involving scientific or technical issues. The description here focuses on review of informal rule-making proceedings by U.S. courts of appeals, which are appellate courts (usually sitting in panels of three judges) located across the country. The basic statutory provision governing this kind of review is section 706 of the Administrative Procedure Act (5 U.S.C. § 706).[3] Section 706 provides in pertinent part:

> To the extent necessary to decision and when presented, the reviewing court shall decide all relevant questions of law, interpret constitutional and statutory provisions, and determine the meaning or applicability of the terms of an agency action. The reviewing court shall—
>
> . . .
>
> (2) hold unlawful and set aside agency action, findings, and conclusions found to be—
>
> (A) arbitrary, capricious, an abuse of discretion, or otherwise not in accordance with law;
> (B) contrary to constitutional right, power, privilege, or immunity;
> (C) in excess of statutory jurisdiction, authority, or limitations, or short of statutory right;
> (D) without observance of procedure required by law;
> (E) unsupported by substantial evidence in a case subject to sections 556 or 557 of this title or otherwise reviewed on the record of an agency hearing provided by statute. . . .
>
> In making the foregoing determinations, the court shall review the whole record or those parts of it cited by a party, and due account shall be taken of the rule of prejudicial error.

A first reading of this provision suggests that the reviewing court is being asked to scrutinize and correct any errors of fact or law committed by an agency in the course of issuing a rule, a process similar to that of a reviewing executive authority that substitutes its judgment on legal factual matters for that of its subordinates. This would be an incorrect understanding of the statute and the review process. Although there is no one agreed law of judicial review, courts have interpreted their powers under the Administrative Procedure Act (which is said to be a codification of common law) in a far more limited fashion. [See, e.g., Citizens to Preserve Overton Park, Inc. v. Volpe, 401 U.S. 402, 416 (1971); Lead Industries Ass'n, Inc. v. EPA, 14 E.R.C. 1906, 1916 (D.C. Cir. 1980), cert. denied, 49 U.S.L.W. 3422 (Dec. 9, 1980); Ethyl Corp. v. EPA, 541 F.2d 1, 34 (D.C. Cir.) (en banc), cert. denied, 426 U.S. 941 (1976)]

Agencies make essentially three kinds of predications: findings of fact, conclusions of law, and policy decisions (although frequently the boundaries between these categories are obscured in rule-making decisions).

Review of Agency Findings of Fact

Courts are directed to set aside findings of fact in informal rule making if they are found to be "arbitrary, capricious, or an abuse of discretion." In addition, in formal rule making and in some special statutory proceedings, the court is directed to set aside findings if they are not "supported by substantial evidence." Whatever may have been the historical distinction between these tests, it is now widely agreed that they are essentially the same and that the nature of judicial review will not differ significantly depending on the statutory rubric to be applied.[4]

The court does not sit as a superagency to appraise an agency's findings de novo (that is, to replicate the agency's process) or to substitute its judgment for that of the agency. [Citizens to Preserve Overton Park, Inc. v. Volpe, *supra*, 401 U.S. at 416] However, a court will require that there be at least some evidence in the record from which an agency could rationally have drawn a factual inference. [Lead Industries Ass'n, Inc. v. EPA, *supra*, 14 E.R.C. at 1916] Substantial evidence means "more than a mere scintilla." The standard entails "such relevant evidence as a reasonable mind might accept as adequate to support a conclusion." [Consolidated Edison Co. v. NLRB, 305 U.S. 197, 229 (1938)] The degree to which a reviewing court is willing and able to probe in depth complex scientific and technical factual evidence is a subject of some controversy.

Review of Agency Conclusions of Law

Section 706 is blunt. It tells a court to "decide all relevant questions of law, interpret constitutional and statutory provisions, and determine the meaning or applicability of the terms of an agency action." The court is also instructed to hold unlawful agency action "contrary to constitutional right, power, privilege, or immunity" and "in excess of statutory jurisdiction, authority, or limitations, or short of statutory rights." These stringent commands have been mitigated in practice, however, by judge-created doctrines calling for deference to agency interpretations of its own statute. [*See* Lead Industries Ass'n, Inc. v. EPA, *supra*, 14 E.R.C. at 1918; Train v. Natural Resources Defense Council, Inc., 421 U.S. 60, 75 (1975)][5] Reviewing courts generally, although not universally, will defer to an agency's statutory interpretation that has some reasonable basis in the statute's language and history, even though it may not be the interpretation that the court itself would prefer. Courts have reasoned that agencies acquire expertise in the subject matter of their statutes, are directly responsible for the administration of the laws enacted by Congress, and are often consulted by Congress in the drafting of statutes that they later administer. Thus courts, at least nominally, are inclined to give the agency the benefit of the doubt if its statutory interpretation has any reasonable basis.

Review of Agency Policy Decisions

Section 706 does not refer to policy decisions as such, but courts do review administrative-policy decisions. Courts recognize that policy is the area in which agencies should be accorded the broadest discretion in the first instance. Courts, however, will determine whether a policy conflicts with or is consistent with, congressional purpose as set out in the governing statute. [Synthetic Organic Chemical Mfrs. Ass'n v. Brennan, 503 F.2d 1155, 1159-60 (3rd Cir. 1974), *cert. denied*, 420 U.S. 973 (1975); Lead Indus. Ass'n, Inc. v. EPA, *supra*, 14 E.R.C. 1906] A policy, however rationally supported, that runs counter to the will of Congress is obviously unlawful. [*See, for example*, Indus. Union Dep't, AFL-CIO v. Am. Petroleum Institute, 100 S. Ct. 2844, 2866-69 (1980)] Second, courts will take a hard look at policy decisions to ascertain whether they are rationally grounded in statutory policies and the evidence of record.[6] The court does not purport to substitute its own judgment for the agency's exercise of discretion in adopting one of a number of policy alternatives. [Citizens to Preserve Overton Park, Inc. v. Volpe, *supra*, 401 U.S. at 416] Rather, it attempts to ensure that the result reached by the agency is not "arbitrary, capricious, or an abuse of discretion," given the facts as the agency has found them and the goals it is called on to reach. A court will insist that "assumptions must be spelled out, inconsistencies explained, methodologies disclosed, contradictory evidence rebutted, record references solidly grounded, guesswork eliminated and conclusions supported in a 'manner capable of judicial understanding.' " [Rogers, *A Hard Look at Vermont Yankee: Environmental Law under Close Scrutiny*, 67 Geo. L.J. 699, 706 (1979) (citing E.I. duPont de Nemours & Co. v. Train, 541 F.2d 1018, 1038 (4th Cir. 1976), *aff'd. in part and rev'd. in part*, 430 U.S. 112 (1977))]

*Review of Procedures Followed in the Issuance of Rules
Involving Scientific and Technical Issues*

Section 706 requires that a court hold unlawful and set aside agency action, findings, and conclusions found without observation of the procedures required by law. The procedures contemplated by informal rule making under section 553 of the Administrative Procedure Act are relatively simple. The agency must give notice of its intention to issue a rule, it must provide an opportunity for written comment, and, when the final rule is issued, this must be accompanied by "concise general statement of their basis and purpose." [5 U.S.C. § 533 (c)]

These procedural requirements have been elaborated by the courts substantially beyond the bare elements of section 553. First, courts have required that agencies assemble a record facilitating judicial review, although section 553 contains no such requirement. Agencies have been told to expand their initial notice to provide a more-detailed statement of the nature of the rule and of materials on which the agency intends to rely. The courts have required republication of rules to permit further opportunity for comment when new elements have been introduced. The final statement of basis and purpose has been expanded to require the agency to respond to significant comments or arguments made with respect to the proposed rule.[7] In addition, the arbitrary and capricious standard under which informal rules are reviewed has been converted into what is essentially a substantial evidence standard, requiring factual support in the record for rules that rest on factual premises. [*See, for example*, Indus. Union Dep't, AFL-CIO v. Am. Petroleum Institute, *supra*, 100 S.Ct. at 2860, 2870-74 (1980); Nat'l Lime Ass'n v. EPA, 627 F.2d 416, 452-53 (D.C. Cir. 1980)]

In addition, a few courts have gone beyond these requirements and directed the agency to conduct oral procedures, including presentation of witnesses and cross-examination, when these were thought essential to illuminate the factual basis of a rule. [Int'l Harvester Co. v. Ruckelshaus, 478 F.2d 615 (D.C. Cir. 1973)] These relatively few decisions were overruled, however, by the Supreme Court's decision in Vermont Yankee Nuclear Power Corp. v. Natural Resources Defense Council, Inc., 435 U.S. 519, 524 (1978), that a reviewing court may not require an agency to utilize procedures that are different from or additional to those described in section 553 of the APA, except in very exceptional circumstances. The Supreme Court recognized, however, the continuing judicial obligation to appraise a record to determine whether a rule was adequately supported in fact and reasoning under the arbitrary and capricious standard.

The *Vermont Yankee* decision has been extensively criticized and supported. [*See, for example*, Stewart, *Vermont Yankee and the Evolution of Administrative Procedure*, 91 Harv. L. Rev. 1805 (1978); Byse, *Vermont Yankee and the Evolution of Administrative Procedure: A Somewhat Different View*, 91 Harv. L. Rev. 1823 (1978); DeLong, *Informal Rulemaking and the Integration of Law and Policy*, 65 Va. L. Rev. 257 (1979)] It is not clear at this stage what effect the case ultimately will have on judicial review of rule making. There is some evidence that the lower courts, while scrupulously adhering to its central holding, have continued to apply essentially the same standards and methods to test the validity of agency rules.[8]

The actual application of these doctrines is not straightforward. The issues confronting a court when reviewing a complex rule-making proceeding are not neatly subdivided into questions of fact, law, policy, and procedure. Usually policy and factual issues are intermingled in ways that make it difficult for a court to sort them into neat categories for appraisal. Questions as to the adequacy of the substance of an agency rule are often enmeshed with questions as to the adequacy of agency procedures since the procedures necessarily generate the substance. Moreover, courts are not uniform in the application of doctrine or even in some instances in agreeing on a bare statement of the doctrine of administrative review. The stringency of review varies with the court, the subject matter, the agency, and other factors, making it difficult to predict the fate of an agency rule at the end of appellate review.

The Interaction between Court and Agency and Its Effect on the Administrative Record

The Competence of Judges to Evaluate Scientific Questions

Running through the development of the modern law of judicial review has been a controversy regarding the competence of federal appellate judges to evaluate scientific and technical questions. The conflict has been encapsulated in the positions of two judges on the D.C. Circuit. Judge David Bazelon, suggesting that "substantive review of mathematical and scientific evidence by technically illiterate judges is dangerously unreliable," believes that a reviewing court should seek primarily to enforce the use of fair and efficient procedures as a means of ensuring reasoned decision making. [Ethyl Corp. v. EPA, *supra*, 541 F.2d at 67 (concurring opinion, Bazelon, C.J.). *See also* AFL-CIO v. Marshall, 617 F.2d 636 (D.C. Cir. 1979), *vacated and remanded sub nom.*, 101 S. Ct. 56 (1980); Smithkline Corp., v. FDA, 587 F.2d 1107 (D.C. Cir. 1978); and Bazelon, *Coping with Technology Through the Legal Process*, 62 Cornell L. Rev. 817, 823 (1977)] Judge Bazelon's colleague, the late Judge Harold Leventhal, objected that substantive review of administrative action "cannot be carried out in a vacuum of understanding" but requires judges to acquire "whatever technical knowledge is necessary as background for decision of the legal questions" in an administrative case. [Ethyl Corp. v. EPA, *supra*, 541 F.2d at 68-69 (Leventhal, J. concurring); *see also* Leventhal, *Environmental Decisionmaking and the Role of the Courts*, 122 U. of Pa. L. Rev. 509, 511 (1974)]

There is something to be said for the Bazelon position in cases where the agency has not been able to organize and articulate scientific questions in a way that makes them readily comprehensible to a lay person. It should be noted, however, that most administrative heads are not scientists. They are much more likely to be lawyers, politicians, or business-persons than persons trained in the scientific or technical subject matter that concerns their agency. Thus, an agency record that is unintelligible to an experienced federal appeals judge is likely to have been unintelligible to the agency head who allegedly made a decision based on it. Such an administrator is thus exposed as having relied on either intuition or experts.

Putting this problem aside, Judge Bazelon's position is troubling for reasons in part articulated by Judge Leventhal. In many instances, the adequacy of procedures used cannot be easily separated from the merits of the decision reached. There are no good or bad procedures in the abstract, if only because the questions an agency must address vary so much. In order to appraise the procedures used, some understanding of the merits (sometimes a relatively sophisticated understanding) of a case is necessary. A court must have a sense of what relevant facts are known or knowable and of what administrative procedures will ensure agency consideration of these facts.

It is also important to recognize that agencies have made decisions that are arbitrary, capricious, or an abuse of discretion while following impeccable procedures. Agencies can fall into error for distinctly different reasons: single-mission blinders or zealotry, ideological bias, political pressure, personal or political animosity, incompetence, or venality or bribery. The basis for this kind of error may not be apparent from the briefs or record. If the result is a decision that, though wrong, is supportable under general standards for review, then the court can and should do nothing. Often, however, a result can be seen to be arbitrary and capricious or factually unsupported when examined on the merits. A relatively straightforward example of this point is provided by Cincinnati Gas & Electric Co. v. EPA [578 F.2d 660 (6th Cir. 1978), *cert. denied*, 439 U.S. 1114 (1979)], involving an EPA order imposing sodium dioxide limits on point sources in Ohio. Petitioners attacked EPA procedures as violative of the Administrative Procedure Act and due process. They also attacked a number of models used by the agency to predict pollution dispersion as invalid on a variety of grounds. The court, while upholding the lawfulness of the agency's procedures, held that use of one of the models was "not a rational decision and is arbitrary and capricious." [Cincinnati Gas & Electric Co. v. EPA, *supra*, 578 F.2d at 664] The ground for the holding was the agency's failure to justify the use of the model in the face of evidence suggesting that it could not predict reality with sufficient accuracy. It can be argued that a limited Bazelon-style review would not discern and reverse this type of error. Thus, if Bazelon's key premise—that judges without scientific or technical training cannot make this analysis on a reliable basis—is assumed away, it can be argued that such a limited review shirks a fundamental responsibility.

The correct answer to this question is of considerable importance since courts play a significant role in shaping the records and thus the results of scientific and technical rule making. It is important to determine whether appellate judges, within the limitations of their experience, time, and resources, are able to become sufficiently versed in scientific and technical material to take the hard look at the substantive content of agency rule making that is called for by Judge Leventhal. If they are not, then we can no longer count on the courts to provide assurance that agency rules based on scientific and technical materials reflect an adequate appraisal of relevant facts and a reasoned analysis of statutory goals and policy. This conclusion would seem to require reevaluation of the nondelegation doctrine, as well as the procedures currently used by agencies to develop their records.

Although the question is open and needs to be examined, I believe that appellate judges can satisfactorily perform the kind of review called for by Judges Leventhal and Wright, if they acquire certain essential skills. By skills, I do not mean a working familiarity with the scientific or technical fields involved in rule making. Science and engineering today are so multifaceted and highly specialized that such an undertaking clearly would be impossible. Rather, it means sufficient familiarity with scientific method to be able to follow and evaluate the analytical processes used by the agency in reaching its decision. Appellate judges should have at least a rudimentary understanding of basic scientific methodologies such as controlled testing, statistical measurement, probability assessment, and modeling. A judge does not need to know how to run a regression analysis but should be able to appreciate its significance, or the lack thereof, if presented with an adequate brief on the subject.

It may be argued that this is too much to expect of judges trained in the law. I would respond that practitioners seeking to deal successfully with these subject matters clearly must acquire such rudimentary skills. Given the importance of this appellate function, such minimal capability is a reasonable skill qualification for a federal appellate judge. These skills can be acquired on the job from study, dealings with more-experienced colleagues, and the day-to-day work.[9] Many federal appellate judges possess such a capacity, which the British call "high vulgarization." This capacity will become more and more widely recognized as a necessary tool for appellate jurists.

Other Institutional Factors Affecting Court Review

Judicial review affects the agency rule-making process in at least two ways, most obviously through its impact on the individual case (that is, by affirming or remanding for additional proceedings with their attendant delay), an impact highly significant where proceedings are polycentric and of great importance. Judicial review has a cumulative effect, which determines to a considerable degree the kinds of proceedings that agencies hold to resolve scientific and technical issues. Thus, the Atomic Energy Commission's procedures for determining the safety of nuclear-power reactors were largely dictated by reviewing courts in the *Calvert Cliffs* and later decisions. [Calvert Cliffs Coordinating Comm., Inc. v. AEC, 449 F.2d 1109 (D.C. Cir. 1971)] Ten years of judicial review drastically changed the procedures followed by EPA under its various environmental statutes.

Basic institutional differences between agencies and courts have an effect on what the court sees and what it does to an agency rule. Courts review rules on a paper record. These rules are the products of institutional decisional processes, and the administrator who ultimately issues them may have played little or no role in their formulation. The agency involved is usually neither one person nor a small collegial group but rather a collection of diverse organizations within a bureaucracy that are working at various levels of expertise, abstraction, and comprehension. [Pedersen, *Formal Records and Informal Rulemaking*, 85 Yale L.J. 38 (1975)] Each of these groups has its own perspective on the record, and in aggregate these viewpoints feed into and often control the final agency judgment about record adequacy. The resulting rule can be a great deal better in practical effect than in written justification.

Appellate judges, in contrast, do their own work, aided only by intelligent but relatively inexperienced law clerks without technical or scientific qualifications. Their review of the agency's paper record is usually supplemented by only brief oral argument. This relative isolation is bound to influence the judge's perception of the record, putting a high value on such factors as immediate intelligibility, convenience, and rigor in exposition. As a result, such factors are elevated to a status that they do not customarily receive in the rough and tumble of regulatory practice.

Perhaps even more important, the record in a particular proceeding is usually only a small piece of a comprehensive program of regulation affecting a whole industry or broad segments of the public. The agency assembles and appraises this record in the context of that entire program; the court sees it in relative isolation. It is an obvious source of strength that the court's view is unitary and isolated. However, there are elements in agency processes significantly affecting records and decisions that courts may find difficult to take account of, even if they are willing to do so.

A contemporary agency has a defined mission and typically limited means to accomplish it. Congress usually is lavish in bestowing goals and responsibilities and parsimonious in supplying resources. Agencies also are often time constained by events or statutory command. Thus, such agencies must continually balance quality against quantity and expedition against both. A record and resulting decision that seems shoddy and inadequate to a court may represent the agency's best judgment as to the resources it can prudently devote to only one of many tasks it is supposed to carry out under its statutory directives within a definable time frame.[10] Courts are neither equipped nor disposed to take account of such limitations and hold agencies to a more-or-less absolute standard in the particular cases that rather fortuitously reach them.[11]

Agencies are also subject to a variety of political pressures that courts consider totally irrelevant. A mission-oriented agency will accommodate its decisional process to such pressures to the extent it perceives that they threaten its ability to carry out its program.[12] These pressures can come from congressional committees with substantive and appropriating power, from state governments, from other parts of the executive branch, or elsewhere. Court interference in the agency process by remands (with their resulting delays) that do not take account of resource limitation and the political environment can produce wholly incalculable results. It has been argued that such piecemeal intervention can induce the exact opposite of the court's intent by injuring the agency's ability to do the best job possible with limited resources.[13]

These inherent limitations to a court's ability to assess a record play a significant role in proceedings involving scientific and technical issues. The scientific questions assessed by various regulatory agencies may arise in appraising an isolated product or process, but they usually are part of, or have implications for, a broad regulatory program designed to achieve public-policy objectives. The evidence and reasoning supporting a particular decision may be found inadequate by a court. However, a decision by the agency to assemble a particular kind of record and to use a particular decisional model can be a programmatic choice reflecting various constraints and goal assessments. The agency may have concluded that its conflicting responsibilities permit it to attack a particular task this way and that if barred from using these procedures, it would not undertake the task.[14] It may be better for the agency to perform within these limitations than not to perform at all. Yet the reviewing court will have no occasion to consider this question.

*Analysis of the Effect of Judicial Review
on Four Types of Administrative Records*

Gelpe and Tarlock identify four categories of information on which a rule making record can be based. [*The Uses of Scientific Information in Environmental Decisionmaking*, 48 S. Cal. L. Rev. 371, 392 (1974)]

Review of Records in which Relevant Information Is Available and Definite: The first category includes cases in which relevant information of a definite nature is reasonably available to the agency. In such a case, courts usually insist that before they finally rule on an issue, the agency gather and analyze the information. If equipment tests are feasible and are relevant to product-safety regulation, the agency must perform them rather than rely upon essentially unsubstantiated opinion of experts. [Aqua Slide 'N' Dive Corp. v. Consumer Prod. Safety Comm'n, 569 F.2d 831, 843-844 (5th Cir. 1978)] If an opposing party has established that there is a relevant form of test methodology, the agency may not base its decision on an assertion that no relevant methodology exists.[15] [Cincinnati Gas & Electric Co. v. EPA, *supra*, 578 F.2d at 663-664] If "facts pertinent to the standard's feasibility are available and easily discoverable by conventional technical means," the agency may not refuse to analyze the accessible evidence without justifying its refusal. [Nat'l Lime Ass'n v. EPA, 627 F.2d 416, 454 (D.C. Cir. 1980)] The Supreme Court in the *Benzene* decision held that OSHA's burden of proof in setting a safe exposure level for benzene requires proof of significant risk based on actual testing rather than assuming that some risk existed based on an "absolute, no-risk policy that [OSHA] applies to carcinogens." [Indus. Union Dep't, AFL-CIO v. Am. Petroleum Institute, 100 S. Ct. 2844, 2860, 2870, 2872, 2874 (1980). *See* Sampson and Perdue, *The Supreme Court's Benzene Decision*, 2 Environmental Regulation Analyst, Feb. 1981, at 7]

The rule that an agency should assemble and consider germane evidence that is readily available may seem virtually self-evident; however, scientific and technical rule makings are consumed with controversies over the germaneness of existing evidence, the accessibility of evidence, and the allowable inferences to be drawn from such evidence.[16] It is the competence of appellate judges to appraise the questions that is called into question by Judge Bazelon's arguments.

Review of Records in which Relevant Information Is Available but Inherently Indefinite: This type of record was presented in Ethyl Corp. v. EPA. [541 F.2d 1 (D.C. Cir.) (*en banc*), *cert. denied*, 426 U.S. 941 (1976)] The inherent uncertainty in projecting health effects from lead particulates resulted from the slow incubation period for lead poisoning and the impossibility of finding a lead-free control group because of the multiple sources of lead pervading the atmosphere. [541 F.2d at 25-26] The court determined that:

> where a statute is precautionary in nature, the evidence difficult to come by, uncertain, or conflicting because it is on the frontiers of scientific knowledge, the regulations designed to protect the public health, and the decision that of an expert administrator, we will not demand rigorous step-by-step proof of cause and effect. . . . The Administrator may apply his expertise to draw conclusions from suspected, but not completely substantiated, relationships between facts, from trends among facts, from theoretical projections from imperfect data, from probative preliminary data not yet certifiable as 'fact,' and the like. [541 F. 2d at 28 (footnote omitted)]

The administrator will have acted properly if he evaluated "all the evidence in a consistent and rational manner" [541 F.2d at 43], applied reasonable methodology [541 F.2d at 42], and relied upon evidence adequately exposed to public critique. [541 F.2d at 47] Thus, in cases of this type, the court will not expect the agency to do the impossible: to establish a concrete, factual basis for a decision that must rest primarily on educated guesses and policy considerations. The court instead will look at two factors. First, the court will determine whether the agency's decision is consistent with or serves to fulfill the statutory goals. [*See, for example*, Synthetic Organic Chem. Mfrs. Ass'n v. Brennan, 503 F.2d 1155, 1159 (3rd Cir. 1974). *See also* Lead Industries Ass'n, Inc. v. EPA, 14 E.R.C. 1906 (D.C. Cir. 1980), *cert. denied*, 49 U.S.L.W. 3422 (Dec. 9, 1980)] Second, the court will scrutinize the reasoning that supports the adoption of one policy initiative as opposed to the alternatives available in order to ensure that there is a rational basis for the rule despite the fact that the existing knowledge does not permit the rule to be firmly based on demonstrable fact. [Indust. Union Dep't, AFL-CIO v. Hodgson, 499 F.2d 467, 474-476 (D.C. Cir. 1974)]

Review of Records in which Relevant Information Is Currently Unavailable but Theoretically Obtainable: Courts customarily apply the tests discussed earlier to these sorts of records as well; they will scrutinize the rule and its reasoned support for consistency with the statute and rationality. The question encountered here is the extent to which the court will require the agency to accumulate information (through additional research, testing, and so forth) likely to throw light on the wisdom of the rule and the extent to which a showing has been made that providing such information is technically feasible. The result in this kind of case usually turns on the court's appraisal of the adequacy of the factual and other support for the existing rule, as compared to the additional expense, delay, and other costs of a remand to assemble additional information. Thus, in Weyerhaeuser Co. v. Costle [590 F.2d 1011 (D.C. Cir. 1978)], the court, although remanding the biochemical oxygen demand limitation on the ground that the agency had not followed correct procedures in resolving this issue, accepted the agency's choice of a particular methodology and refused to require the collection of the additional information necessary to provide a more-concrete basis for the rule, although such information theoretically could have been assembled. [590 F.2d at 1054 n.70] The decision was grounded on a finding that the agency's methods were reasonable, and its explanation for proceeding on the basis of imperfect information was sufficient. Where the collection of theoretically available information involves data so massive as to be administratively infeasible, the agency may rely on the reasonable amount of data readily available. Environmental Defense Fund v. EPA, 598 F.2d 62, 84-85 (D.C. Cir. 1978);

Cleveland Electric Illuminating Co. v. EPA, 572 F.2d 1150, 1161 (6th Cir.), *cert. denied*, 439 U.S. 910 (1978)]

The court's determination that the data gathered is reasonably sufficient essentially applies a balancing test. If the court is sufficiently dissatisfied with the basis for the rule, it is likely to require assemblage of additional information if this apparently can be done given the existing state of the art. Obviously such decisions can have profound effects on the distribution of agency resources and on the pace and impact of agency programs.

Review of Records in which Potentially Relevant Information Is Neither Currently Available Nor Attainable under Existing Scientific Techniques: The courts have not habitually attempted to force the agencies to do the impossible: to provide a factual basis for a rule incorporating a factual predicate where a convincing showing has been made that the facts are unascertainable according to the current state of the art. Courts, however, do scrutinize such rules for consistency with the statute, and they will give particularly intensive consideration to whether such rules are rationally supported. It is generally recognized that Congress has and will require agencies to reach decisions based on whatever combinations of guess, intuition, and policy predilections are available to them. This type of record was considered in Amoco Oil Co. v. EPA [501 F.2d 722 (D.C. Cir. 1974)], where the court found that key factual elements determining the lead-content levels to be set by rule were not currently available. The agency necessarily was proceeding on an "informed hunch or guess." [501 F.2d at 742] The court found that the agency had studied all accessible information and had selected a relatively low lead ceiling based upon a sustainable policy judgment in favor of overprotection when considering issues of public health. [501 F.2d at 742-743] In this kind of case, if an agency makes a respectable showing that it has attempted unsuccessfully to develop the factual basis, that it has considered all of the policy implications of various approaches proposed, and that it has selected a policy alternative that appears reasonably consistent with statutory goals, the court is unlikely to interfere with the resulting rule.

Conclusion and Overview

Judicial review of agency regulation serves a number of social purposes. It enhances general acceptance of government, provides a public-policy enforcement mechanism, and tends to prevent individual injustice. Courts operate as an elite body, interfering sporadically and unpredictably with regulatory processes that reflect a multiplicity of often low-visibility pressures. Courts operate within structured prescripts and follow procedures that have little relationship to the agency process they are reviewing. They enforce statutes, often taking the will of Congress more seriously than would any Congress. They sometimes reverse agencies for shortcomings that no involved party would consider reprehensible, absent the appeal context. They often require agencies to take seriously words that Congress has spoken but did not mean, and most often Congress does not correct them. Courts thus play a legitimating role—imposing a standard of accuracy, fairness, and rationality on an inherently irrational process.

There can be little doubt that reviewing courts will continue to have a profound effect on the nature of rule-making records. The effect thus far, and on balance, has been salutary. Our current structure of economic, health, and environmental regulation would neither be politically acceptable nor socially desirable without it. These chapters recognize a need to develop innovative ways of making policy based on scientific and technical knowledge, ways that will permit more-expeditious, accurate, and acceptable decisions. Such innovations must produce records acceptable to reviewing courts under current standards, or appellate judges must be willing to revise their thinking and standards to accommodate them. New approaches may result in records differing from those currently compiled by agencies such as the Nuclear Regulatory Commission (NRC) and the Occupational Safety and Health Administration (OSHA), which may present novel problems of comprehension and evaluation. For example, agencies may decide to use innovative modeling techniques or novel forms of policy analysis to assess risk or compare costs and benefits. Such records may impose unusual, although not wholly unprecedented, demands on the courts' ability to understand and evaluate processes that are opaque to nonspecialists.[17]

The courts at a minimum will surely continue to require that the results of such studies be presented in a way that permits rational evaluation under the conditions of an appeal.[18] If the agency's lawyers cannot explain and justify the results on the basis of the existing record, the courts will continue to remand for further explanation by the agency. If the techniques involved become sufficiently complex and alien to nonspecialist judges, the resulting reversals and delays could have an inhibiting effect on agency experimentation with decisional modes, an effect that has rightly concerned Judge Bazelon. On the other hand, any relaxation of review standards in the face of increased technicality would be self-defeating.

In short, although it is impossible to foresee agency developments, I do not anticipate a necessary change in the methodology of review. What I do look for is an increasingly demanding burden on the courts to read, mark, learn, and inwardly digest more and more complicated records so as to ensure a hard look at the resulting rule.

Notes

1. Congressional action can have an impact on agency records, a subject not discussed in this chapter; however, most legislation regarding administrative procedure more or less codifies court decisions rather than innovating new procedures.

2. Fuller's polycentric proceedings involve a complex variety of issues and affect large numbers or groups, giving rise to considerable variability in procedures and results. Most significant rule makings involving scientific or technical issues have these characteristics. Fuller, *The Forms and Limits of Adjudication*, 92 Harv. L. Rev. 353, 394-404 (1978).

3. There are, in addition, a variety of review schemes within specific statutes that typically do not depart materially from the Administrative Procedure Act. For the sake of simplicity, the description of procedure in this chapter will assume that the APA applies.

4. *See* Pacific Legal Foundation v. Dep't of Transp., 593 F.2d 1338, 1343 n.35 (D.C. Cir.), *cert. denied*, 444 U.S. 380 (1979); Associated Indus. of N.Y. State, Inc. v. Dep't of Labor, 487 F.2d 342, 349-350 (2d Cir. 1973). Some courts and commentators have perceived a procedural difference between the two tests, observing that the substantial-evidence test requires evidentiary support from a record developed as a result of formal hearings, whereas evidence under the arbitrary and capricious test is not so limited. Ethyl Corp. v. EPA, 541 F.2d 1, 37 n.79 (D.C. Circ.) (*en banc*), *cert. denied*, 426 U.S. 941 (1976); Scalia and Goodman, *Procedural Aspects of the Consumer Product Safety Act*, 20 U.C.L.A. L. Rev. 899, 934-935 (1973).

5. The so-called Bumpers amendment introduced into the 96th, and again in the 97th, Congress (*see* S. 67 and H.R. 746, 97th Cong., 1st Sess. (1981)) would eliminate these presumptions.

6. The phrase "hard look" originally described the agency's obligation to support its decisions, but it evolved into a "rigorous standard of judicial review applied to increasingly utilized informal rulemaking proceedings or to other decisions made upon less than a full trial-type record." Nat'l Lime Ass'n v. EPA, 627 F.2d 416, 451 n.126 (D.C. Cir. 1980) (citations omitted). *See also* Kleppe v. Sierra Club, 427 U.S. 390, 410 n.21 (1976)(court must ensure that agency has taken a "hard look" at the environmental effects of the proposed action). In essence, the court is to engage in a "substantial inquiry" and a "thorough, probing, in-depth review" of the evidence on which decisions are based. Citizens to Preserve Overton Park, Inc. v. Volpe, 401 U.S. 402, 415 (1971).

7. U.S. v. Nova Scotia Food Prods. Corp., 568 F.2d 240, 252-3 (2d Cir. 1977); Office of Communication of United Church of Christ v. FCC, 560 F.2d 529, 532-3 (2d Cir. 1977); Nat'l Resources Defense Council, Inc. v.

NRC, 547 F.2d 633, 644 (D.C. Cir. 1976) *rev'd on other grounds sub nom.*, Vermont Yankee Nuclear Power Corp. v. Nat'l Resources Defense Council, Inc., 435 U.S. 519 (1978); Portland Cement Ass'n v. Ruckelshaus, 486 F.2d 375, 393 (D.C. Cir. 1973), *cert. denied*, 417 U.S. 921 (1974).

8. The Court's proscription of the requirement of additional procedures may be limited to cross-examination and other formal adjudication requirements spelled out in §§ 554 and 555 of Title 5. In the recent *Benzene* case, Industrial Union Dep't, AFL-CIO v. Am. Petroleum Institute, 100 S. Ct. 2844, 2872 (1980), the Court condemned OSHA's failure to gather knowable facts, suggesting that the agency required regulated industries to maintain monitoring and testing programs to supplement available information. The Court is apparently unwilling to impose trial-type procedures in an attempt to augment an inadequate record, but it does go so far as to suggest appropriate substantive information-gathering procedures. *See also* Nat'l Lime Ass'n v. EPA, 627 F.2d 416, 454-455 (D.C. Cir. 1980).

9. It is becoming generally appreciated that a judge should possess some familiarity with economic concepts. Scientific methodology seems equally important.

10. Such time restraints are sometimes imposed by courts, further complicating the agency's problems. *See e.g.*, MCI Telecommunications Corp. v. FCC, 627 F.2d 322 (D.C. Cir. 1980); Nader v. FCC, 520 F.2d 182 (D.C. Cir. 1975).

11. Courts have conceded the play of administrative limitations in some cases, recognizing that the impossible cannot be imposed. However, this recognition has been on an ad hoc basis, and no generally applicable principle of administrative convenience or necessity has developed in the law of judicial review.

12. Boyer, *Alternatives to Administrative Trial-type Hearings for Resolving Complex Scientific, Economic, and Social Issues*, 71 Mich. L. Rev. 111, 141 (1972).

13. It may be argued that court reversals stemming from poor performance due to resource limitations are justified as an inducement to Congress to modify either the agency's mission or its means, however, there are very few instances in which Congress has taken this salutory step.

14. Agencies pragmatically are allowed broad discretion to exercise or not exercise delegated powers, despite the seeming rigidities of statutory commands. This is the case not only in law-enforcement type regulation but in economic and standard-setting regulation as well.

15. The court's requirement that available methodology be considered does not extend to requiring an agency to use any available methodology or to conduct individual tests in lieu of making categorical determinations. An agency, in establishing a margin of safety, may use the most-sensitive member of a group to establish standards applicable to the group in general,

and it may make reasonable statistical assumptions. *See* Hercules, Inc. v. EPA, 598 F.2d 91, 106 (D.C. Cir 1978). The court will decide whether the numbers used by the agency are within a "zone of reasonableness," and this flexibility should free the court from "the minutiae of particular calculations" and allow an agency "the discretion to adopt a general formula or methodology to the aspects of a particular case." 598 F.2d at 107.

16. *See* McGarity, *Substantive and Procedural Discretion in Administrative Resolution of Science Policy Questions: Regulating Carcinogens in EPA and OSHA*, 67 Geo. L.J. 729, 740-741 (1979). For example, identification of statistical significance can be an issue of pure policy that is often mistaken for a factual matter. *Id.* at 748. *See also* Martin, Note, *Procedures for Decision-making under Conditions of Scientific Uncertainty: The Science Court Proposal*, 16 Harv. J. on Legis. 443, 485-490 (1979).

17. A classic example of an esoteric decisional tool is the fault tree-event tree analysis used by the AEC-NRC to evaluate the risk to the public of the ultimate nuclear accident, a core meltdown. The merits of this study were extensively debated by experts. (2 Nuclear Reg. Rep. (CCH) ¶ 20,094; Letter from NRC to Jeannie Honicker (Sept. 7, 1978), *see* Honicker v. NRC, 590 F.2d 1207 (D.C. Cir. 1978), *cert. denied*, 441 U.S. 906 (1979).) Executive Order 12291, 46 Fed. Reg. 13193 (1981), just issued by President Reagan, ensures that there will be a plethora of cost-benefit analysis presented to the federal courts in the coming years.

18. In this regard, I see no reason why a court, confronted with a particularly impenetrable technical question, could not invite the parties to an informal conference with their experts. The panel would question the experts, and the lawyers would comment on and argue the merits of the experts' comments. If this is a consensual procedure, the only problem I see, other than time and expense, is exposure to factual assertions de hors the record. This could possibly be dealt with by a strict rule precluding any reliance on extrarecord fact assertions in deciding the appeal.

Comment

Stephen G. Breyer

Bill Ross's chapter is very useful as a brief account of the role of the courts. The main issue is highlighted with great skill: should judges seek to review the substance of agency decisions more closely, or should they try to control the outcome of agency decisions by insisting upon fair agency procedures?

I agree with the general theme of the chapter. It says, "Get the courts out. The less, the better." As a practical or logistical matter, it is nearly impossible for courts to become deeply involved in agency work. The First Circuit, which consists of four judges on active status, hears oral argument one week each month. Typically, each judge sits on three or four of those days as a member of a three-judge panel. Before argument, he or she must become familiar with anywhere from twenty to thirty cases, a task that involves digesting voluminous briefs and appendixes and examining leading authorities. Upon completion of the week of oral argument, each judge is assigned to write from six to nine opinions. This often requires a reading of trial transcripts or records of agency proceedings amounting to thousands of pages. In short, the magnitude of the demands on judicial resources is quite apparent.

Looking at the matter logistically, one might think that there would be public pressure that the courts undertake less review of what agencies are doing. Instead, the clamor at present is in the opposite direction. At least Congress seems to be saying that judges should become more involved in what the agencies are doing. When the Bumpers amendment, which provided that judges should subject agency action to greater scrutiny, without deference to the agency in certain areas, was on the Senate floor, the Judiciary Committee staff did not believe it would pass. The White House did not feel that the amendment was a matter of concern, nor did the EPA. But Senator Bumpers said that those for regulatory reform should vote for it, and the amendment passed, fifty-six to twenty-two.

The force behind the Bumpers amendment and other such proposals is fairly evident. It is not that agency decisions are becoming increasingly more technical but that agencies are making more important decisions now using informal rule making than previously; they are "legislating" far more. Thus, rules emanate from the Federal Trade Commission on undertakers, from the National Highway Transportation Safety Administration on auto safety, and from the Environmental Protection Agency on water pollution. These rules are highly significant, perhaps more significant than most of the laws that Congress may enact in a typical session.

At the same time, people feel that the agencies are out of control. They are skeptical about various possible checks on agency decisions. The "discipline of the science of management," as a check, is not credible, and the informal rule-making procedure itself provides little check. The agency rule-makers are not elected; the inadequacy of these checks may lead to a feeling that agency decisions lack legitimacy. The public currently is placing its hope for reform in a solution that states: "Let's get somebody with authority to look at what the agency is doing." In the United States, there are only three sources of authority: the executive branch, personified by the president, the Congress, and the judiciary.

The call for presidential control of the agencies is exemplified by the Cutler and Johnson[1] and similar proposals. Their sponsors believe that they will bring about more-responsible agency decision making. However, certain arguments made against greater control by the president have lessened the popularity of this approach. First, the president, in his decision making, will arguably be too political. Second, increased control will result in replication of the staffs of the agencies themselves inside the president's own executive office. There is much to be said for increased presidential authority, but the spotlight is elsewhere at the moment.

A second candidate to control the agencies is the Congress, with its legislative veto. Proponents believe that the legislative veto is a healthy way to get the public's view before the agency before it issues regulations. But opponents ask whether the staffs of Congress should start running the agencies.

A third possible locus for control of the agencies is the courts, and this currently is the popular approach. Thus judges are being urged to review agency decisions more closely. Given the increasingly legislative activity of the agencies, exercised through unelected officials, that judges should review the result more stringently to check abuse of agency power is not surprising. But how are judges to exercise their own responsibility?

As Bill Ross has pointed out, there are two main forms that increased judicial review of agency rule making might take. First, judges might examine more closely the procedures that agencies use in reaching their decision. Second, they might examine more closely the substance of the decision itself.

The procedural direction has been very much influenced by Judge David Bazelon. It is based upon the view that courts do not, or cannot, know much about the substance of what agencies do but they do know about procedures. To a judge, fair procedure means courtlike procedure. I am not certain that courtlike procedure is always the right procedure for an agency. Scientists in fact may believe that fair procedure means something very different. In any event, at the moment, pursuit of this approach without new legislation has been hindered by the Supreme Court, which apparently disapproved it in the *Vermont Yankee* case.[2]

The second approach, associated with Judge Harold Leventhal, is less concerned with procedure. It urges the judge conscientiously to determine whether the agency decision was rational and not arbitrary. And at least in important cases, it would have the judge look more deeply into the underlying facts.

Before I became a judge, I tended to favor the second approach strongly. Insofar as my brief experience as a judge has changed my views, it has made me somewhat more aware of the wisdom of the procedural approach. I am far less certain than I was that judges have the time sufficient to make the second approach work. On the other hand, my preliminary experience has served to reconfirm my view that court procedure is often not the best model for agencies seeking to formulate rules.

The lawyers' instinct, and the judges' instinct, is to favor procedure that requires that a matter be decided on a record, giving each side an opportunity to present evidence and argument, followed by decision. This is what judges do for the most part: they review records, where the parties have had an opportunity to present evidence and to make arguments.

That system has strengths and weaknesses. Its primary strength is that it is fair, assuming roughly equivalent resources for the parties. Both sides have an equal opportunity to present arguments and to counter the arguments of others. Court procedure also tends to ensure that a controversy is definitely settled, and it yields fairly accurate results. Court procedure seems to work best where what is important is that a matter be settled, in a manner perceived as fair, and where the matter rests upon individual (adjudicative) facts that can be placed in a record.

The major weakness of court procedure is that the more the issue is one of general policy, the less reason there is to believe that courts can find the truth, given their limited sources of information and dependence upon a record. Is carnauba wax really dangerous, or not? Will a record created by paid advocates reveal, or hide, the truth? Will a record remain accurate? A record is made over a long period of time and is difficult to update. I am not convinced that on matters of general policy, a formal legal record produces accurate results as opposed to fair results. In adjudication or dispute settlement, settling the dispute fairly may be more important than getting the right result. However, in a rule-making context, accuracy is important, and getting the right rule may be more important than getting a rule quickly or even getting one at all.

These facts suggest that, on balance, a substantive approach to court review of agency rule making is preferable to the imposition of more-courtlike procedures. The substantive approach allows the agency more procedural freedom, permitting it to go outside the record, where necessary, but it still provides some court control, to the extent needed to determine whether the agency result is reasonable. There are still many serious problems in giving a judicial hard look to many scientifically based agency decisions. One major difficulty arises from the fact that many technical agency decisions involve lawyers and scientists working together. Lawyers and scientists are governed by different canons of good performance. Thus, an agency might reach results that would look irrational to a judge but are rational from the scientist's perspective.

Let me give an example. Lawyers, judges, or policymakers must take all relevant factors into account, even if only superficially, when making a decision. They are faulted for omitting from their account any important factor that may bear upon the ultimate legal issue or the ultimate policy judgment. If they fail to consider whether saccharin promotes weight loss—even if they do not know anything about the questions—they are criticized, and their policy result is attacked. Scientists, on the other hand, are trained to hold other things equal and to go into one issue thoroughly. They are faulted if they do not treat thoroughly the matter that they do not hold constant. Therefore, scientists are more likely to characterize the evidence—for example, as good evidence or slight evidence—and they will leave the policy conclusion to the policymaker. A scientist who is asked whether saccharin should be banned might reply, "Speaking as a scientist, I do not know. But I am happy to state what studies show—whether they constitute good evidence, or bad evidence, or evidence that means nothing."

Since the scientist's scientific judgment is often limited to characterizing some of the evidence in accordance with scientific canons, the agency and the judge may find it particularly difficult to decide what reasonably follows from the scientist's conclusion. If the scientist determines that saccharin may be dangerous to health, does that mean that the product should be available to the consumer? If the agency decides to ban it, can the judge easily determine whether the decision maker, who is a lawyer or an agency head, was rational or irrational when accepting the scientist's statement as a basis for the ban? The question is a vexing one.

The problem is made still more difficult by the fact that scientists often have strong feelings about the proper policy outcome. In principle, scientists only give opinions on the state of the evidence, but in fact, they may try to sway policy judgment. Thus, scientists who evaluate drugs know what the words "there is good evidence," or "there is not good evidence," or "there is slight evidence" will signify to the head of the Food and Drug Administration. If they say there is slight evidence of safety, they may know that means (to the FDA) "ban the product"; if they state that there is something more than slight evidence, they may know that means "don't ban the product." Hence, scientists may develop a series of coded understandings, highly relevant to the final resolution of a matter by the decision maker, yet not articulated in the record, and thus not visible to the reviewing judge. Similarly unarticulated but fundamental are the different philosophical viewpoints from which people approach a problem, the differing value judgments and assumptions about the role of science, and the choices society should make. All of these features play a role in the agency's decision. Perhaps they should do so, but they make it difficult for a reviewing judge to assess a decision's rationality. Indeed, the closer the judge examines the decision, the less rational it may appear.

Hard look review is difficult for other reasons as well. Scientists and agencies are often working in areas in which there is great scientific uncertainty, such as those involving the relationship of pollution, drugs, or chemicals with cancer. Rationality of a decision would be easier to assess if we knew what causes cancer, but we do not. Neither economics nor cost-benefit analysis offers any easy answer to the problem. Cost-benefit analysis is time-consuming; it involves complex proceedings; it raises difficult questions of valuation, risk, and evidence. And its postulates are subject to change.

Despite these and other problems, I still favor the hard look approach, for I fear the overjudicialization that the procedural approach might bring about. Also, I am intrigued by Bill Ross's notion that we should bring scientific experts into the courts of appeal. Finally, although these remarks are highly impressionistic, they should point out that regulatory reform is not likely to be much affected one way or the other by tinkering with standards of judicial review. If agencies go wrong, I doubt that one can rely upon a judge to set the matter straight by reviewing a record for the use of proper procedure or for the rationality of the agency's conclusion.

Notes

1. Cutler and Johnson, *Regulation and the Political Process*, 84 Yale L.J. 1395, 1414-1418 (1975).

2. I have written about Vermont Yankee in *Vermont Yankee and the Courts' Role in the Nuclear Energy Controversy*, 91 Harv. L. Rev. 1833 (1978).

4 Some Thoughts on Science and Scientists in the 1980s

J. William Haun

The Scientific Method and Ethos

The Method

The scientific method and science as we think of it evolved as a way of evading the endless circular debates of the philosophers over the way the universe is structured and operates. Like many other disciplines, it is simple in concept but extremely difficult in practice.

The essence of the method is straightforward:

1. Out of experience, theory, speculation, or a flash of inspiration, the scientist forms a hypothesis.
2. An experiment is planned to test the hypothesis. Part of a rigorous experimental plan is the decision in advance as to the possible outcomes, specifically that outcome that will support the original hypothesis.
3. The experiment is conducted. The rules of sound practice require sufficient documentation of the apparatus, the technique, and the environment so that any other trained person could exactly reproduce the experiment.
4. The experiment, regardless of outcome, must be replicated enough times to eliminate the possibility of chance.
5. The hypothesis is confirmed, proved wrong, or an unexpected outcome results, in which case nothing useful about the hypothesis has been learned. Note, though, that unexpected outcomes are a fertile source of truly new thinking.

A hypothesis that has some basis in abstract thought or observation becomes a theory. Most theories remain just that because they cannot be unambiguously tested experimentally, even though they may be widely accepted and even believed passionately. Darwin's theory of natural selection is an example. The deductive proof from many sources of evidence and reason support it, but no experiment can be devised that will finally prove Darwin was right.

A theory that has been proved adequately, or at least has been around long enough to be acceptable, may gradually become a law; we all know the law of gravity, at least in our sensory experiential world. Many know the laws of thermodynamics, and there are other such laws. What is hard to accept is that once the laws were merely theories competing for proof among others and that at another level, where Einstein lived and worked, the law of gravity is only a limiting simplification of an immensely complex relationship nearly impossible to confirm or deny by experiment.

The difficult concept that delimits the validity of scientific laws or theories is the framework within which they are set. The laws of thermodynamics, for example, apply only to bodies of finite size and break down utterly at molecular and atomic levels until they are mere probabilistic statements.

Thus the only scientific facts ever to have existed are the raw data collected by the same methods in a repeated experiment. Everything else in science is inferential, descriptive, and the product of a human mind.

The Ethos

Scientific work in its truest sense can proceed only in a framework in which every step, every conclusion, is subjected to rigorous challenge and defense. The classic way to do this was the presentation of the thesis in an open meeting, followed by discussion, question and answer, and leaving to each participant the resolution of the issue. There are no judges. As the numbers of scientists have grown, the process has become institutionalized in the refereed journal. Such a journal accepts a responsibility to ensure that articles submitted for publication are significant, reporting some significant information that may be of value to other scientists, and that the quality of work and conclusions are suitable to be relied upon by others.

The referees are authoritative, accepted workers who have agreed to review, comment upon, and advise the editor on the value of the work reported for publication. Most recognized journals guard this process with great care, and it is an excruciating one for the aspiring author.

The idea is that every published article meets at least minimum standards of quality and reliability. Many articles are rejected. Usually only a few people would know of a rejection, and the author may try to submit the work to another publication.

Big Science and the Deterioration of the System

As the recognition of science has grown in this century and the scale of research has increased, changes have occurred that have nearly extinguished science in the classic mold.

Increasing costs have almost eliminated the independent investigator. When simple analytical instruments costs $100,000 or more and require full-time specialists to maintain and operate them, the free investigator is unable to work. Some experiments in physics may cost millions of dollars just to obtain the equipment. Thus, the opportunity to do research is conditioned on finding a sponsor to support the work financially, and in modern science, that sponsor makes the rules.

The reality of modern science also has other facets. Funding is dependent on someone's concept of value received, so results must be forthcoming. Publishing is a matter of institutional prestige. A contribution is from NCI, Sloan Kettering, Dow Chemical, or some other sponsor. The actual author may be (usually is) a graduate student or postdoctoral fellow, although the principal investigator's name is the one on the paper, and often for good reason: it was that person's idea. Funds come often from short-term grants or project budget authority, and the sponsor expects regular progress reports. Finally, most of the scientists often called as authorities are full-time research directors; almost never are they full-time researchers. Their role is to pull in the sponsors and keep them happy with their investments.

The result is that there are many scientists and little science to be found in the world of big science, making it ever more difficult to differentiate between science and the opinion of scientists. Public statements and publications or both that will alienate the powers of the granting agencies will be unlikely to survive the review process.

The independent scientist is rare. Overall approximately 80 percent of funding for basic research comes from the federal government. It is very difficult to oppose a granting agency publicly. Even Leonardo spent most of his life making toys.

Comment

Clifford Grobstein

Editors' Note: The following excerpts from Clifford Grobstein's work, which appears in full in chapter 6, are presented here because they relate directly to the subject of this chapter and illustrate how science has evolved new responsibilities.

The scientific contribution to policy and decision making, whether in regulation or other areas, has three conceivable components. The first is substantive, having to do with assembly and interpretation of relevant scientifically valid information. A second is transitional in the sense that it proceeds beyond the strictly substantive but is not truly decisional. The third component is the decision process itself, occurring in the complex context of the social arena with conflicting values and interests playing their roles in a structured political framework.

    The generality of the phenomenon [of science in the policy mode] is indicated by the establishment of the National Institute for Occupational Safety and Health (NIOSH) and the National Center for Toxicological Research, federal scientific agencies created to provide accurate information on materials primarily of policy interest. The expanded need for scientific analysis of policy issues also is well illustrated by the expanded and altered activities of the NAS. It is my impression that the legitimate scope of these activities necessarily goes beyond the simple assembly and interpretation of existing data, the first and essential scientific contribution to policymaking. Beyond this, scientific expertise is necessary to recognize the need for new data accumulation to anticipate emerging issues, to point to possible or probable implications of new courses of action of changes of circumstance, to interpret for various audiences the scientific and technical content of political issues, and to provide access to decision makers to the best and latest technical information. This is the content of the transitional component. It is the province of policy-centered and decision-oriented science, bridging into the decision process but stopping short of the decision itself. Such science in the policy mode must remain free of advocacy but must also be free of constraints that limit its effectiveness in substantially enriching decision arenas, with equal access to all contending parties. The practice of such science requires something different from the usual characteristics of either fundamental or technologically oriented applied science. Greater resolution of and attention to this emergent scientific area is a task for the immediate future.

    .

Part II
Five Case Studies of
Special Mechanisms

Part II
First-Line Strategies:
Social Interaction

5

OSHA's Generic Carginogen Policy: Rule Making under Scientific and Legal Uncertainty

Thomas O. McGarity

Cancer is a major health problem in the United States. Although scientists have known since at least 1775 that exposure to chemicals in the work place can cause cancer in workers, serious governmental efforts to reduce the incidence of cancer in the work place did not begin until the early 1970s after the enactment of the Occupational Safety and Health Act of 1970 (OSH Act).[1] Even with a strong mandate from Congress, the Occupational Safety and Health Administration (OSHA) found the process of setting standards for carcinogens in the work place tedious and controversial. The job was tedious because it required lengthy public hearings and detailed explanations; it was controversial because many of the issues that the agency had to resolve were on "the frontiers of scientific knowledge."[2] Most of the important questions that arise in attempts to regulate potential carcinogens generate robust scientific disagreements that are difficult, if not impossible, for nonscientist decision makers to resolve.

If the scientific uncertainties were not difficult enough, OSHA's regulatory actions have also been on the cutting edge of administrative law. Virtually all of OSHA's standard-setting actions have been challenged in court,[3] and the Supreme Court's recent decision in the *Benzene* case, *Industrial Union Department, AFL-CIO* v. *American Petroleum Institute*,[4] guarantees that OSHA's standards will continue to be litigated.

Despite the obvious difficulties that OSHA faced in attempting to implement the OSH Act, the agency was heavily criticized in the mid-1970s for failing to promulgate a generic rule to guide future standard-setting actions for carcinogens. The substance of the generic carcinogen policy (GCP) that resulted reflected the efforts by several civic-minded scientists to codify for

I would like to express my gratitude to Mary Lewis Janes and Monique Ferrell, both of the class of 1981, University of Texas School of Law, for their assistance in the preparation of this chapter.

regulatory purposes a body of cancer principles. OSHA applied its technology-based regulatory approach to the principles to yield a mechanism under which definite, preordained regulatory consequences attached to the classification of a substance as a carcinogen. Not surprisingly this far-reaching generic rule has also been challenged in court, and after a year spent in deciding which court would hear the challenge, the validity of OSHA's generic approach should be decided shortly.

History of the OSHA Generic Carcinogen Policy

Pressures to Articulate a Carcinogen Policy

In the first four years of OSHA's existence, the agency had proposed only four complete standards and had completed administrative proceedings for only three of those four.[5] In the next two years, OSHA proposed standards for five more chemicals[6] but promulgated final standards for only one. Mounting criticism of the agency's glacial pace[7] culminated in a 1976 report of the House Government Operations Committee[8] and an investigation by the General Accounting Office (GAO). Both reports criticized OSHA for concentrating on minor safety problems at the expense of larger health problems.[9] The GAO investigation concluded that neither OSHA nor the National Institute for Occupational Safety and Health (NIOSH) "had an adequate policy and guidelines on the evidence needed to regulate a substance as a cancer-causing agent,"[10] and the GAO recommended that the agencies establish "a common policy and guidelines for developing and reviewing evidence and deciding whether a substance should be regulated as a carcinogen."[11] By the time that the GAO report was completed for submission to Congress, a generic cancer policy was already germinating in OSHA, and on January 20, 1977, a draft GCP was transmitted to the National Advisory Committee for Occupational Safety and Health for review.[12] The assistant secretary could then in subsequent oversight hearings point to the development of the GCP in answering criticisms that the agency was not moving quickly enough to promulgate health standards.[13]

Origins of the Content of the GCP

Although various scientific bodies had for years been articulating principles for evaluating the carcinogenic risk of chemicals,[14] a key historical document for OSHA and EPA was a Report to the surgeon general, "Evaluation of Chemical Carcinogens," prepared in 1970 by a panel of scientists from government and academia assembled by National Cancer Institute scientist

Dr. Umberto Saffiotti at the request of the surgeon general.[15] Although never formally published in a scientific journal,[16] the document (hereinafter referred to as the ad hoc committee report) accompanied Saffiotti's testimony in two 1971 Senate hearings.[17] The report recommendations articulate the conservative, risk-averse approach toward regulating potential carcinogens that ultimately became regulatory policy in OSHA:

> Any substance which is shown conclusively to cause tumors in animals should be considered carcinogenic and therefore a potential cancer hazard for man. . . .

> No level of exposure to a chemical carcinogen should be considered toxicologically insignificant for man. For carcinogenic agents a "safe level for man" cannot be established by application of our present knowledge. The concept of "socially acceptable risk" represents a more realistic notion. . . .

> Evidence of negative results, under the conditions of the test used, should be considered superseded by positive findings in other tests. . . .

> The implication of potential carcinogenicity should be drawn both from tests resulting in the induction of benign tumors and those resulting in tumors which are more obviously malignant. . . .

> The principle of zero tolerance for carcinogenic exposures should be retained in all areas of legislation presently covered by it and should be extended to cover other exposures as well. . . .

> An ad hoc committee of experts should be charged with the task of recommending methods for extrapolating dose-response bioassay data to the low response region.[18]

The document is as much a statement of a prudent regulatory policy as it is a compendium of scientific principles.[19] In addition to prescribing criteria for identifying carcinogens and assessing their risks, the document prescribed a regulatory policy of zero tolerance for carcinogens.

In promulgating emergency temporary standards for fourteen potential carcinogens, OSHA relied heavily upon the ad hoc committee report to justify its use of laboratory animal data to support its conclusion that the chemicals posed carcinogenic risks to humans.[20] It neglected, however, to place the report in the rule-making record. The third circuit therefore remanded twelve of the standards to the agency and vacated the other two.[21] In the rule making on the permanent standards for the fourteen carcinogens, however, OSHA was careful to include the ad hoc committee report. Quoting from the report, the Third Circuit upheld the standards with one minor exception.[22] Recognizing that the mouse-to-man question was highly policy

dominated, the court opined that "what the Secretary has done in extrapolating from animal studies to humans is to make a legal rather than a factual
determination."[23]

The ad hoc committee report next made its appearance in the Environmental Protection Agency's (EPA) DDT cancellation hearings conducted
under the Federal Insecticide, Fungicide, and Rodenticide Act (FIFRA).[24]
Saffiotti testified at the hearing and read portions of the ad hoc committee
report into the record.[25] EPA lawyers then drew on Saffiotti's testimony in
their brief, which listed seven "general principles applicable to determination of carcinogenic hazards."[26] Saffiotti testified again in the hearing that
followed EPA's notice of intent to suspend the registrations of aldrin-
dieldrin,[27] and lawyers for EPA drew on his testimony to summarize nine
cancer principles.[28]

In the notice of intent to suspend the registrations of heptachlor-chlordane, the administrator set out his "basis for evaluating the carcinogenicity
of pesticides," which very closely resembled the nine cancer principles
listed in the aldrin-dieldrin brief.[29] Nevertheless, EPA again presented
testimony from cancer experts, many of whom had testified at the aldrin-
dieldrin suspension hearings in support of its conservative approach
toward identifying and assessing the risks of potential carcinogens.[30] The
D.C. Circuit on appeal rejected the pesticide registrant's argument that the
administrator's adherence to the cancer principles improperly biased him
against the registrant's position on those principles, pointing out that the
agency had relied on expert reports and the testimony of expert witnesses
and that EPA had given the registrant an opportunity to present its own
witnesses.[31]

The administrator's express adoption in his heptachlor-chlordane suspension notice of a "basis for evaluating the carcinogenicity of pesticides"
generated concern among some agency scientists that agency lawyers had
articulated an agency cancer policy without sufficient scientific help. The
nine cancer principles had also attracted criticism from organizations outside EPA.[32] In preparation for a meeting with the administrator and agency
scientists, the associate general counsel for pesticides asked Saffiotti to summarize the principles that EPA witnesses had articulated in the various pesticide hearings.[33] Saffiotti responded with a draft for discussion that listed
seventeen principles of carcinogenesis, which stressed the environmental
origins of a majority of human cancers, the presumptive applicability of
laboratory animal bioassays to humans, the irreversibility of the carcinogenic
process, the lack of any demonstrated threshold for carcinogenesis, the
limited usefulness of most negative epidemiological studies, and the absence
of any clear-cut distinction between a benign tumorigen and a malignant
tumorigen.[34] Draft principle 5 probably best summarizes the thrust of Saffiotti's draft: "Any substance which has been shown to cause tumors in any

mammalian species in adequately conducted studies at any dose level must be considered a carcinogenic hazard to humans, unless proven otherwise."

EPA lawyers then attempted to secure explicit agency recognition of the seventeen cancer principles by filing a motion for official notice of the seventeen principles in the pending hearing involving the pesticide mirex.[35] The motion precipitated a flood of protests that lasted for seven months, during which the seventeen principles were reduced to "three basic facts."[36]

While the official notice motion and the heptachlor-chlordane suspension case were pending, an EPA scientist requested that the National Cancer Institute review EPA's nine cancer principles for scientific validity. Although this request was quickly withdrawn, the matter was nevertheless referred to the Subcommittee on Environmental Carcinogenesis of the National Cancer Advisory Board,[37] chaired by Dr. Phillippe Shubik. On November 10, 1975, the subcommittee met to consider EPA's cancer principles and to attempt to arrive at a functional definition of a chemical carcinogen.[38] Saffiotti's draft for discussion was circulated and criticized by Shubik. Other members of the subcommittee, however, seemed favorably disposed toward the Saffiotti document.[39] Saffiotti agreed that his principles did not adequately define chemical carcinogen for all purposes but stressed that they were based on the testimony of expert witnesses in EPA pesticide hearings. The subcommittee finally, at Shubik's insistence, decided to attempt its own definition.[40] One of the subcommittee members, Dr. Norton Nelson, later observed that though it was impossible, lawyers and regulators "would like to have an easy black and white answer."[41]

The nuances of the apparent rejection of the Saffiotti principles were not lost on lawyers for the pesticide companies. After Shubik announced to the full National Cancer Advisory Board that the subcommittee was of the opinion that the Saffiotti draft was not "an adequate definition of a carcinogen for use by regulatory agencies for legislative purposes,"[42] lawyers for Velsicol Chemical Company in the heptachlor-chlordane litigation and for Allied Chemical Company in the mirex litigation immediately seized upon this statement as a rejection of the seventeen principles by the subcommittee, and this apparently had a significant impact on the administrative law judge (ALJ) in the heptachlor-chlordane case.[43] Soon thereafter, he recommended that the agency not suspend heptachlor-chlordane.[44]

The document that finally emerged from the subcommittee in June 1976 did not depart in any significant degree from the Saffiotti draft.[45] The document did, however, contain a prefatory warning that is germane to attempts to address chemicals generically:

> The complexity of the problem dictates that the evaluation of the potential human hazards of a given agent must be individualized in terms of the chemical and metabolic aspects of that agent, its intended and other factors

pertinent to the case under consideration. Each case must be considered on
its own and criteria appropriate for one agency may not necessarily apply
to another.[46]

In April 1976 the EPA administrator rejected the Office of General
Counsel's attempt to have the seventeen principles officially noticed as
facts.[47] The administrator explained that "while I am convinced that the
proposed facts reflect the best available evidence . . . , a firm degree of
scientific certainty does not yet appear to have been achieved in this
area. . . . I remain convinced that [the] proposed 'facts' are valid principles
to support regulatory and adjudicatory actions under a public health statute
such as FIFRA. . . . However, I am not prepared at this time to elevate
these principles to officially noticed facts."[48]

Although the mirex official-notice motion was pending before the administrator, the agency was internally preparing a carcinogen policy. On
May 19, 1976, the agency circulated for comment its "Interim Procedures
and Guidelines for Health Risk and Economic Impact Assessments of Sus-
pected Carcinogens."[49] The document prescribes a weight-of-the-evidence
approach for assessing carcinogenic risks according to which the best evidence of human carcinogenicity consists of epidemiological studies in conjunction with confirmed animal tests. Animal tests in which the chemical-
induced malignant tumors, including benign tumors that are generally
recognized as early stages of malignancies, constitute substantial evidence.
In vitro tests and animal tests in which the chemical induces only benign
tumors that are generally accepted as not progressing to malignance constitute suggestive evidence of carcinogenicity. In addition to articulating a
flexible mechanism for classifying potentially carcinogenic chemicals, the
document further stated EPA's intention to utilize quantitative risk-assessment models for performing individual risk-benefit balances.[50]

Although the EPA document, which was the product of compromise
among the competing factions within EPA, does not depart dramatically
from the ad hoc committee's risk-averse approach toward carcinogen regulation, it is definitely not a strong statement of regulatory principles of carcinogenicity. For example, the document partially adopts the Shubik committee's
distinction between benign and malignant tumorigens, and for the first time,
it announces the agency's intent to rely upon quantitative risk assessment for
evaluating carcinogenic risks.[51] Many of the document's important aspects,
however, are almost lost in its excessive preoccupation with internal agency
procedures. One principle, however, clearly emerges from the document: the
agency's commitment to proceed on a case-by-case basis under its various
statutes. Since the weight of the evidence presumably will vary from chemical
to chemical, the administrative response can similarly vary. This first attempt
by a regulatory agency to articulate a clear regulatory policy on carcinogens

(other than the zero-risk approach of the Delaney clause) was obviously intended to maintain maximum regulatory flexibility.

The Development of the GCP in OSHA

The EPA interim guidelines did not satisfy those, like Saffiotti, who were convinced that a strong carcinogen policy could be articulated and applied in a regulatory context. Although the current administrator, Russell Train, seemed willing to apply conservative cancer principles on a case-by-case basis, he was apparently less willing to commit the institution to a generic regulatory policy of the sort advocated in the ad hoc committee report.[52] Hence although Train might be depended upon to render risk-averse decisions with respect to carcinogens, there were no guarantees that his successors would not weigh the evidence differently. The focus of the effort to articulate on across-the-board regulatory policy therefore shifted from EPA to OSHA.

The soil at OSHA was fertile. The agency had won several important appeals on its early carcinogen standards, one of which had relied heavily upon the ad hoc committee report. OSHA's reading of its statutory mandate, which had been approved in three circuits, precluded the agency from weighing the risks against benefits in setting standards for carcinogens. Hence, EPA's weight-of-the-evidence approach, which seemed more appropriate for risk-benefit balancing, did not fit well into OSHA's existing regulatory scheme. OSHA was under a great deal of pressure to speed up its issuance of health-based standards and was therefore not anxious to pursue difficult scientific and policy questions on a case-by-case basis. Finally, and perhaps most importantly, Anson Keller, who had been associate general counsel for pesticides in EPA during the DDT and aldrin-dieldrin hearings, was a special assistant to the assistant secretary of labor for OSHA. By the fall of 1976 Keller had drafted a proposed generic cancer policy, which was circulated for public comment.

The Proposed GCP: The detailed preamble to the proposed GCP generally adopted the conservative approach advocated by the ad hoc committee.[53] The essence of the GCP proposal was a four-part categorization scheme and a set of model regulations to match that scheme. The agency proposed to take immediate action only with respect to chemicals that fell into category I. Substances that caused an increased incidence of benign or malignant tumors or that reduced the latency period between exposure and tumor onset in humans, two mammalian test species, a single mammalian test species in more than one experiment, or a single mammalian test species if supported by short-term tests were presumed to fall into category I.[54] The presumption could be rebutted by showing: (1) that the tumors were caused by a physical rather than chemical stimulus; (2) that the route of exposure in animals was "grossly disproportionate relative to potential occupational routes of exposure"; (3) that the data were only "suggestive"; (4) that the data were "totally inadequate to establish any conclusion with respect to the carcinogenicity or non-carcinogenicity" of the substance; or (5) that for some other reason, the positive results in animals were "not scientifically relevant" to humans.[55] In addition, the assistant secretary also had discretion to place any other chemical into category I on the basis of any other sufficient evidence.[56] Any interested person could petition the agency to place a chemical into category I, and the agency was required to respond within specified time limits. If the agency, pursuant to request or on its own motion, classified a chemical as in category I, it was required to issue immediately an emergency temporary standard (following the format of the model emergency temporary standard detailed in the proposed GCP) and within sixty days issue a notice of proposed rule making in accordance with a model proposed standard that specified various labeling, monitoring, surveillance, and housekeeping requirements. In addition, the model standard required employers to reduce employee exposure to the lowest feasible level, unless there were less-hazardous substitutes for the chemical, in which case no exposure would be allowed.[57] At the rule-making hearing that followed, the issues would be limited to: (1) whether the substance was correctly placed in category I; (2) whether the classification had been rebutted according to the specified rebuttal criteria; (3) review of the determination of the lowest feasible level or the availability of less-hazardous substitutes; (4) whether the substance possessed unique properties that would make specific protective measures inappropriate or infeasible; and (5) the environmental impact of the regulation.[58] If the assistant secretary determined after the hearing that the agency position had prevailed, the agency was required to promulgate a standardized final regulation, which would be subject to judicial review.[59]

The Emergence of Other Government-Wide Carcinogen Policies: While OSHA was occupied with the GCP rule-making hearing, events were moving forward on other fronts. On November 7, 1977, the Environmental Defense Fund (EDF) petitioned the EPA to establish a policy governing the classification and regulation of carcinogenic air pollutants under the Clean Air Act closely resembling OSHA's proposed GCP.[60] On June 13, 1978, the Consumer Product Safety Commission (CPSC) issued an "Interim Policy and Procedure for Classifying, Evaluating and Regulating Carcinogens in Consumer Products."[61] CPSC, however, made its policy effective immediately. The chemical industry quickly persuaded a federal district court to enjoin the policy on the ground that it was really a rule requiring notice-

and-comment rule-making procedures.[62] After the same court rejected CPSC's attempt to clarify the nonregulatory character of its policy,[63] it was withdrawn.[64]

At the same time, other broader-based efforts to set government-wide carcinogen policies were germinating. Soon after the Carter administration was in place, the heads of OSHA, EPA, CPSC, and the Food and Drug Administration formed the Interagency Regulatory Liaison Group (IRLG).[65] This group adopted as one of its highest priorities the establishment of a general cancer policy to guide all four agencies. An IRLG working group, on July 6, 1979, completed a document entitled "Scientific Bases for Identification of Potential Carcinogens and Estimation of Risks."[66] Publication of this document was crucial to the completion of the OSHA GCP because the White House had signaled OSHA that it should not promulgate a final generic regulation on its own unless it could be made consistent with the IRLG's product. Therefore it was important to OSHA to have the IRLG document resemble the OSHA GCP as closely as possible.

Although the IRLG document adopted the same risk-averse approach toward identifying carcinogens as did the OSHA GCP,[67] it did not advocate the same regulatory scheme. At numerous junctures, the document stressed the need for individualized scientific judgment. For example, in summarizing the considerations necessary to determine whether a chemical poses a carcinogenic risk to humans, the document concluded:

> The judgment that a substance poses a carcinogenic hazard derives from the evaluation of the total evidence provided by all of the sources. Different data sources may not contribute equally to the cumulative evaluation, depending on the specific nature and extent of the data, the scientific quality of the studies, and the adequacy of their documentation.[68]

This statement, and others like it in the IRLG document, seem much closer to the EPA weight-of-the-evidence approach than to the OSHA presumption-rebuttal approach. Another point of apparent disagreement is the IRLG's tacit endorsement of risk-assessment models, which seems to conflict with the proposed GCP's major premise that carcinogenic risk quantification is so beclouded with uncertainties as to be virtually worthless as a regulatory device.

A second multiagency attempt to state a cancer policy originated in the Regulatory Council,[69] which was created by President Carter to aid in the coordination of federal regulatory initiatives.[70] The Regulatory Council effort, however, relied almost exclusively on the IRLG document for its scientific and regulatory conclusions.[71]

One final candidate for the government-wide carcinogen policy was an attempt by the President's Office of Science and Technology Policy (OSTP) to create a framework for federal decision making on carcinogens.[72] This document came as close to advocating the typical industry position on identifying carcinogens and assessing carcinogenic risk as any recent independent report. The framework accepted the relevance of animal tests to humans but only when the chemical is tested at a dose that would not have "measurably altered the metabolic or immune processes of the test animal."[73] OSTP even questioned the need to take immediate action on the basis of positive epidemiological data in the absence of confirming animal studies. The report advocated the use of risk-assessment models and suggested that best estimates rather than conservative estimates be used in risk assessments. Finally, OSTP agreed with the industry-created American Industrial Health Council that all of the evaluations and risk assessments should be performed by scientists, not policymakers, on a case-by-case basis.[74] The role of the public policymaker should be limited to weighing the scientifically assessed risks against the chemical's benefits.

The Final GCP: At the same time that the various carcinogen policies were receiving intensive attention from OSTP and the various other multiagency bodies, OSHA was reformulating its GCP.

The January 22, 1980, Final GCP: On January 22, 1980, OSHA issued its final GCP.[75] The preamble to this document, which was a virtual encyclopedia of scientific and economic information, analyzed in great detail the massive hearing record, drawing extensive quotes from the testimony of the various witnesses to the proceeding. The document reaffirmed the generally conservative approach toward occupational carcinogens that the proposed GCP expressed. The agency, however, made several significant changes in its regulatory approach.

Perhaps the most-significant change was the elimination of the automatic trigger for OSHA action. Rather than requiring OSHA to respond within thirty days to any petition to place a substance in category I, the final GCP established a priority-setting mechanism under which the agency may choose at its leisure from a priority list of ten candidates.[76] The final GCP otherwise retained the presumption-rebuttal format with some significant refinements. For category I chemicals,[77] the agency must at some point issue a proposed permanent standard that must contain specified requirements for exposure limits, monitoring, methods of compliance, housekeeping, waste disposal, and so forth.[78] The January 22, 1980, version of the GCP, like the proposed GCP, required that the exposure limit be set at the lowest feasible level, to be achieved primarily through engineering and work-practice controls, except that no exposure would be permitted where a suitable substitute substance exists.[79] The broad category I rebuttal criteria of the proposed GCP, however, were replaced in the final GCP by stringent threshold requirements specifying in great detail the kinds of rebuttal evidence that the agency would consider.[80] Many of these new criteria may have erected insurmountable barriers for parties who would attempt to rebut a category I classification.[81]

The Benzene *Case:* The OSHA GCP rule making did not take place in a regulatory vacuum. Although OSHA's technology-based regulatory approach had survived judicial scrutiny in three circuits, the appeal from the benzene standard, through a strange procedural quirk,[82] was heard in the unsympathetic Fifth Circuit. That circuit overturned the standard, ruling that OSHA must weigh the potential benefits of a permanent standard against its costs before imposing those costs upon the regulated industry.[83] The Supreme Court affirmed the Fifth Circuit, but for different reasons. Declining to decide whether the OSH Act required OSHA to balance costs against benefits in promulgating permanent standards, the plurality opinion held that before OSHA requires that exposure to a carcinogen be reduced to the lowest feasible level, the agency must make the threshold finding that a status quo exposure to a substance "poses a significant health risk in the workplace."[84] Because the January 22, 1980, version of OSHA's final GCP did not recognize a significant-risk threshold to prescribing its feasibility-limited exposure limit, it was apparently inconsistent with the Supreme Court's *Benzene* decision.[85]

The January 1981 Amendments to the GCP: The agency reacted to the *Benzene* decision during the waning moments of the Carter administration. On January 19, 1981, OSHA published deletions to the GCP that were to take effect immediately.[86] The deletions eliminated all reference to requirements that exposure levels for carcinogens be set at the lowest feasible level. The agency, therefore, signaled a willingness to consider evidence on risk-related matters other than the feasibility of alternative exposure levels. Since a risk-assessment model is the most obvious mechanism for determining the significance of the risk of a particular exposure, this indicates that OSHA will hear evidence on the merits of various risk-assessment models on a case-by-case basis.

On January 23, 1981, the agency published a notice of proposed rule making suggesting additional language that would require the agency to set exposure levels at "the lowest feasible level which is necessary to eliminate significant risk."[87] The agency further decided not to promulgate generic policies for determining whether a risk is significant or for evaluating specific risk-assessment models. Hence, evidence relevant to risk assessments will be considered in individual proceedings for purposes of assessing a chemical's risks, even if it will not be considered for purposes of identifying the chemical as a carcinogen.[88] An obvious example of such evidence would be the dose level of an animal test. That level would generally be irrelevant under the GCP for purposes of placing a chemical in category I; nevertheless, it would be quite germane to an assessment of the risk that the chemical posed to workers at low exposure levels. The *Benzene* case thus worked a profound change in the GCP.

Appropriateness of Generic Resolution of Legal, Policy, and Factual Questions in Carcinogen Regulation: OSHA's adoption of a generic approach toward carcinogen regulation is consistent with a judicially approved administrative trend away from case-by-case consideration of issues that arise repeatedly in individual rule makings or adjudications.[89] Generic resolution of recurring questions has at least three major advantages. First, it increases the efficiency of the administrative process by eliminating the need to consider the same questions over and over again in individual hearings.[90] Second, it offers an opportunity for broad public participation in the regulatory process by allowing parties who might not otherwise have the resources to participate in many individual cases to prepare a single thorough presentation to the agency.[91] In addition to ensuring more-accurate generic factual findings and better-balanced policy determinations, those who ordinarily do not participate in individual hearings are more likely to accept the results.[92] A third advantage of generic rule making is the limits it imposes upon administrative arbitrariness. Once the agency has articulated the principles that it proposes to depend upon in the future and has subjected those principles to public and judicial scrutiny, the agency has the burden of justifying any departures from those principles. This should discourage the agency from treating a similar case differently for political or other reasons.

Generic proceedings do, however, have significant disadvantages. To the extent that the answer to a generically resolved question varies from case to case, generic rule making reduces the accuracy of the resulting individual decisions. The agency can meet this objection by agreeing to waive the general rule in cases in which it is demonstrably inappropriate, but even this ameliorating feature can sacrifice accuracy to the extent that the threshold waiver requirements are excessively burdensome. Generic rule making on highly complex scientific and technological questions has the additional disadvantage of discouraging further research on the crucial factual issues.[93] In the words of the American Industrial Health Council, generic fact finding can "freeze science."[94] This objection can be met by a liberal willingness to amend the generic determination as more evidence accumulates but only to the extent that the agency is perceived to be open-minded toward new evidence. Moreover, an agency's inflexible adherence to generic determinations may contribute to a perception of unfairness among the regulatees or other interested groups. Finally, even efficiency can be sacrificed by generic determinations that ultimately cannot withstand review. An agency's generic efforts may be wasted if a reviewing court rules that they are unlawful or arbitrary and capricious. The courts may be expected to view more carefully the products of broad generic rule makings because the consequences of the administrative decisions are generally more far-reaching.[95]

Legal Questions

Generic resolution of basic legal questions is generally appropriate because an agency's interpretation of its statute is not likely to change from case to case. Moreover, generic rule making on legal questions raises none of the disadvantages of generic rule making. OSHA attempted to resolve at least one important legal question in the final GCP: whether the agency was legally authorized to take a technology-based approach toward setting exposure limits for carcinogens.[96] The Supreme Court in the *Benzene* case, however, rejected OSHA's pure technology-based approach and interposed a significance threshold to the agency's invocation of its feasibility requirement.[97] In addition, the Court has signaled that it will soon decide whether the technology-based approach has any applicability to OSHA's promulgation of health standards.[98] While the agency was unquestionably correct in attempting to resolve this key legal question generically, it discovered in midstream that its answer to the question was erroneous, and it was required to make time-consuming corrections to the GCP.[99]

Science-Policy Questions

The GCP attempts to resolve several questions that appear to be questions of scientific fact but actually require the application of regulatory policy. I have elsewhere referred to such questions as science-policy questions, and I have argued that agencies must carefully identify such questions and resolve them in accordance with result-oriented policies, the content of which must derive primarily from the agency's statute.[100] The agency can, as OSTP and the AIHC have suggested, defer to scientists to make these difficult determinations, but in doing so the agency is, in my judgment, impermissibly delegating its policymaking functions to a group of unaccountable experts. Since policy judgments must fill the factual voids, the scientists to whom such decisions are delegated will simply apply their own result-oriented policy preferences, which may or may not have a statutory basis. Scientists can be chosen for expert bodies on the basis of their political and ideological views, and the ad hoc committee and Shubik committee experiences illustrate how expert panels can be used by adversaries in the broader regulatory context.

The OSH Act prescribes a risk-averse policy according to which the agency is obliged to "err on the side of safety" in resolving science-policy questions.[101] Although the *Benzene* case appears to hold that the statute does not support agency action requiring the expenditure of gross sums of money to eliminate de minimis risks, the case does support a risk-averse approach toward identifying carcinogens.

Transscientific Questions: The no-effect-level question is a classic example of a transscientific question, which, until a great deal more is known about carcinogenesis, is purely a question of regulatory policy that should not vary from case to case. Since the experiment that would verify the existence of a no-effect level is impossibly impractical,[102] OSHA determined as a policy matter that it would not assume that exposure to a carcinogen below some threshold level is safe. The Supreme Court in the *Benzene* case did not directly address the question whether the OSH Act supports this policy determination, but it stated in dicta that "so long as they are supported by a body of reputable scientific thought, the Agency is free to use conservative assumptions in interpreting the data with respect to carcinogens, risking error on the side of over-protection rather than under-protection."[103] This language supplies strong support for OSHA's application of a risk-averse policy to transscientific questions.

Although the Court apparently accepted the agency's judgment that no no-effect levels exist for carcinogens, it demanded that OSHA do more than jump from this policy determination to a conclusion that any exposure to a carcinogen poses a significant risk.[104] Yet for the same reason that the no-effect level question is transscientific, the general shape of the carcinogenic dose-response curve at low doses is similarly transscientific. Since OSHA must now assess a chemical's risks to determine whether they cross the Court's significance threshold, the agency could generally address this transscientific question as well.[105] However, the agency has decided against doing this at the present time because it believes that it lacks sufficient experience with risk-assessment models to make a generic choice.[106]

Lack of Available Information: In many cases, the scientific uncertainty that plagues an agency's attempts to regulate chemicals is attributable largely to the lack of available information on a particular factual issue.[107] If the necessary information could be forthcoming within a relatively short time span, generic resolution of the issue is generally unwarranted because the acquisition of further data over a relatively brief period of time might significantly reduce the need for policy judgment to fill the factual gap. Moreover, generic resolution of such questions might discourage further research efforts aimed at reducing the uncertainty surrounding the issue. Probably the most-appropriate agency response to this kind of science-policy question is to specify generically in as much detail as possible the nature of information required to resolve the question in individual cases.

For example, OSHA might confront a study in which the chemical was introduced into an animal system in an unconventional manner such as subcutaneous injection. A straightforward application of the GCP would result in that chemical's being placed in category I. Yet scientists would probably disagree on whether the test demonstrated that the chemical posed a carcinogenic risk to humans by normal exposure routes. Presumably, further testing by normal routes could aid significantly in resolving the dispute. If that information is likely to be forthcoming within a reasonable period of time, it would probably be unwise for OSHA to resolve the dispute generically. However, OSHA might generically specify in detail the kind of data that would generally resolve the issue in individual cases. OSHA has in fact done this by determining generically that the oral, respiratory, or dermal routes are never irrelevant to human experience and that other routes will be considered inappropriate if the tumors are induced only at the site of administration and if evidence is provided that establishes that the induction of such tumors is related to the physical configuration of the substance and that tumors are not induced when the same material is administered in a different configuration.[108] This appears to be a reasonable approach, which ought to survive judicial review.

Varying Scientific Interpretations: Occasionally scientists interpret the same scientific data differently. Each scientist can objectively explain his or her interpretation of some kinds of data only to a point; past that point subjective considerations play an important role. This quasi-subjective process is occasionally referred to as the exercise of scientific judgment. Examples of issues requiring the exercise of scientific judgment include disagreements among pathologists as to the nature of the lesions caused by a chemical, varying interpretations of retrospective epidemiological studies, and disputes over the adequacy of laboratory-test methodologies. In all of these cases, policy considerations must fill the factual gap left by the scientific dispute.[109] The agency can, of course, allow an appointed group of scientists to fill in the gaps with their subjective policy preferences.[110] However, if the agency desires to control the policy input into such judgments, it must attempt to apply its own policy judgements to the factual uncertainties. Unfortunately, this can rarely be done generically without sacrificing a great deal of accuracy and perceived fairness to gain little administrative efficiency.

OSHA could, for example, promulgate detailed specifications for interpreting pathological data,[111] epidemiological studies,[112] and animal bioassays,[113] and simply refuse to acknowledge the existence of any data that do not meet the generically prescribed criteria. The agency would, however, be ill advised to adopt such an inflexible approach toward questions that depend so heavily upon scientific judgment. General criteria may simply not exist. Each scientist's evaluation may be based on the particular application of his or her own experience to the information so that each scientist's opinion would be sui generis. This might be the case should an agency decide to prescribe in detail how a pathologist should diagnose lesions produced by chemicals in particular organs. Presumably each pathologist currently applies subjective criteria to evaluate the tissues observed. Occasionally pathologists disagree with one another.[114] The disagreements probably do not stem from erroneous application of accepted diagnostic criteria; rather, the differences are probably due to the lack of any accepted criteria. Even if an agency could articulate result-oriented conservative or liberal criteria, it would be very difficult to determine whether one scientist's diagnoses differed from another's because of a disagreement over the application of the prescribed criteria or because of a disagreement over the criteria. To avoid this problem the agency might certify, according to result-oriented criteria, a group of scientists whose diagnoses would be accepted to the exclusion of all others. Although listening only to scientists who shared the agency's policy preferences would eliminate the need for time-consuming presentation and cross-examination of conflicting scientific testimony, such an approach would deprive the agency of participation by an informed group of scientists, and the accuracy and acceptability of agency decisions would thereby suffer. Moreover, both of the two suggested result-oriented policies would probably hinder future research and efforts to arrive at more-accurate and accepted diagnoses.

Even where scientifically accepted generic criteria exist, blind adherence to the criteria in individual cases may obscure scientific analysis. For example, even though several accepted statistical techniques exist for analyzing epidemiological and bioassay data, application of a particular technique in all cases may obscure important data such as the existence of very rare tumors or other factors not related to the test substance that could explain the statistical results. Unless biological as well as statistical considerations play a role in bioassay and epidemiological analyses, the accuracy of agency decisions will suffer with few corresponding efficiency gains.

For the most part, OSHA has wisely refrained from attempting to specify generic interpretational criteria, preferring instead to resolve interpretational debates as they arise in individual cases.[115] The GCP does, however, attempt generic resolution of at least one interpretational question: the criteria to be applied in interpreting negative epidemiological studies. The criteria that OSHA specifies for such studies are so stringent that any test that meets them almost certainly poses a low carcinogenic risk to humans. On the other hand, the stringent criteria may well deprive the agency of relevant information. The GCP preamble, however, appears to support adequately OSHA's contention that negative epidemiological studies that do not meet the criteria have very little information to convey.[116]

Curiously OSHA has specified no corresponding criteria for interpreting positive epidemiological studies, preferring instead to evaluate any arguably positive studies on a case-by-case basis. This one-sided approach rather clearly reflects the conservative policy of erring on the side of safety that OSHA has traditionally espoused. Whether that policy is strongly enough articulated in the OSH Act to justify OSHA's generic conclusion is an important question for judicial review.

Conflicting Inferences: Scientists occasionally agree upon a single interpretation for existing data but disagree over the proper inferences to draw from that interpretation. Examples of such disputes that have arisen in attempts to regulate carcinogens include the inference that substances that are carcinogenic in laboratory animals will be carcinogenic in humans, the inference that a substance that causes benign tumors will also cause malignant tumors, and the inference that a chemical that causes cancer in a large percentage of heavily exposed individuals will cause cancer in a smaller percentage of lesser-exposed individuals.[117] Since inferences are always based upon assumptions about the way the universe generally behaves, lay administrators are often capable of evaluating inferences. However, lay decision makers can evaluate inferences only to the extent that they are competent to evaluate the assumptions that undergird them. The administrative process can test those assumptions only to the extent that common sense is an appropriate litmus. Since a lay person's understanding is not always sufficient to dictate a choice between two competing assumptions, the regulator is occasionally forced to choose on the basis of policy considerations.[118] Normally this can be done generically because the assumptions that underly the competing inferences rarely vary from case to case.

Like generic specification of interpretational criteria, generic adoption of particular inferences can reduce the accuracy with which agencies make regulatory decisions. For example, a generic rule that laboratory animal studies be used to predict cancer risks in humans (which would be based on the assumption that chemicals are metabolized roughly the same way in most mammalian species or that differences in metabolism are irrelevant to chemical carcinogenesis) could result in erroneous decisions in cases where it could be shown that differences in metabolism between the test species and humans rendered the animal data irrelevant to human experiences.

Another potent objection to applying the generic approach to scientific inferences is the danger that adopting a single inference generically might discourage future research that could in turn undermine the assumptions underlying the inference. For example, an agency that refused to acknowledge any distinction between benign and malignant tumors might discourage research for benign tumorigens or for ways to halt the progress of benign tumors to malignancies.

OSHA has applied its quasi-generic presumption-rebuttal approach to both metabolism and the benign-malignant issues. The final GCP establishes a generic presumption that high-dose tests in laboratory animals will place a chemical in category I. The regulatee may rebut the presumption, however, by demonstrating, in accordance with generically specified criteria, that metabolic differences render the animal test irrelevant for assessing human risks.[119] Similarly, OSHA will presume that a substance that apparently causes only benign tumors is a malignant tumorigen, unless the regulatee can make certain generically prescribed showings that in essence undermine the assumption that a chemical that causes benign tumors will also cause malignant tumors.[120]

OSHA's presumption-rebuttal approach to inferential science-policy questions seems well conceived. OSHA appears to be eminently reasonable in agreeing to waive application of generic inferences if participants can meet designated criteria for demonstrating that the assumptions undergirding the inferences are erroneous. A presumption-rebuttal mechanism must pass three tests to avoid claims of arbitrariness, however. First, the assumptions underlying the agency's presumptions must be firmly grounded in fact and policy. Otherwise it makes little sense to presume their validity. Second, the rebuttal criteria must include all reasonably foreseeable instances where the generic assumptions will not hold. The agency should not, absent compelling efficiency needs, screen out legitimate exceptions to its presumptions. Finally, the rebuttal criteria should not be so stringent as to preclude attempts at rebuttal that have a reasonable basis in fact. Overly stringent rebuttal criteria will hamper needed research.[121]

Although the Fifth Circuit will ultimately decide the matter, OSHA's attempt to apply its presumption-rebuttal approach to inferential science-policy questions should survive the application of these tests. The preamble to the final GCP sets out in great detail the factual and policy bases for the assumptions underlying its presumptions. The agency seems to have identified all of the available rebuttal arguments. While the rebuttal criteria are quite stringent, the stringency seems justified in light of the current scientific uncertainties and OSHA's risk-averse policy preferences. As the Supreme Court has observed,[122] OSHA's preference to "err on the side of safety" has a reasonable basis in the OSH Act. Indeed OSHA's presumption-rebuttal format very closely resembles the Supreme Court-sanctioned summary judgment approach adopted by FDA for determining whether to deprive litigants of statutorily prescribed hearings.[123] Finally, the GCP's lenient amendment provisions should adequately protect against the possibility that some unanticipated scientific development will render the agency's inferences invalid in some or all cases.[124]

Effectiveness of the GCP Effort

OSHA's attempt to promulgate a generic carcinogen policy has already consumed substantial quantities of agency and private resources, and the end is not yet in sight.[125] At this point it is appropriate to ask whether the gains to the agency and the public have been worth the resource expenditures. In a sense, it is unfair to ask this question today because OSHA could not have anticipated many of the events, such as the formation of the IRLG and the Supreme Court's *Benzene* decision, that ultimately redirected and sometimes hindered its efforts. Moreover, the agency cannot now predict how many more hurdles it will be required to leap successfully in pursuit of the GCP. Yet the question can appropriately be asked at this juncture for two reasons: an administration much less sympathetic to the OSH Act's goals than the Carter administration might decide to forgo further expenditures on the effort and proceed as before on a case-by-case basis, and the OSHA experience up to this point should be relevant to other agencies (including OSHA itself) that are contemplating reducing administrative costs by adopting generic rules.

It is, of course impossible to determine whether the effort has been worthwhile without knowing what the goals for the GCP were and are. The history of the GCP reveals several possible goals for that effort ranging from the narrow practical goal of reducing the resources expended upon individual hearings by focusing them on the feasibility question, to the broader institutional goal of issuing more proposed and final health standards in less time, to the more-cosmic goal of forging a coherent government-wide carcinogen policy.

Increasing Hearing Efficiency

According to Anson Keller, the primary architect of the GCP, the immediate aim of the GCP was to refocus attention in individual hearings from the recurring scientific questions to the important nongeneric question of economic feasibility.[126] Conceptually the agency attempted to accomplish this through a two-step process. First, OSHA would specify generic criteria for identifying carcinogens. Second, since the OSH Act required, in OSHA's opinion, that worker exposure be reduced to the no-effect level if feasible, the agency applied the no no-effect level hypothesis for carcinogens to reach the generic conclusion that exposure to carcinogens must be reduced to the extent feasible. Therefore, meeting the modest goal of increasing hearing efficiency requires the agency to meet three tests: the definitional criteria must have an adequate basis in fact and policy; the no no-effect level hypothesis must have an adequate basis; and the agency's legal conclusion that, under the OSH Act, only feasibility concerns can limit OSHA's mandated reduction of health risks must be correct.

All of OSHA's definitional criteria and its no no-effect level determination should survive judicial review. OSHA seems to have done a reasonably good job at isolating for generic resolution recurring issues for which newly emerging scientific information is not likely to be critical and for which repeated litigation would be wasteful. Moreover, the agency has made reasonable provisions for rebuttal of those criteria in cases that do not fit the general pattern, although there is certainly room for debate on this point. Finally, the agency has made liberal provisions for amending the policy should its general prescriptions not fit an individual case. On the other hand, many of the issues that OSHA has generically resolved have large policy components, and courts are generally less reluctant to overturn agency policy prescriptions than they are to overturn agency factual determinations for which an agency's expertise is more relevant.[127] The GCP will pass the first two of the three tests only if it can persuade the Fifth Circuit that the OSH Act generally allows the agency to err on the side of protecting worker health. The Fifth Circuit has not been notably deferential to OSHA's policy judgments in the past, and it does not have a general reputation for deference to regulatory agencies.[128] Yet the court presumably will not ignore the Supreme Court's dicta to the effect that OSHA may risk "error on the side of over-protection rather than under-protection."[129] The final answer may well depend on how the Supreme Court resolves the pending cotton dust cases.[130]

Even if OSHA's definitional criteria pass judicial scrutiny, their utility will be limited if a large number of chemicals arguably meet the rebuttal criteria. Unlike other Court-approved generic rules,[131] the GCP is not intended to eliminate entirely the need for a hearing.[132] Since OSHA must use rule-making procedures to promulgate health standards,[133] it has no apparent mechanism for excluding irrelevant information that does not meet the rebuttal criteria. Hence, that information will find its way into the record, and OSHA personnel will have to at least acknowledge its existence. Although OSHA can respond to such information by brief reference to the GCP, even this takes time, and agency efficiency will thereby suffer.

Although the GCP definitional criteria and the generic no no-effect level finding have a good chance of surviving judicial review, the agency's legal conclusion quite clearly will not survive because it is inconsistent with the *Benzene* case. The Supreme Court in *Benzene* has held that before OSHA can require a regulatee to reduce health risks to a feasible level, the agency must make a determination that the risks were significant in the first place. The lynchpin of the pre-*Benzene* GCP regulatory scheme was the automatic triggering of the feasibility requirement once a chemical had met the category I criteria and survived rebuttal attempts. Not only was this the key time-saving mechanism, but it also shielded the agency from the complicated necessity of placing value on life.[134] Now OSHA must add a third step to its traditional two-step regulatory process. It must identify a chemical as a carcinogen and determine that the carcinogen poses a significant risk at present exposure levels. Finally, OSHA may reduce exposure to the lowest extent feasible.[135]

The addition of the middle step will increase the time and resources that health-standards hearings will consume. The pertinent question here is whether the second step is so intertwined with the first step as to render arbitrary any attempt to distinguish between the classifying chemicals and assessing their risks. Although it is difficult to speculate on this matter in the absence of any relevant OSHA experience, my initial assessment is that the two steps are conceptually distinct and that the GCP can be a valuable time saver. The evidence concerning a chemical's purported carcinogenicity is typically so sketchy as to permit few firm distinctions among chemicals on the basis of the strength of the evidence. An agency could therefore rationally decide to treat all chemicals that meet certain threshold tests as carcinogens for purposes of risk assessments, even though the existing evidence on one chemical appears to support that conclusion more firmly than the evidence on another chemical. An agency could equally rationally decide, as has EPA, to weigh the evidence of carcinogenicity subjectively into the assessment of the risk that each chemical poses to exposed humans.[136]

The OSHA generic identification approach allows the agency to avoid time-consuming arguments on whether chemicals for which positive epidemiological studies exist are more likely to be carcinogenic than chemicals for which only positive animal studies exist; whether chemicals that have been tested positive in three species are more likely to be carcinogenic than those that have been tested positive in only one species; and whether chemicals that have produced some benign and some malignant tumors are more likely to be carcinogenic than those that cause only malignant tumors.[137] On the other hand, the weight-of-the-evidence approach permits flexibility. It allows the agency to mix policy and evidence on a case-by-case basis. Yet the subjective weighing of indefinite evidence invites arbitrariness, and over time the agency may face the embarrassing question of why it is attempting to reduce exposure to a chemical that apparently poses a lower risk than one that it failed to regulate.[138]

It is not yet clear how OSHA plans to implement the middle step. The January 1981 changes to the GCP indicate only that OSHA seems willing to consider, for purposes of risk assessment, evidence that it would not consider for purposes of identification. Unfortunately, the amendments do not attempt to delineate which evidence that is irrelevant for identification is relevant for risk assessment. If OSHA is now willing to entertain all of the arguments that the GCP previously proscribed, then the agency has in effect adopted a weight-of-the-evidence approach. The identification aspect of the GCP will do little more than create a class of chemicals that the agency will examine more closely at the risk-assessment stage. OSHA could, however, decide to consider for risk-assessment purposes only evidence relevant to extrapolating from high doses to low doses. Under this approach, the characteristics of a chemical that caused it to be placed into category I would not be reevaluated for purposes of determining significance. The significance stage of the regulatory evaluation would consist only of the application of one or more risk-assessment models to the existing data. If the agency is unwilling to draw a firm line of this sort between the indentification stage and the risk-assessment stage of its evaluation of individual chemicals, then it can expect virtually no resource savings from its GCP.

The agency could improve efficiency still further by specifying generically a particular dose-response model for predicting carcinogenic effects at low exposure levels and by generically prescribing a risk level that the agency will always consider significant. The agency, however, has so far declined to extend its generic approach this far because it has had insufficient experience with the risk-assessment models to form a basis for choosing among the available alternatives. In any event, this logical extension of the generic approach to the Supreme Court-mandated risk-assessment phase of OSHA's regulatory process would seem to put OSHA in the position of placing values on lives threatened or lost, which it has vigorously avoided in the past. Rather than follow its generic approach to its logical conclusion, the agency may, in light of the dramatic shift in focus brought about by the *Benzene* case, decide to abandon the GCP in favor of the more-flexible, and hence more-discretionary, weight-of-the-evidence approach.

Increasing the Number of Standards

If OSHA's principal goal was to reduce outside criticism and pressure to issue more health standards, then the GCP has been a great success, even if it never goes into effect. The pressure to issue more standards virtually ceased when OSHA announced the proposed GCP.[139] Yet it is doubtful that the agency would have committed such an extraordinary amount of energy to the GCP effort if its predominant goal was merely to deflect outside criticism. It is probably best to take at face value the statement in the preamble to the final GCP that the primary purpose of the GCP was to speed up the issuance of health standards.[140] According to the proposed GCP's preamble, the speed-up would be accomplished in two ways. First,

OSHA would voluntarily require itself within a specified period of time to respond to petitions requesting that standards be proposed for particular chemicals. Second, since the more-efficient hearings would consume fewer agency resources, more resources presumably be available for additional hearings.

The automatic trigger, however, is not likely to accelerate the pace at which the agency issues standards, for a very simple reason: the agency eliminated it from the final GCP.[141] Moreover, while the generic determination of some issues should increase the efficiency with which the agency can conduct individual hearings, this will probably not appreciably affect the agency's overall pace. Even if hearings were eliminated entirely, the pace at which OSHA proposes and issues regulations would probably not accelerate appreciably. Table 5-1 shows that the time consumed in actual hearings is a miniscule proportion of the time consumed between the moment the agency is asked to promulgate a standard and the time it issues a final standard. The glacial pace at which the agency has issued health standards has deeper reasons, including White House pressure to delay issuance of standards,[142] inadequate and/or incompetent staff in the Standard Division,[143] poor management,[144] rapid turnover in leadership,[145] poor interaction between managers in OSHA and scientists in the National Institute for Occupational Safety and Health,[146] poor interaction between OSHA and its lawyers in the Office of the Solicitor of Labor,[147] and the requirement that OSHA perform lengthy regulatory analyses before it issues standards.[148] While streamlining the hearings will probably enhance the agency's efficiency somewhat, it is not likely to aid the agency greatly in reaching its goal of increasing its output of health standards, if indeed that is any longer a goal for the agency.[149]

Forging a Consistent Intra-Agency Carcinogen Policy

Another less-obvious goal of the GCP was to mandate a consistent carcinogen policy for the agency itself. Although many different assistant secretaries had at one time or another signed final standards with preambles that adopted risk-averse regulatory principles, the broad contours of the agency's evolving policy and the details of that policy were not available to agency employees in a single place. Long-time agency personnel understood the agency's policy, but newcomers could not rapidly absorb it. A written uniform policy could be absorbed and applied by all employees, thus ensuring consistency of approach throughout the agency. Moreover, if the policy were promulgated as a rule, it would be binding upon future assistant secretaries.

It is difficult to assess whether the GCP will meet this goal. If the GCP is pursued through the courts and it remains more or less intact, one

Table 5-1
Chronology of GCP and Related Hearings

	DBCP	Asbestos	Cotton Fiber Dust	Beryllium	Sulfur Dioxide	Noise	Lead	Acrylonitrile	Benzene	Arsenic	Coke Oven Emissions	Vinyl Chloride	Fourteen Carcinogens
Criteria Document or petition	None	None	Sept. 26, 1974		June 1974		Jan. 1973	Sept. 29, 1977	Aug. 1976	Nov. 8, 1974	Feb. 1973	Jan. 22, 1974	Jan. 4, 1973
ANPR	None	Jan. 12, 1972	Dec. 27, 1974				None	None	None		None	None	July 16, 1973
Proposed standard	Nov. 1, 1977	Jan. 12, 1972	Dec. 28, 1976	Oct. 17, 1975	Nov. 24, 1975	Oct. 1974	Oct. 3, 1975	Jan. 17, 1978	May 27, 1977	Jan. 21, 1975	July 24, 1975	May 10, 1974	July 16, 1973
Beginning of hearing	Dec. 13, 1977	Mar. 14, 1972	April 5, 1977 April 10, 1977 May 10, 1977	Aug. 1977	May 3, 1977	June 23, 1975 Sept. 21, 1976	May 3, 1977	Mar. 21, 1978	July 19, 1977	April 8, 1975 Sept. 8, 1976	Nov. 4, 1975 May 4, 1976	June 25, 1974 July 8, 1974	Sept. 11, 1973
End of hearing	Dec. 15, 1977	Mar. 17, 1972	April 8, 1977 April 12, 1977 May 12, 1977	Sept. 1977		July 30, 1975 Oct. 8, 1976	(7 weeks)	April 4, 1978	Aug. 10, 1977	April 14, 1975 Sept. 14, 1976	Jan. 8, 1976 May 14, 1976	June 28, 1974 July 11, 1974	Sept. 14, 1973
Final standard	Mar. 15, 1978	June 7, 1972	June 19, 1978	Pending		Pending	Nov. 14, 1978	Oct. 3, 1978	Feb. 10, 1978	May 5, 1978	Oct. 22, 1976	Oct. 4, 1974	Jan. 29, 1974
Conclusion of judicial review	Not appealed	1974	Pending before the Supreme Court				Pending before the Supreme Court	Not appealed	July 2, 1980 Overturned	Pending before 9th Circuit	Sept. 10, 1980 Upheld	May 27, 1975 Upheld	Oct. 6, 1975 Upheld

suspects that the encyclopedic preamble will become closely followed by agency employees. Policy disputes and turf battles will get resolved by reference to the GCP, and the agency's approach will be more consistent overall. Yet although internal consistency is certainly a valuable agency goal, that goal alone cannot justify the massive public effort that was poured into developing and defending the GCP. A general statement of policy circulated to all current and incoming agency employees could probably perform the same function at a fraction of the cost.

Forging a Consistent Interagency Carcinogen
Policy in a Public Forum

Although the preambles to the proposed and final GCPs make no mention of an agency effort to take the lead in molding government cancer policy, this may have been one of the agency's hidden agendas. Scientists who wanted the federal government to articulate a strong policy on carcinogen regulation abandoned their attempts at EPA after the administrator refused to take official notice of Saffiotti's seventeen principles. Many of these scientists had a great deal of respect for Anson Keller's political and bureaucratic judgment. Soon after Keller left EPA to become a special assistant to the assistant secretary for OSHA in the spring of 1975, he began drafting the proposed GCP. Keller was unhappy with the way the EPA cancer policy was evolving. In the early days, EPA had developed its cancer policy by recruiting sympathetic expert witnesses to testify in quasi-public hearings about cancer principles. The attorneys incorporated those principles into briefs, and they ultimately found their way into the administrator's opinions.[150] This litigation-oriented process, in which Keller played a major role, had unnecessarily precipitated heavy criticism from outside the agency and bitterness within the agency.

The administrator's rejection of the mirex official notice motion signaled an end to this lawyer-dominated process, but the process that took its place was in many ways no improvement. The interim guidelines that emerged from internal EPA debates about substance, procedure, and territory were signed by the administrator without the benefit of outside scrutiny from environmental groups and industry trade associations. In Keller's mind, both decision-making processes lacked crucial public participation. Keller hoped that the OSHA GCP effort would, by contrast, precipitate a full-scale public shootout, an effort in which all interested parties could aid the agency in forging a policy that could serve as a model for all other government agencies. Since Keller agreed with Saffiotti and others that there was a body of scientific knowledge on carcinogenesis that could be codified in a single document,[151] he drew heavily upon his experience in EPA to draft a proposal that was squarely within the tradition of the ad hoc committee report, the nine aldrin-dieldrin principles, and the seventeen Saffiotti principles. He hoped that the preamble that would ultimately emerge from this process would summarize the state of the art of carcinogen regulation in a manner that could be relied upon by other federal agencies.[152] Dr. Eula Bingham, who became assistant secretary for OSHA in early 1977, agreed with Keller on the role that the GCP could play in forging a general federal policy toward carcinogens and testified in House oversight hearings that the GCP "is a far-reaching proposal that will have a significant effect upon the Federal Government approach to regulating cancer-causing chemicals."[153]

Industry representatives easily perceived this broader underlying purpose for the GCP[154] and responded by forming the American Industrial Health Council (AIHC) to formulate and present a unified industry position on regulatory policy toward carcinogens.[155] Agreeing that some government-wide approach was needed, AIHC proposed an alternative, less-conservative approach, which would delegate decisions on scientific issues to a body of independent scientists for case-by-case resolution.[156]

For a time, it appeared that the OSHA GCP would be adopted as the predominant model for regulating carcinogens. CPSC quickly adopted a similar policy, and EPA agreed to consider adopting the same categorization scheme for regulating carcinogens under the Clean Air Act, despite the fact that it had already forged a weight-of-the-evidence approach out of its pesticides experiences. The IRLG, however, ultimately gained White House recognition as the principal forum for promulgating a federal cancer policy. The GCP then assumed the status of merely one of several competing regulatory approaches that included EPA's weight-of-the-evidence guidelines and OSTP's leave-it-to-the-scientists scheme.

With the Regulatory Council's endorsement, the IRLG document apparently has become the multiagency carcinogen policy that OSHA had hoped to articulate. OSHA succeeded in precipitating the government-wide policymaking process, but the final product in many ways more closely resembles EPA's weight-of-the-evidence guidelines than the GCP's presumption-rebuttal approach. Nevertheless, the IRLG document does incorporate most of the key principles that were summarized a decade earlier in the ad hoc committee report. More importantly, the IRLG document, like the GCP, rejects OSTP's suggestion that a body of government scientists be charged with the primary responsibility for assessing carcinogenic risks. Publicly accountable decision makers, not a group of scientists, will continue to make the difficult policy judgments concerning the classification and regulation of potential carcinogens.

Yet the process through which the IRLG document was promulgated did diverge significantly from the wide-open public discussion that the OSHA policy precipitated. It was therefore difficult for participants in the

GCP hearings to avoid the conclusion that government carcinogen policy was being generated on two levels: a for-show level in which all interested parties were encouraged to participate, and a for-real level in which government bureaucrats debated policy behind closed doors.[157] The massive record of the GCP hearings amply demonstrates that the agency achieved its goal of securing broad public participation in designing its regulatory policy toward carcinogens. However, because the policymaking initiative slipped out of OSHA's hands, one can legitimately question whether the public display was worth the major effort that went into it.

A partial answer to that question is that the OSHA GCP differs from the IRLG document in one fundamental regard: it is a rule; the IRLG document is just a policy. The GCP's presumption-rebuttal approach toward identifying carcinogens, along with all of its risk-averse science-policy determinations, will be binding on all regulatees if it survives judicial review. While the IRLG document by and large makes the same risk-averse science-policy determinations, the policy content of those determinations does not necessarily derive from any particular statute. An agency attempting to rely on the IRLG document for resolving critical science-policy questions in individual cases may be vulnerable to a challenge based on the IRLG's failure to promulgate its document as a rule.[158] The CPSC experience with its cancer policy demonstrates the reality of this possibility. To the extent that the IRLG document cannot be relied upon in individual cases, it has little practical value. Moreover, the err-on-the-side-of-safety policy that the IRLG document reflects can also be characterized as err on the side of regulation, and an administration more sentitive to the costs that health and safety regulation impose on businesses could easily resolve the science-policy questions differently and produce a dramatically different document. Individual agencies can ignore the IRLG document if they find it convenient to do so, or they can weight the evidence in a way that leads them to less-risk-averse decisions. The OSHA GCP, on the other hand, draws its policy directly from a statute. In addition, it was forged in the furnace of a public rule making. Although the GCP makes liberal provision for its own amendment, the amending process too must be public, and the amended product must be capable of surviving judicial review. Hence the GCP is built upon a much firmer foundation than is the IRLG document.

Even if the agency, after its *Benzene* setback, ultimately adopts a weight-of-the-evidence approach toward identifying carcinogens and assessing their risks, the critical science-policy questions involved in identifying carcinogens have been publicly articulated and resolved in the preamble to the final GCP in a way that reflects the OSH Act's err-on-the-side-of-safety regulatory philosophy. At the very least, the GCP rule-making process has produced a preamble that the agency can conclusively rely upon when these questions arise again in individual cases.

Lessons for the Future

OSHA's GCP rule-making process has not yet run its full course. The *Benzene* decision required significant changes in the GCP, and the forthcoming cotton dust decision may require still further amendments. Ultimately the GCP itself will be reviewed in the Fifth Circuit and perhaps in the Supreme Court. Given OSHA's rocky regulatory road, it is particularly risky at this juncture to attempt to draw lessons from the GCP experience, nevertheless, a few broad generalizations may be attempted.

The clearest lesson to draw from the GCP experience is that an agency should be very hesitant to initiate a large-scale rule-making process until it is quite sure that the legal framework for that initiative will survive judicial review. Despite protestations to the contrary, reviewing courts are not always deferential to an agency's interpretation of its own statute. The agency should at least secure judicial approval of the legal basis for its regulatory approach in one or two circuits in individual cases before embarking on a major regulatory initiative. Indeed the GCP experience suggests that the agency should be loathe to inaugurate a major rule-making initiative until the Supreme Court has approved its interpretation of its statute.

This lesson applies equally to reviewing courts. To the extent that agencies are fearful that forum-shopping regulatees can find some court to dismantle the legal framework for their regulatory approaches, the agencies are likely to continue to make policy cautiously on a case-by-case basis. This deprives regulatees and others of the opportunity to engage in major shootouts with agencies on important regulatory initiatives, and it ultimately results in agencies' exercising more case-by-case administrative discretion.

The second lesson of the OSHA experience is similar to the first. Since many recurring questions in highly technical regulatory fields must be answered in the face of great scientific uncertainty, policy must guide the decision maker as much as scientific expertise. Since that policy must draw its content primarily from the agency's statute and since courts are not overly deferential toward an agency's interpretation of its statute, generic resolution of science-policy question is vulnerable on appeal. OSHA's presumption-rebuttal approach to generic resolution of unsettled science-policy questions offers a reasonable mechanism for waiving generic determinations when the evidence in a particular case undercuts the generic assumptions. However, the agency must take care to avoid specifying rebuttal criteria that in practice deprive the agency of the benefits of the generic presumption.

Finally, OSHA's experience teaches that a broad generic rule-making hearing is an excellent vehicle for precipitating a public forum on important issues of regulatory policy. Generic rule making puts all interested parties on notice that their interests may be affected by the agency's decision, and this can motivate the participants to produce higher-quality contributions than could be forthcoming in individual proceedings. However, the OSHA experience also indicates that if the agency's hidden agenda includes influencing policy beyond its own bureaucratic baliwick, its efforts may take unexpected turns, and the agency may well lose control of the initiative. Yet if the agency does stick to its own turf, generic proceedings seem very well suited for generating broad public debates. At the very least, the wide-ranging debates that took place at the OSHA GCP hearings produced a 280-page preamble containing the most thorough analysis of the various principles of chemical carcinogenicity and related regulatory options that currently exists.

Even if the Supreme Court continues to read the OSH Act to signal less risk-averse policies than OSHA has traditionally applied, the effort will not have been a complete failure. The conservative principles that the ad hoc committee advanced in 1970 for the most part have become national policy. OSHA can claim some credit for this accomplishment because it initiated the interagency consensus-building process in an open, public forum.

Notes

1. 29 U.S.C. §§ 761-678 (1976).

2. Industrial Union Dep't. AFL-CIO v. Hodgson, 499 F.2d 467, 474 (D.C. Cir. 1974).

3. *See e.g.,* United Steelworkers v. Marshall, 8 OSHC 1810 (D.C. Cir. 1980); AFL-CIO v. Marshall, 7 OSHC 1775 (D.C. Cir. 1979), *cert. granted,* 49 U.S.L.W. 3245 (1980); Am. Iron and Steel Institute v. OSHA, 6 OSHC 1451 (3d Cir. 1978); Am. Petroleum Institute v. OSHA, 581 F.2d 493 (5th Cir. 1978), *aff'd sub nom.* Industrial Union Dep't. AFL-CIO v. Am. Petroleum Institute, 100 S. Ct. 2844 (1980).

4. 100 S. Ct. 2844 (1980). By the end of 1974, OSHA had promulgated proposed standards only for asbestos, 37 Fed. Reg. 466 (1972); cotton fiber dust, 39 Fed. Reg. 44769 (1974); vinyl chloride, 39 Fed. Reg. 16896 (1974); fourteen carcinogens, 38 Fed. Reg. 18900 (1973). *See* App. I.

5. The final standards issued by the end of 1974 were for asbestos, 37 Fed. Reg. 11318 (1972); vinyl chloride, 39 Fed. Reg. 35890 (1974); and fourteen carcinogens, 39 Fed. Reg. 3756 (1974). Although OSHA was slow in promulgating standards, it compiled a remarkably successful record in reviewing courts. OSHA standards for carcinogens were either affirmed or affirmed with minor exception in Industrial Union v. Hodgson, 499 F.2d 467 (D.C. Cir. 1974) (asbestos); Synthetic Org. Chem. Mfrs. Ass'n v. Brennan 503 F.2d 1155 (3d Cir. 1974) (ethyleneimine [one of the fourteen carcinogens]); Synthetic Org. Chem. Mfrs. Ass'n v. Brennan, 506 F.2d 385

(3d Cir. 1974) (fourteen carcinogens minus ethyleneime); Soc' of Plastics Indus., Inc. v. OSHA, 509 F.2d 1301 (2d Cir. 1975) (vinyl chloride). All of these courts found substantial evidence in the record and a basis in the statute to support OSHA's conservative approach toward regulating carcinogenic risk.

6. OSHA proposed standards during 1975-1976 for beryllium, 40 Fed. Reg. 48814 (1975); sulfur dioxide, 40 Fed. Reg. 54520 (1975); lead, 40 Fed. Reg. 45934 (1975); arsenic, 40 Fed. Reg. 3392 (1975); and coke-oven emissions, 40 Fed. Reg. 32268 (1975).

7. *See, e.g.,* Hearings before the Subcommittee on Oversight and Investigations of the House Committee on Interstate and Foreign Commerce on Environmental Causes of Cancer, 94th Cong., 2d Sess. (1977); Oversight Hearings before the Subcommittee on Labor of the Senate Committee on Labor and Public Welfare, 94th Cong., 2d Sess. (1976); Hearings before a subcommittee of the House Committee on Government Operations on Control of Toxic Substances in the Workplace, 94th Cong., 2d Sess. (1976); Hearings before the Subcommittee on Labor of the Senate Committee on Labor and Public Welfare, 93rd Cong., 2d Sess. (1974).

8. Chemical Dangers in the Workplace, thirty-fourth Report by the House Committee on Government Operations, H. Rept. No. 94-1088, 94th Cong., 2d Sess. (1976) [hereinafter cited as Chemical Dangers].

9. U.S. General Accounting Office, Delays in Setting Workplace Standards for Cancer-Causing and Other Dangerous Substances (1977) [hereinafter cited as GAO Delays Report].

The House Committee Report concluded, *inter alia,* that:

[f]or the first five years of its existence, [OSHA] emphasized safety issues while paying little attention to occupational health . . . the present OSHA administration is now giving greater attention to occupational health. But it has yet to devise a strategy adequate to deal with the occupational health crisis facing the nation today.

Chemical Dangers, *supra* note 8, at 4.

10. GAO Delays Report, *supra* note 9.

11. *Id.* at iii.

12. 42 Fed. Reg. 54148, 54182 (1977).

13. *See, e.g.,* Oversight Hearings before a subcommittee of the House Committee on Government Operations 98, 95th Cong., 1st Sess. (1977); Hearings before the Subcommittee on Labor of the Senate Committee on Human Resources on Occupational Diseases, 1978 (1978). Failure to Meet Commitments Made in the Occupational Safety and Health Act, Tenth Report by the House Committee on Government Operations, H. Rept. No. 95-710, 95th Cong., 1st Sess. (1977).

14. *See, e.g.,* Food Protection Committee, National Research Council, Problems in the Evaluation of Carcinogenic Hazard from Use of Food Additives (1960); Joint FAO/WHO Expert Committee on Food Additives, Evaluation of the Carcinogenic Hazards of Food Additives, Evaluation of the Carcinogenic Hazards of Food Additives (Org. Tech. Rept. Series No. 220 1961); WHO Expert Committee on the Prevention of Cancer, Prevention of Cancer (WHO Tech. Rep. Ser. No. 276 1964).

15. Hearings before the Subcommittee on Executive Reorganization and Government Research of the Senate Committee on Government Operations on Chemicals and the Future of Man, 92nd Cong., 1st Sess. 173 (1971) [hereinafter cited as Hearings on Chemicals and the Future of Man].

16. The document was submitted to the Journal of the National Cancer Institute, Hearings on Chemicals and the Future of Man, *supra* note 15, at 173, but, curiously, it was never published.

17. Hearings on Chemicals and the Future of Man, *supra* note 15, at 180. Hearings before the Subcommittee on Agricultural Research and General Legislation of the Senate Committee on Agriculture and Forestry, 92nd Cong., 1st Sess. 677 (1971).

18. Hearings on Chemicals and the Future of Man, *supra* note 15, at 180-181. The Ad Hoc Committee was composed of Dr. Umberto Saffiotti, associate scientific director for carcinogenesis, etiology, National Cancer Institute (now a research scientist with NCI); Dr. Hans L. Falk, associate director for laboratory research, NEIHS; Dr. Paul Kotkin, director NEIHS (now with Johns-Manville); Dr. William Lijinsky, professor of biochemistry, the Eppley Institute for Research on Cancer, University of Nebraska (now with Litton Bionetics); Dr. Marvin Schneiderman, associate chief, Biometry Branch, NCI (now with Clement Associates); Sidney Weinhouse, director, Fels Research Institute, Temple University School of Medicine; Gerald Wogan, professor of food toxicology, MIT.

19. The ad hoc committee report apparently was drafted in response to a 1969 report of the Food Protection Committee of the National Research Council of the National Academy of Sciences. National Academy of Sciences, National Research Council, Evaluating the Safety of Food Chemicals (1969). The Food Protection Committee report was, like the ad hoc committee report, as much a statement of regulatory policy as it was a statement of scientific principles. The content of the policy, however, was dramatically different. While recognizing the difficulty in designing and implementing adequate epidemiological studies and the consequent need for relying on laboratory animal data for assessing human risk, the report also suggested that regulators allow exposure to potentially carcinogenic chemicals in foods at toxicologically insignificant levels. Among its "Guidelines for Estimating Toxicologically Insignificant Levels of Chemicals in Foods" were several suggestions for avoiding testing

altogether. One guideline, for example, suggested that "[i]f a chemical has been in commercial production for a substantial period, *e.g.,* 5 years or more, without evidence of toxicological hazard incident to its production or use, if it is not a heavy metal or a compound of a heavy metal, and if it is not intended for use because of its biological activity, it is consistent with sound toxicological judgment to conclude that a level of 0.1 ppm of the chemical in the diet of man is toxicologically insignificant." *Id.* at 53. Recommendation 3 of the ad hoc committee report urged that "[t]he statement made in 1969 by the Food Protection Committee, National Research Council, that natural or synthetic substances can be considered safe without undergoing biological assay should be recognized as scientifically unacceptable."

Although not specifically addressed in the report of the ad hoc committee, the Food Protection Committee report also included other statements inconsistent with the conservative approach advocated by the ad hoc committee. The committee suggested that a "no carcinogenesis level" may be shown for a species (*id.* at 36), although it recognized that "there is as yet no generally accepted way of quantitatively extrapolating dose-response data in predicting a noncarcinogenic level for man." *Id.* at 47-48.

20. The Occupational Safety and Health Administration's

> entire case depends on an extrapolation from the data gathered in rodent experiments, and to justify that extrapolation [OSHA] relies heavily on the April 22, 1970, Report of the Ad Hoc Committee on the Evaluation of Low Levels of Environmental Chemical Carcinogens to the Surgeon General.

Dry Color Mfrs. Assn. v. Dept. of Labor, 486 F.2d 98, 103 (3d Cir. 1973).

21. *Id.* at 108-109.

22. Synthetic Organic Chem. Mfrs. v. Brennan, 503 F.2d 1155 (3d Cir. 1974). The standard was remanded for further evidence insofar as it applied to laboratories.

23. *Id.* at 1159.

24. 7 U.S.C. § 136 *et seq.* (1976). The cumbersome adjudicatory hearing required "seven months of testimony from a broad spectrum of the public." Environmental Defense Fund v. EPA, 489 F.2d 1247 (1973) (EPA cancellation of DDT registration affirmed).

25. Also testifying in the DDT hearing on the carcinogenicity issue were Dr. Marvin Schneiderman, a member of the ad hoc committee, and Dr. Samuel Epstein, who was at that time senior research associate in pathology at the Children's Research Foundation in Boston.

26. Brief of Respondent, Consolidated DDT Hearings. The seven principles are almost verbatim from the recommendations section of the report of the ad hoc committee. The EPA administrator later replied on

Saffiotti's testimony in concluding that "DDT poses a carcinogenic risk." Consolidated DDT Hearings, I.F.&R. (Insecticide, Fungicide & Rodenticide) Docket Nos. 63 etc., 37 Fed. Reg. 13369, 13375 (1972).

27. 39 Fed. Reg 37246 (1974). Other EPA witnesses included Drs. Schneiderman and Epstein, as well as Dr. Walter E. Heston, chief of the Laboratory of Biology of the National Cancer Institute, and Dr. Arthur C. Upton, who was at that time dean of the School of Basic Health Sciences at the State University of New York at Stony Brook.

28. In re: Shell Chemical Company *et al.,* FIFRA (Federal Insecticide, Fungicide & Rodenticide Act) Docket No. 145 *et al.,* Respondent's Brief, Proposed Findings, and Conclusions on Suspension 31 (filed September 16, 1974). The principles listed in the EPA brief are as follows:

(1) A carcinogen is any agency which increases tumor induction in man or animals.

(2) Well-established criteria exist for distinguishing between benign and malignant tumors; however, even the induction of benign tumors is sufficient to characterize a chemical as a carcinogen.

(3) The majority of human cancers are caused by avoidable exposure to carcinogens.

(4) While chemicals can be carcinogenic agents, only a small percentage actually are.

(5) Carcinogenesis is characterized by its irreversibility and long latency period following the initial exposure to the carcinogenic agent.

(6) There is great variation in individual susceptibility to carcinogens.

(7) The concept of a "threshold" exposure level for a carcinogenic agent has no practical significance because there is no valid method for establishing such a level.

(8) A carcinogenic agent may be identified through analysis of tumor induction results with laboratory animals exposed to the agent, or on a post hoc basis by properly conducted epidemioloigcal studies.

(9) Any substance which produces tumors in animals must be considered a carcinogenic hazard to man if the results were achieved according to the established parameters of a valid carcinogenesis test.

Among the attorneys for EPA in the aldrin-dieldrin proceeding were Anson Keller and John C. Kolojeski; Dr. Ian Nisbet was listed as a scientific consultant.

Although neither the ALJ nor the administrator explicitly adopted the nine cancer principles, their written opinions adopted the same conservative approach toward identifying and regulating chemical carcinogens.

Shell Chemical Co. *et al.,* Consolidated Aldrin/Dieldrin Hearing, 39 Fed. Reg. 37246, 37249, 37265 (1974). The administrator's decision was affirmed by the D.C. Circuit. Environmental Defense Fund v. EPA, 510 F.2d 1292 (D.C. Cir. 1975).

29. Consolidated Heptachlor/Chlordane Hearing. 41 Fed. Reg. 7552 (1976).

30. Witnesses included Saffiotti, Schneiderman, Epstein, and Heston.

31. We start by rejecting Velsicol's argument that the "cancer principles" EPA relied on in structuring its analysis of the mice and rat studies improperly biased the agency's open-minded consideration of the evidence. In brief form, the principles accept the use of animal test data to evaluate human cancer risks; consider a positive oncogenic effect in test animals as sufficient to characterize a pesticide as posing a cancer risk to man; recognize that negative results may be explained by the limited number and sensitivity of the test animals as compared to the general human population; note that there is no scientific basis for establishing a no-effect level for carcinogens; and view the finding of benign and malignant tumors as equally significant in determining cancer hazard to man given the increasing evidence that many "benign" tumors can develop into cancers. The Agency's reliance on these principles did not come as a surprise to Velsicol; they were included in the Administrator's Notice of Intent to Suspend; and . . . from part of the Agency's "scientific expertise." Velsicol was properly given an opportunity to put in evidence contesting those principles, but failed to demonstrate anything more than some scientific disagreement with respect to them.

Environmental Defense Fund v. EPA, 548 F.2d 998, 1006 (D.C. Cir. 1976).

32. *See, e.g.,* Lehnert, *Cancer: EPA Uses this Fear-Inspiring Word to Attack Important Ag Chemicals,* Mich. Farmer, Nov. 20, 1976 at 6; Plant, *A Dangerous Definition,* Chem. & Engr. News, Oct. 20, 1975 at 4.

33. Memorandum to the Administrator from Jeffrey Howard re: Basis for Evaluation of Chemical Carcinogens—August 27, 1975 Meeting dated August 26, 1975 (copy on file with author). This meeting was one skirmish in a larger battle between lawyers in the Office of General Counsel and scientists and managers in the Office of Pesticides Programs over whether the agency's cancer policy was to be based on the testimony of outside experts in adjudicatory hearings or on the initiatives of in-house scientists. The battle ultimately ended with the protest resignations of three agency lawyers and the establishment of an in-house carcinogen assessment group.

34. The draft "Statements on Principles of Chemical Carcinogenesis in Relation to the Evaluation of Carcinogenic Hazards" is reproduced in Appendix E to the Post Hearing Brief for the American Industrial Health Council submitted at the end of the hearings on OSHA's GCP, where the

principles are compared with statements in the preamble to OSHA's proposed GCP.

35. Motion to Take Official Notice of Certain Facts, Public Hearing to Determine Whether or Not the Registration of Mirex Should Be Cancelled or Amended, FIFRA Docket No. 293 (Sept. 9, 1975). Apparently because the doctrine of official notice applies only to facts, *see* K. Davis, Administrative Law Text § 15.03 (1958), the motion labeled the seventeen principles "facts."

36. Supplemental Memorandum in Support of Respondent's Motion for Reconsideration of Denial of Respondent's Motion to take Official Notice of Certain Facts, Public Hearing to Determine Whether or Not the Registrations of Mirex Should Be Cancelled or Amended, FIFRA Docket No. 293 (Nov. 26, 1975). The "three basic facts" are as follows:

(1) There is presently no scientific basis concluding that there is a "no effect" level for chemical carcinogens.

(2) Experimental data derived from mouse and rat studies can be used to evaluate whether there is a cancer risk to man.

(3) All tumorigens must be regarded as potential carcinogens. For purposes of evaluating carcinogenicity hazard, no distinction should be made between the induction of tumors diagnosed as benign and the induction of tumors diagnosed as malignant.

37. The National Cancer Advisory Board is part of the National Cancer Institute at NIH and is composed of twenty-nine presidental appointees. It is authorized to review research projects relating to the cause, prevention, or methods of diagnosis and treatment of cancer and to collect information on cancer studies and generally to make recommendations to the secretary of health and human services on cancer research. 42 U.S.C. § 2866 (1976).

38. The description of the NCAB subcommittee meeting is drawn from S. Epstein, *The Politics of Cancer* 277-278 (1978); Zinman, Wyrick, & Hevesi, *Scientist's Role Is Questioned,* Newsday, Jan. 18, 1977; and the Transcript of the National Cancer Advisory Board (NCAB) Subcommittee Meeting.

39. Dr. Norton Nelson stated at the meeting, "I find it pretty difficult to disagree with these general principles." Transcript of NCAB Subcommittee Meeting at 16.

40. This was apparently not meant as a rejection of Saffiotti's draft. Rather, one subcommittee member urged that the Saffiotti document not be used as a starting point because if it were modified, "it will be interpreted as a criticism of it and I don't think that this is what we would want to do nor is it warranted." Transcript of NCAB Subcommittee Meeting at 21-22.

41. Zinman, Wyrick, & Hevesi, *supra* note 38.

42. *Id.*

43. *See* S. Epstein, *supra* note 38, at 279. A key issue in the heptachlor-chlordane proceeding was whether observed metastasis or invasion, or both, was necessary to a proper definition of a carcinogen, since few instances of metastasis or invasion had been reported in heptachlor-treated mice. At the time the ALJ issued his proposed decision, the NCAB subcommittee working draft stated that bioassays in which compounds cause "a significant and reproducible increase in only benign neoplasms . . . do not in themselves constitute definitive evidence of carcinogenicity." Although he disavowed relying on the working draft, the ALJ did allude to the NCAB subcommittee's efforts to "better define, in functional terms a chemical carcinogen" and to develop "general guidelines which can be used for interpreting carcinogenicity data." 41 Fed. Reg. 7567 (1976).

Later the subcommittee eliminated the above-quoted phrase and substituted the following statement:

> The carcinogenicity of a substance is established when the administration to groups of animals in adequately designed and conducted experiments results in increases in one or more types of malignant neoplasms [or a combination of benign and malignant neoplasm]. . . .
>
> The occurrence of benign neoplams raises the strong possibility that the agent in question is also carcinogenic since compounds that induce benign neoplasms frequently induce malignant neoplasms.

National Cancer Advisory Board Subcommittee on Environmental Carcinogenesis, General Criteria for Assessing the Evidence for Carcinogenicity of Chemical Substances 5 (1976) [hereinafter cited as Shubik Committee Report].

44. Velsicol Chemical Corp. *et al.,* Preliminary Statement; Recommended Decision, 41 Fed. Reg. 7555 (1976). The administrator later reversed the ALJ and ordered most uses of heptachlor-chlordane suspended. Velsicol Chemical Corp. *et al.,* Decision of the Administrator on the Suspension of Heptachlor/Chlordane, 41 Fed. Reg. 7572 (1976). The administrator was not swayed by Shubik's attempt to draw a distinction between benign and malignant tumorigens, concluding, "I cannot give the draft subcommittee report significant weight." *Id.* at 7577. The administrator's decision was affirmed in all significant respects in Environmental Defense Fund v. EPA, 548 F.2d 998 (D.C. Cir. 1977).

45. Since the Shubik committee report was aimed at addresssing only the question of the definition of a carcinogen, it did not address issues identified by the seventeen cancer principles such as the proportion of death attributable to cancer, the latency period of a carcinogen, the number of chemicals that cause cancer, the comparative susceptibility of humans and

laboratory animals, or the existence of no-effect levels. The two documents are in almost precise agreement on the mouse-to-human question and the validity of short-term tests, although the subcommittee document is more explicit in specifying examples of animal tests for which extrapolation to humans might be inappropriate. Both documents caution against using negative epidemiological studies to refute positive animal studies. The subcommittee draft further cautions that "quantitative extrapolation from animal studies for the purpose of evaluating human risks entails large uncertainties at the present time." Shubik committee report, *supra* note 43, at 8.

The only possible difference in approach between the two documents is the somewhat greater emphasis placed on benign tumors in the Shubik committee report. *See* note 43, *supra*. Since few, if any, agents have been shown to produce only benign tumors in laboratory animals, this difference in emphasis is very minor.

46. Shubik committee report, *supra* note 43, at 1.

47. Public Hearing to Determine Whether or Not the Registration of Mirex Should Be Cancelled or Amended, FIFRA Docket No. 293, Administrator's Decision on Interlocutory Appeal Affirming Denial of Respondent's Requests to Take Official Notice, dated April 22, 1976 [hereinafter cited as Administrator's Official Notice Decision].

48. Administrator's Official Notice Decision, *supra* note 47, at 7-9. The administrator expressed some doubt about the proposed statement that "no distinction should be made between the induction of tumors diagnosed as benign and the induction of tumors diagnosed as malignant." He cautioned that while he would draw no such distinctions in determining whether a chemical poses a cancer hazard to humans, he might distinguish between benign and malignant tumors in choosing among his regulatory options. *Id.* at 10.

49. This document was published in the Federal Register, 41 Fed. Reg. 21402 (1976).

50. This additional focus does not contradict any of the ad hoc committee recommendations or the Saffiotti principles, indeed, it is responsive to the ad hoc committee's suggestion that "[a]n ad hoc committee of experts should be charged with the task of recommending methods for extrapolating dose-response bioassay data to the low response region." Ad Hoc Committee Report, *supra* note 15, at 2.

51. The administrator previously had rejected attempts by pesticide registrants to require the agency to engage in quantitative risk assessment.

52. As a legal matter, the weight-of-the-evidence approach that EPA's interim guidelines adopted made a good deal of sense in the pesticides context that generated that approach. The Federal Insecticide Fungicide and Rodenticide Act, 7 U.S.C. § 136 *et seq.* (1976) mandates that EPA weigh the risks of a pesticide's use against the benefits. The weight-of-the-evidence

approach makes less sense when applied to the Clean Air Act, which speaks of margins of safety. 42 U.S.C. §§ 7409(b)(1), 7412 (1979 Supp.).

53. The only point at which the preamble to the proposed GCP differed with the ad hoc committeee report was in its failure to adopt the ad hoc committee's suggestion that experts be employed for the purpose of recommending methods for extrapolating dose-response bioassay data to the low-response region.

54. Identification, Classification and Regulation of Toxic Substances Posing a Potential Occupation Carcinogenic Risk, 41 Fed. Reg. 54147, 54149 (1977) [hereinafter cited as Proposed GCP].

55. Proposed GCP, *supra* note 54, at 54185.

56. *Id.* at 54185. Category II substances include those that produce only suggestive results, those that have induced tumors in an unreplicated experiment in a single mammalian species, and those for which sufficient evidence exists to justify the classification. *Id.* at 54185-54186. No action is taken with respect to category II substances based on their carcinogenicity. *Id.* at 54186. A category III substance is any potential carcinogen that is not included within category I or category II. *Id.* No action is taken with respect to category III substances other than listing them for possible reconsideration in light of additional information. *Id.* Category IV substances are potential carcinogens that are not found in the American work place. *Id.* These substances also are simply listed. *Id.* at 54187.

57. *Id.* at 54185.

58. *Id.*

59. *Id.*

60. Environmental Defense Fund, Inc., Petition for the Initiation of Rule-making Proceedings to Establish a Policy Governing the Classification and Regulation of Carcinogenic Air Pollutants under the Clean Air Act, Nov. 7, 1977. EPA finally responded to the petition on October 10, 1979, with a proposed rule that would establish generic standards under Section 112 of the Clean Air Act, 42 U.S.C. § 7412 (1970), for source categories producing or handling "significant quantitites" of air pollutants that posed "a significant carcinogenic risk to human health." Environmental Protection Agency, National Emission Standards for Air Pollutants; Policy and Procedures for Identifying, Assessing, and Regulating Airborne Substances Posing a Risk of Cancer, 44 Fed. Reg. 58642 (1979).

61. 43 Fed. Reg. 23658 (1978).

62. Dow Chemical, U.S.A. v. CPSC, 459 F. Supp. 378 (W.D. La. 1978).

63. Dow Chemical, U.S.A. v. CPSC, 464 F. Supp. 904 (W.D. La. 1978).

64. 44 Fed. Reg. 28821 (1979). CPSC at the same time announced its intention to adhere to the policy expressed in the Interagency Regulatory

Liaison Group cancer-assessment document. *See* text accompanying n. 65-68, *infra*.

65. Report of the Work Group on Risk Assessment, Interagency Regulatory Liaison Group, 44 Fed. Reg. 39858 (1979) [hereinafter cited as IRLG Report].

66. *Id.*

67. The IRLG document specifies in some detail criteria for assessing epidemiological and laboratory animal studies. *Id.* at 39861-71. The document concludes that animal tests conducted at the maximum tolerated doses (MTD) are acceptable qualitative predictors of carcinogenic response in humans. *Id.* at 39864. It goes on to specify three cases in which MTD animal studies might not be relevant to human experience, including indirect mechanisms of action, action of promoting agents only on tissues previously initiated by carcinogens, and carcinogenic activity through unusual metabolic pathways. *Id.* at 39868. Unlike the proposed OSHA GCP, the IRLG document addresses directly the question of statistical significance and concludes that 95 percent confidence is the generally accepted test. *Id.* at 39868-69. However, since the strength of the conclusion depends upon the statistical significance of the results, the document suggests that in each case the level of significance be reported. *Id.* The document stresses that negative animal tests and epidemiological studies "do not deny the conclusions of carcinogenicity on the basis of animal bioassays." *Id.* at 39871. The IRLG's conclusions with respect to the benign-malignant distinction are similar to those of EPA; it is unlikely that a benign tumorigen exists, but a chemical that causes mostly benign tumors is less dangerous than a chemical that causes only malignant tumors. The IRLG also cautions against qualitative assesssments of carcinogenic potency, since "one could refer to weak evidence of a strong effect or strong evidence of a weak effect." *Id.* While the document examines in great detail several models for quantitative estimation of carcinogenic risk, it recognizes that such estimates are clouded by large uncertainties and recommends that conservative assumptions be used in assessing risks. *Id.* at 39870-71.

68. *Id.* at 39870.

69. Regulatory Council Statement on Government Policy for Regulation of Chemical Carcinogens, reprinted in 9 OSH Rptr. 442 (1979).

70. The Regulatory Council was created by executive order to coordinate federal regulatory policy among all federal agencies. [1979] U.S. Code Cong. & Ad. News 502, 503.

71. 9 OSH Rptr. at 445.

72. Office of Science and Technology Policy, Identification and Control of Potential Human Carcinogens: A Framework for Federal Decision-making (1979).

73. *Id.* at 10.

74. *Id.* at 22-23. The major difference between the OSTP framework and the AIHC proposal is the locus of the scientific risk assessment. OSTP would have government scientists perform this task. AIHC would have a panel of scientists appointed by the National Academy of Sciences do the job.

75. Occupational Safety and Health Administration, Identification, Classification and Regulation of Potential Occupational Carcinogens, 45 Fed. Reg. 5002 (1980).

76. Although the final GCP does not force the agency to take any particular regulatory action, it does list the factors that shall guide the agency in setting priorities. *Id.* at 5285. These factors are almost identical to those listed in the Regulatory Council Statement.

77. The final GCP amended the definition "potential occupational carcinogen" (and hence expanded category I) to include substances that cause tumors in a single species. Moreover, OSHA may on a case-by-case basis eliminate the requirement that a single test's results be verified before being placed in category I. In addition, the definition of potential occupational carcinogen now includes any substance that is metabolized into one or more potential occupational carcinogens by mammals. *Id.* at 5283-84.

78. *Id.* at 5285-86.

79. *Id.* at 5286.

80. For example, the agency may consider nonpositive epidemiological studies to rebut positive animal studies if the study followed the subjects for thirty years after initial exposure, predicted the site at which the chemical would cause cancer if it were carcinogenic in humans, and involved a sufficient number of participants that it could detect an increase in incidences of 50 percent. *Id.* at 5287. OSHA may also consider arguments that differences in metabolic characteristics between humans and animals demonstrate that an animal carcinogen is not a human carcinogen if the evidence meets stringent criteria for demonstrating that the carcinogenic animal metabolite is not produced in humans. *Id.* Similarly, the agency may hear arguments that high-dose experiments are irrelevant to assess human risks at lower exposure levels if the regulatee can produce data that demonstrate that a metabolite that is produced only at high doses in animals is the carcinogenic agent. *Id.* Indeed, the agency may even consider evidence that a substance is capable of producing only benign tumors, if experiments in at least two mammalian species produce, in the minds of at least one qualified pathologist and OSHA scientists, only benign tumors of the type that do not progress into malignancies. *Id.* The agency further replaced its improper-route-of-exposure rebuttal criteria with a presumption that carcinogenicity via any route of exposure would place a substance in category I unless the regulatee could show that the route was not oral or inhalation and that the tumors resulted only at the site of administration and that the tumor induction is related to the physical configuration of the substance.

Id. Finally, the catch-all rebuttal criteria of the proposed GCP that would allow a regulatee to argue that "[f]or some other reason, the positive results in the experimental animal species are not scientifically relevant to man" (*Id.* at 54185) is eliminated in the final GCP and replaced by a provision allowing regulatees in individual proceedings to present substantial new evidence that may warrant the amendment of the GCP. *Id.* at 54286. The threshold requirement that the evidence was not considered in the massive GCP rule-making hearing may be stringent enough to preclude substantial use of the substantial-new-evidence route to raising science-policy issues in individual cases. *See* Zener, *Cancer Policy: Extreme Regulatory Philosophy,* Legal Times of Washington, Feb. 4, 1980, at 11.

81. Telephone interview with Robert C. Barnard, Jan. 27, 1980. *See* Zener, *supra* note 80.

82. Industrial Union, AFL-CIO v. Bingham, 470 F.2d 965 (D.C. Cir. 1977). The strange history of this classic race to the courthouse is recounted in detail in McGarity, *Multiparty Forum Shopping for Appellate Review of Administrative Action,* 129 U. Penn. L. Rev. 302 (1980).

83. Am. Petroleum Institute v. OSHA, 581 F.2d 493 (5th Cir. 1978).

84. Industrial Union Dep., AFL-CIO v. Am. Petroleum Institute, 100 S. Ct. 2844, 2850 (1980). Justice Stevens wrote the plurality opinion for three justices. Justice Powell concurred, although he "would not rule out the possibility that the necessary findings could rest in part on generic policies properly adopted by OSHA." 100 S. Ct. at 2875.

85. One could, however, argue that the GCP adequately provided the findings of significant risks for carcinogens that Justice Powell was apparently willing to accept. *See* note 84, *supra.* If Justice Powell could be won over, the four *Benzene* dissenters would presumably join him to make a majority. However, Justice Powell also would require OSHA to balance costs against benefits once it had crossed the significant-risk threshold. Since the final GCP explicitly rejects his cost-benefit approach, the possibility of winning Justice Powell over seems remote.

86. Occupational Safety and Health Administration, Identification, Classification and Regulation of Potential Occupational Carcinogens; Conforming Deletions, 46 Fed. Reg. 4889 (1981) [hereinafter cited as GCP Conforming Deletions].

87. Occupational Safety and Health Administration, Identification, Classification and Regulation of Potential Occupational Carcinogens; Proposed Amendments, 46 Fed. Reg. 7402 (1981) [hereinafter cited as GCP Proposed Amendments].

88. The proposed amendments promise that OSHA will consider arguments based on evidence that do not meet the threshold critiera "to the extent justified by its relevance in assessing the risk of a substance for purposes of regulation." GCP Proposed Amendments, *supra* note 87, at 7407.

89. The Supreme Court on numerous occasions has encouraged agencies to promulgate general rules to guide their decisions in individual cases. *See, e.g.*, Vermont Yankee Nuclear Power Corp. v. Natural Resources Defense Council, Inc., 435 U.S. 519, 545-46 (1978); FPC v. Texaco, Inc., 377 U.S. 33, 39-44 (1964); U.S. v. Storer Broadcasting Co., 351 U.S. 192, 201-205 & 201 n.9 (1956). The lower courts also have upheld general rules that resolve questions with high factual content. *See, e.g.*, Nat'l Petroleum Refiners' Ass'n v. FTC, 482 F.2d 672, 678 (D.C. Cir. 1973); WBEN, Inc., v. U.S. 396 F.2d 601, 617-19 (D.C. Cir.) *cert. denied*, 393 U.S. 914 (1968); Air Line Pilots Ass'n v. Quesada, 276 F.2d 892, 895-98 (2d Cir. 1960).

OSHA's attempt to promulgate a generic cancer policy in many ways mirrors the attempts by the Atomic Energy Commission (later the Nuclear Regulatory Commission) in the early 1970s to resolve generically specific issues that arose repeatedly in trial-type hearings concerning nuclear-power-plant licensing. The legal literature on the developments in AEC-NRC, which was generally supportive of that agency's generic efforts, offers excellent insights into the generic versus case-by-case question. The following discussion draws heavily upon that literature. *See* Recommendations of the Administrative Conference of the United States, 1 C.F.R. § 305.73-6 (1980); Crampton, *A Comment on Trial-Type Hearings in Nuclear Power Plant Siting*, 58 Va. L. Rev. 585 (1972); Murphy, *The National Environmental Policy Act and the Licensing Process: Environmentalist Magna Carta or Agency Coup de Grace?* 72 Mich. L. Rev. 963, 988 (1972); Comment, *Judicial Review of Generic Rulemaking: The Experience of the Nuclear Regulatory Commission*, 65 Geo. L.J. 1295 (1977); Note, *The Use of Generic Rulemaking to Resolve Environmental Issues in Nuclear Power Plant Licensing*, 61 Va. L. Rev. 819 (1975). I have also drawn heavily upon my own work in this area. *See* McGarity, *Substantive and Procedural Discretion in Administrative Resolution of Science Policy Questions: Regulating Carcinogens in EPA and OSHA*, 67 Geo. L.J. 729 (1979). In the interest of conserving space, I will forgo extensive citation to these sources in the material that follows.

90. Since the prospect of lengthy hearings often is a significant brake upon agency initiatives, generic rulemakings have the related advantage of helping the agency pursue its regulatory mandate. *See* McGarity, *supra* note 89, at 754 n.115.

91. *See generally* Shapiro, *The Choice of Rulemaking or Adjudication in the Development of Administrative Policy*, 78 Harv. L. Rev. 921 (1965).

92. I am borrowing here from Professor Crampton's criteria for evaluating administrative procedures: accuracy, efficiency, and acceptability. Crampton, *supra* note 89, at 591-93.

93. *See* Final GCP, *supra* note 75, at 5212; Hearings on Chronic Hazard Programs before the Subcommittee for Consumers of the Senate

Committee on Commerce Science and Transportation, 96th Cong., 1st Sess. 29 (1979) (testimony of Chemical Specialties Manufacturing Association).

94. *See* Final GCP, *supra* note 75 at 5029-35. AIHC Recommended Alternatives to OSHA's Generic Carcinogen Proposal 1-10 (July 9, 1978) [hereinafter cited as AIHC Alternative]; in re: Proposed Regulations of the United States Occupational Safety and Health Administration for the Identification, Classification and Regulation of Toxic Substances Posing a Potential Occupational Carcinogenic Risk to Humans, Post Hearing Brief for the American Industrial Health Council 18-35 (October 23, 1978) [hereinafter cited as AIHC Post Hearing Brief]. The American Industrial Health Council is a group of industry scientists that was formed "to assist the U.S. Occupational Safety and Health Administration in developing a national and practical standard for regulating carcinogens in the workplace." American Industrial Health Council, Background Information, December 1977 (copy on file with the author).

95. *See generally*, Note, *Judicial Review of Generic Rule-making: The Experiences of the Nuclear Regulatory Commission*, 65 Geo. L.J. 1295 (1977).

96. Another important legal question that OSHA attempted to resolve in the GCP proceedings concerned whether the agency had authority to forbid employers to reduce compensation or seniority for employees who had to be removed from certain jobs because of particular susceptibility to hazardous substances or because of inability to wear personal protective devices. *See* Final GCP, *supra* note 75, at 5261. This issue undoubtedly will be litigated on appeal.

97. *See* text accompanying notes 82-85, *supra*.

98. Am. Textile Mfrs. Inst. v. Marshall, 49 U.S.L.W. 3245, Oct. 7, 1980.

99. *See* text accompanying notes 86-88, *supra*.

100. To a large degree the exercise of regulatory policy judgment in resolving science policy questions must be result-oriented. For example, an agency may decide as a policy matter whether results from mouse experiments may be used to estimate carcinogenic risk to man. There is no ascertainable public policy on this narrow issue that is independent of the policies that will be furthered by the agency's decision to regulate. The regulator can predict that if he uses mouse experiments to predict risk to man he is more likely to reduce human exposure to chemicals in general than if he does not. He can then search for sources of public policy, including statutes, court decisions, and the political environment, for indications whether he should choose that result. From this result-oriented perspective, he can ultimately decide how to resolve the original question whether to extrapolate from mouse to man in each specific case.

McGarity, *supra* note 89, at 781-782. Reprinted with the permission of the publisher, © 1979 The Georgetown Law Journal Association. The Supreme

Court recognized this result-oriented approach in the *Benzene* case when it said that OSHA may risk "error on the side of over-protection rather than under-protection." Industrial Union Dep't, AFL-CIO v. Am. Petroleum Institute, 100 S. Ct. 2844, 2871 (1980).

101. Industrial Union Dep't, AFL-CIO v. Am. Petroleum Institute, 100 S. Ct. 2844, 2871 (1980).

102. *See* McGarity, *supra* note 89, at 733-736; Weinberg, *Science and Trans-Science*, 10 Minerva 209 (1972). The reason that the no-effect level is transscientific is because, in the absence of any accepted biochemical model for chemical carcinogenesis, the only way to test the threshold hypothesis for an animal carcinogen would be an experiment requiring millions of laboratory animals. This experiment would obiously be impractical even if it were affordable. *See* Schneiderman, Mantel & Brown, *From Mouse to Man—Or How to Get from the Laboratory to Park Avenue and 59th Street*, 246 Annals of the N.Y. Academy of Sci. 237, 241 (1975).

Another pure policy question that OSHA could have resolved generically is the question of statistical significance. Clearly the magnitude of the risk of error in drawing a factual inference from which regulatory judgments are made is purely a question of regulatory policy. This question apparently eluded OSHA in its proposed GCP. *See* McGarity, *supra* note 90, at 755-756 n.124. Comments at the hearing, however, apparently brought the matter to OSHA's attention, and it resolved in the final GCP not to establish any particular cutoff for statistical significance. Rather, OSHA recognized, apparently for the first time, that considerations in addition to statistical analysis of test results were important in assessing their significance. Therefore, OSHA concluded that statistical analysis would be performed on human, animal, and short-term studies, but they "will not be the exclusive means for such evaluation." Final OSHA GCP, *supra* note 75, at 5100.

103. Industrial Union Dep't, AFL-CIO, v. Am. Petroleum Institute, 100 S. Ct. 2844, 2871 (1980).

104. This is not the place for a detailed critique of the plurality opinion in the case. However, one particularly glaring weakness should be pointed out. Justice Stevens (100 S. Ct. at 2871 n.63, 2874) apparently suffered from a fundamental misconception of the nature of OSHA's feasibility approach. Justice Stevens seemed to be of the erroneous opinion that the feasibility approach demanded absolute safety. OSHA was under no illusion that feasible engineering controls would render workers absolutely safe. Only where another product could be substituted would absolute safety be possible, and even then the workers would be exposed to the lesser risks posed by the substitute.

105. *See* McGarity, *supra* note 89, at 757 n.132.

106. Proposed GCP Amendments, *supra* note 87, at 7403.

107. *See* McGarity, *supra* note 89, at 736-740. One example of a case where scientific uncertainty is attributable to the lack of available information is the extent to which dermal exposure to a liquid carcinogen results in systematic absorption of the chemical. *Cf.* Am. Petroleum Inst. v. OSHA, 581 F.2d 493, 604-610] (5th Cir. 1978), *aff'd sub nom.* Industrial Union Dep't, AFL-CIO v. Am. Petroleum Inst., 100 S. Ct. 2844 (1980). The Supreme Court did not reach the dermal exposure issue. *Id.* at 2874.

108. Final OSHA GCP, *supra* note 75, at 5287.

109. *See* McGarity, *supra* note 89, at 740-743. The American Industrial Health Council failed to recognize this crucial point when it recommended that OSHA establish a body of independent scientific experts, appointed by the National Academy of Sciences, to determine whether individual chemicals are carcinogenic and made that panel's findings binding on the agency. For science-policy questions that are highly policy dominated, OSHA adoption of this suggestion would be a delegation of its policymaking functions to an unaccountable group of scientists who presumably are no more competent than anyone else to make regulatory policy.

110. Post Hearing Brief, *supra* note 94, at 118-119. *See generally* Hoerger, *The Need for Experienced Judgment in Risk Assessment*, paper presented at the Symposium on Health Risk Analysis, Gatlinburg, Tennessee (Oct. 27-30, 1980).

111. For example, the IRLG attempted to specify detailed criteria for interpreting pathological data. IRLG Report, *supra* note 65, at 39865. Yet except for certain general statistical considerations, the criteria offer little more than guidance to the expert pathologists who must observe the lesions on a chemical-by-chemical basis.

112. Several reports have attempted to articulate general criteria for evaluating epidemiological data. *See, e.g.,* Shubik committee report, *supra* note 43, at 4; IRLG Report, *supra* note 65, at 39861-62.

113. For example, EPA has proposed detailed protocols for carcinogenicity tests in its guidelines for registering new pesticides. *See* 2 Chem. Reg. Reptr. (BNA) 569 (1978). The IRLG document also contains detailed "criteria for evaluation of experimental design and conduct." IRLG Report, *supra* note 65, at 39863.

114. *See, e.g.*, Takayama, Variations of Historical Diagnoses of Mouse Liver Tumors by Pathologists, in Mouse Hepatic Neoplasia, app. I (Butler & Newborne eds. 1975).

115. Indeed, the agency rejected a suggestion that it decide as a generic matter not to consider positive bioassay results in animal strains that were subject to a high incidence of spontaneous tumors at the site at which the chemical caused tumors. This generic prescription, which has a sound statistical basis (IRLG Report, *supra* note 65, at 39863), could prove very efficient to the agency. It might eliminate the need for a hearing altogether

if no other positive carcinogenicity data existed for a chemical. However, OSHA apparently decided that the enhanced accuracy that would result from rejecting a categorical rule against considering such data outweighed the efficiency gains. This again is consistent with the OSHA's reading the OSH Act to tell the agency to err on the side of safety. However, another secretary of labor might read that policy differently and, applying a less-conservative approach, promulgate such a generic rule. The ultimate test, of course, is whether Congress meant for the agency to have leeway to adopt one or the other or both rules, and the final arbiter of this test is the reviewing court.

116. Final GCP, *supra* note 75, at 5047-5058.

117. *See* McGarity, *supra* note 89, at 743.

118. *See id.* at 746-747.

119. *See* note 80, *supra*.

120. *See* note 80, *supra*.

121. Although not required to survive arbitrary and capricious review, an agency might for administrative reasons desire to add a fourth test for rebuttal-presumption criteria: the presumptions should not be so broad as to include an unwieldy number of cases. For example, some industry representatives have argued that the number of chemicals that ultimately meet the GCP's category I criteria may be so large as to overwhelm the agency's capacity to deal with them in a rational way. *See* Barnard, *The Emerging Regulatory Dilemma*, New York Academy Work Shop on the Management of Assessed Risk for Carcinogens (March 17, 1980); Hoerger, *The Need for Experienced Judgment in Risk Assessment*, paper presented at the Symposium on Health Risk Analysis, Gatlinburg, Tennessee (October 27-30, 1980). If this is true, then the GCP will have little impact on OSHA's announced goal of issuing more standards in less time. Moreover, the GCP ultimately may slow down the issuance standards still further.

122. *See* note 103 *supra*.

123. *See* Weinberger v. Hynson, Westcott & Dunning, Inc., 412 U.S. 609 (1973). *See generally* Ames & McCracken, *Framing Regulatory Standards to Avoid Adjudication: The FDA as a Case Study*, 64 Calif. L. Rev. 14 (1976).

124. Final OSHA GCP, *supra* note 75, at 5283, 5287-5288.

125. OSHA's attempt to delete certain aspects of the GCP without further hearings may or may not survive Fifth Circuit scrutiny. The agency will have to hold further hearings on its January 1981 amendments to the GCP, and the result of that hearing may be appealed. Finally, the unamended portions of the GCP must still survive the Fifth Circuit's scrutiny.

126. Telephone interview with Anson Keller, Jan. 21, 1981. *See also Government Tackles Tricky Question of How to Regulate Carcinogens*, 1978, Cong. Q. Weekly Rept. 957.

Occasionally, concern for the limited amount of time that busy expert witnesses have for testifying has been cited as a reason for the GCP; however, this could not have been a very large consideration. At most, testifying at individual hearings would have required five or six days per year. The agency's outside expert witnesses probably do not tire of receiving large consulting fees for repeating the same prepared testimony.

127. *See generally* Weyerhauser Co., v. Costle, 590 F.2d 1011, 1057 (D.C. Cir. 1978); McGowan, *Congress, Court and Control of Delegated Power*, 77 Colum. L. Rev. 1119, 1125-27 (1977); Bazelon, *The Impact of the Courts on Public Administrators*, 52 Indiana L.J. 101, 103-105 (1976).

128. *See* McGarity, Forum Shopping, *supra* note 82, at 310 n.42.

129. Industrial Union Dep't, AFL-CIO v. Am. Petroleum Inst., 100 S. Ct. 2844, 2871 (1980).

130. Am. Textile Mfrs. Institute v. Marshall, 49 U.S.L.W. 3245, Oct. 7, 1980.

131. *See* cases cited in note 89, *supra*.

132. Many issues remain to be litigated in individual hearings after the GCP is in place. *See* Zener, *supra* note 80, at 10.

133. Although the statute prescribes informal rule-making procedures for setting health standards, the agency has in the past voluntarily adopted hybrid rule-making procedures with opportunity for oral presentation and limited cross-examination. *See* McGarity, *supra* note 89, at 753.

134. A subsidiary advantage of OSHA's traditional technology-based approach was the absence of any need to perform detailed worker-exposure analyses prior to taking regulatory action.

135. It is not clear to me at this juncture that OSHA can simply reduce risks to the lowest feasible level after it makes its significance determination. Arguably, after *Benzene*, the agency must only reduce risks to some ill-defined "insignificant" level. If "insignificance" is reached before "infeasibility," then only reduction in exposure to the insignificant level would be proper.

136. For a cogent criticism of the yes-or-no categorization approach toward carcinogen risk assessment *see* Hoerger, *The Need for Experienced Judgment in Risk Assessment*, Presentation at the Symposium on Health Risk Analysis, Gatlinburg, Tennessee (Oct. 27-30, 1980). Hoerger suggests that OSHA's yes-or-no categorization approach is in the same family of regulatory philosophies as the Delaney amendment.

137. Even if the agency adheres to its generic approach to identifying carcinogens, it must still devote hearing time to rebuttal attempts. To the extent that the generic criteria allow leeway for rebuttal attempts, efficiency will suffer, although accuracy should increase.

138. EPA has already faced this embarrassing prospect. In the 2, 4, 5-T cancellation hearings, the chairman of EPA's carcinogen-assessment group,

Dr. Roy Albert, was cross-examined on why the agency allowed exposure to a chemical that appeared to pose a much higher carcinogenic risk than 2, 4, 5-T. Albert explained that "it gave certain parts of the agency apoplexy when they heard about this." In re: Hearing of 2, 4, 5-T and SILVEX, Docket Nos. 415 *et al.*, Transcript at 11627.

139. The reduction in pressure to issue more health-based standards has other explanations in addition to the promulgation of the proposed GCP. In 1977 a new administration committed itself to protecting worker health, and the newly appointed assistant secretary took a hard line in her confirmation hearings and later oversight and appropriations hearings. Yet in most of these hearings and in speeches to labor organizations and health groups, the assistant secretary referred to the GCP as evidence of her efforts to reduce occupational-health risks.

140. Final OSHA GCP, *supra* note 75, at 5011.

141. The preamble to the final GCP is evasive on the reasons for eliminating the automatic trigger. Interviews with persons close to the decision, however, reveal that the chief reason was the fear that the agency would be inundated by requests from labor or (in the minds of the more conspiracy-oriented participants) industry to promulgate standards. An unfocused blitz such as this could wreak havoc on agency priorities. The agency decided instead to specify in the GCP a mechanism that it would follow in setting priorities for proposing standards. *See* final GCP, *supra* note 75, at 5207.

142. It has been pointed out that political considerations intruded into the administration of the act with the result that the standard-setting process had been deliberately slowed.

Hearings on OSHA Oversight before the Subcommittee on Labor of the Senate Committee on Human Resources, 95th Cong., 2d Sess. 36 (1978) (testimony of Labor Secretary Ray Marshall); House Committee on Government Operations, Chemical Dangers in the Workplace, House Rept. No. 94-1688, 94th Cong., 2d Sess. 16-17 (1976); Speakers at Union's Pro-OSHA Meeting Say Critics Fail to See Agency Benefits, 9 OSH Rptr. 1628 (1979).

143. *See* Hearings on the Performance of the Occupational Safety and Health Administration before a Subcommittee of the House Committee on Government Operations; 95th Cong., 1st Sess. 100-101 (1977) (testimony of Dr. Eula Bingham); Hearings on Departments of Labor and Health, Education and Welfare and Related Agency Appropriations before the Senate Appropriations Committee, 95th Cong., 2d Sess. 447 (1978); Hearings on Departments of Labor and Health, Education and Welfare Appropriations for 1977, 94th Cong., 1st Sess. 581 (1976).

144. *See* House Committee on Government Operations, Failure to Meet Commitments Made in the Occupational Safety and Health Act, House Rept. No. 95-710, 95th Cong., 1st Sess. 17-19 (1977) [hereinafter cited as Failure to Meet Commitments]; GAO Delays Report, *supra* note 9, at 23-25; *Management Problems in Key Areas Noted by Contractor Study of OSHA,* 7 OSH Rptr. 307 (1977).

145. *See* Failure to Meet Commitments, *supra* note 143, at 17.

146. *See* GAO Delays Report, *supra* note 9, at 56-60; Chemical Dangers in the Workplace, *supra* note 8, at 14-20. Failure to Meet Commitments, *supra* note 143, at 5.

147. *Conference Speakers Say OSHA Will Improve Its Image,* 7 OSH Rptr. 1359 (1977); *Presidential Task Force Recommendations to OSHA Transmitted to President,* 7 OSH Rptr. 1039 (1977); Hearings on Departments of Labor and Health, Education and Welfare Appropriations before a Subcommittee of the House Committee on Appropriations, 95th Cong., 2d Sess. 667-668 (1978) (testimony of Dr. Eula Bingham and Mr. Benjamin Mintz).

148. *See* GAO Delays Report, *supra* note 9, at 61-66; Hearings on Occupational Diseases before the Subcommittee on Labor of the Senate Committee on Human Resources, 95th Cong., 1st Sess. 88 (1977); *Steelworkers, Bingham Share Concern about Delays of Issuance of OSHA Standard,* 8 OSH Rptr. 827 (1978); *Meany Urges Corn to Join Labor in Opposing Preparation of Statements,* 6 OSH Rptr. 520 (1976).

149. Some critics at the time OSHA proposed its GCP predicted that it would have little impact on the agency's overall output. Indeed, even OSHA's own employees from its region I commented to OSHA that "[i]t seems extremely idealistic to suppose that OSHA's glacial progress in the past will be accelerated by the issuance of this standard." Letter to Joanne A. Blayne from Gilbert J. Saulter dated Dec. 13, 1977, *reprinted in* Cancer Policy Final Environmental Impact Statement (OSHA). Years before the GCP effort, Professor Robinson had wisely observed:

> Even accepting the time-honored view that delay is a major problem, it is still questionable how much of it is attributable to reliance on formal procedures. Many of the common complaints about delay relate to routine agency administration—processing of applications, petitions, and the like. Here delay is not a product of the choice of procedure, but a product of managerial organization and operation.

Robinson, *The Making of Administrative Policy: Another Look at Rulemaking and Adjudication and Administrative Procedure Reform,* 118 U. Penn. L. Rev. 485, 523 (1970).

150. Telephone interview with Anson Keller, Jan. 21, 1981.

151. Telephone interview with Dr. Ian Nisbet, Jan. 19, 1981.

152. Others in the agency, including Assistant Secretary Bingham, hoped that the OSHA GCP would serve as a model for other agencies.

153. Hearings on Occupational Safety and Health Administration—State Plans, Federal Agencies and Toxic Substance Identification before a Subcommittee of the House Committee on Government Operations, 95th Cong., 2d Sess. 41 (1978). Other OSHA employees agreed. *See* OSHA Cancer Policy Could Provide "Model" for Others, ACS is Told, 9 OSH Rptr. 340 (1979).

154. Dr. Ronald Lang, head of the newly formed AIHC, told *Business Week* that the GCP's importance reached well beyond OSHA. "It should be looked at as the spearhead of the whole government approach to carcinogens." Business Week, May 29, 1978, at 32. A CPSC commissioner told the same magazine that the GCP "could work across the board." Business Week, Oct. 27, 1977, at 38. Another industry spokesman opined that "[i]t's the domino theory. . . . If OSHA goes, so go EPA, CPSC and others." Cong. Q. Weekly, April 22, 1978, at 961. *See also* OSHA's Action Plan on Cancer, Wall Street J., Oct. 11, 1978, A18, col. 3; OSHA's Ill-Conceived Crusade against Cancer, Fortune, July 3, 1978, at 86, 89.

155. The American Industrial Health Council was assembled "to assist the U.S. Occupational Safety and Health Administration in developing a rational and practical standard for regulating carcinogens in the workplace." AIHC, Background Information, December, 1977.

156. *See* note 94, *supra.* The AIHC proposal would categorize chemicals into three categories: human carcinogens, animal oncogens, and substances for further testing. Each of the first two categories would be subdivided into three subcategories: high potency, intermediate potency, and low potency. OSHA would be required to begin risk-benefit analyses immediately for chemicals in category I, with an eye toward issuing an emergency temporary standard and ultimately a permanent standard. For category II chemicals, OSHA would be required to decide "as soon as possible" whether to issue emergency temporary and permanent standards.

157. The AIHC argued that this two-level approach to forging government-wide carcinogen policy violated due process. *See* Post Hearing Brief, *supra* note 94, at 53-62.

158. The IRLG published its document in the *Federal Register* for comment, 44 Fed. Reg. 39858 (1979), but it did not purport to be a rule. No hearing was held, and comment was invited only "in order to give interested persons an opportunity to express their views on the validity and appropriateness of the concepts and methods described for identifying and evaluating carcinogens." *Id.*

Comment

Richard A. Merrill

Several facets of the OSHA experience continue to be intriguing, and they are the main subject of these comments, which also explore more broadly the use of generic rule making to decide scientific questions.

Tom McGarity has suggested that the rules of the game have changed, which makes it somewhat unfair to reach judgments about the utility of OSHA's exercise, to which it devoted four years and uncounted dollars.

The OSHA cancer policy itself has been challenged in court. Whether those challenges will yield decision is unknown. One suspects it is as likely that OSHA itself will decide what changes it wants to make and then seek a remand from the Fifth Circuit Court of Appeals of the policy itself. That seems to be what OSHA has invited the Supreme Court to do in the cotton-dust case. This raises the next question: of whether the agency is obligated to perform cost-benefit analyses. Even though they seem premature, some preliminary judgments may be made about the utility of OSHA's rule-making exercise.

My first conclusion is tentative. It does seem that this exercise has not been successful as an exercise in efficient gathering of facts that will ultimately underlie individual regulatory decisions. But on that score the jury is still out, because the policy has not been affirmed, much less implemented.

It seems evident that the carcinogen policy has not been successful as an exercise in political accommodation. The adoption of the policy produced no concert of views on the regulatory approach OSHA has followed: it reaffirmed the position that the agency had taken since the mid-1970s and produced a cascade of opposition that was reflected not only in the challenges in court but in efforts in Congress and the executive branch, both before and since the election, to effect changes. In short, the rule-making proceeding was not a forum in which the competing interests were able to achieve agreement on any important issue.

Finally, it would be essentially accurate, although possibly unfair, to say that OSHA's proceeding never purported to be an exercise in scientific decision making. From the beginning, it was an exercise in regulatory policy formulation. And if one steps back and puts aside the policy's ambition and its scope, what OSHA was doing was not novel in terms of process or objective.

OSHA's generic rule making was emphatically a lawyer's process. Anson Keller was undoubtedly influenced by Umberto Saffiotti and other scientists of like mind. But the conception of the cancer policy as a possible vehicle for generic resolution of issues that had come up in past and would unpredictably arise in future proceedings to regulate carcinogens, was a lawyer's inspiration. It drew on well-established administrative law principles.

OSHA's process was traditional quasi-formal rule making. Any departures from the standard model tended in the direction of judicialization rather than in the direction of more-informal attempts to invite the participation of scientists and facilitate resolution of scientific issues.

Anson Keller and other agency lawyers, in advance of the rule-making hearing, prepared witnesses that the agency intended to put on, much as an antitrust lawyer would in an antitrust trial. The witnesses appeared live after the submission of written statements and were subjected to occasionally vigorous but seldom prolonged cross-examination. Their testimony filled the record that was collected by the administrative law judge. Up to that point, there had been no deviations from the norm, except for some greater expenditure of effort to ensure that witnesses were well prepared.

The ultimate policy promulgated in early 1980 does not deviate in important respects from the original proposal, suggesting to me that the agency had largely made up its mind. The agency viewed the rule-making hearing as an exercise in confirmation rather than in exploration.

Rule making typically is not an exercise in discovery in which the agency sets out to find the facts before embracing them in regulations. This was an exercise in policy formulation and the agency knew what policy it wanted to implement when it issued its proposal in 1977.

The centerpiece of the agency's policy had already been confirmed by three or four courts of appeals in roughly half a dozen cases. That policy is the occupational-health version of the Delaney clause. OSHA believes that its statute obligates it to reduce exposure to carcinogens to the lowest feasible level. Feasibility is measured by the potential of bankruptcy of the industry and the availability of technology for achieving the desired exposure. These are important limitations; and in this respect, OSHA's policy is a departure from the Delaney clause. But in terms of the scientific underpinnings that led OSHA to assume that any level of exposure to a carcinogen is likely to be hazardous to some individuals, the agency's posture is consistent with the posture reflected in the Delaney clause and taken by the other regulatory agencies. OSHA has been successful in the Third, Second, and D.C. circuits in sustaining that position.

In this respect, OSHA's assumption that the law was fairly well established was legitimate. The discovery in the *Benzene* case that it was not is a forgivable oversight on its part.

The ostensible objective of OSHA's rule making is to take advantage of familiar administrative law precedents. These precedents established that if an agency had heard and resolved issues of fact or of policy in prior rule-making proceedings open to all potential participants, it could thereafter refuse to rehear those issues in individual cases where they might otherwise be pertinent. It is essentially in narrowing the legal standard that the agency has to apply.

OSHA's generic rule making was a proceeding in which everybody would have a shot at being heard on the central issues that the agency would ultimately thereafter treat as foreclosed in standard-setting proceedings. Theoretically this objective was sensible, and it has a lot of case-law support, but the complexity of OSHA's rule making may have exceeded the reach of those prior precedents.

It was important, therefore, for OSHA to arrive at decisive answers to the issues posed by its proposal. An unsatisfactory outcome from the vantage point of efficiency would have been to come away with conclusions that left a lot of these issues open for reexamination in subsequent standard-setting proceedings. If the rule-making exercise did not narrow the issues open in later cases, the exercise probably was not worth the effort.

But it was also important to OSHA that the answers to those issues be compatible with the policy that it had espoused since the early 1970s: no exposure is tolerable when it can feasibly be reduced. Otherwise, I have no doubt but that Assistant Secretary Bingham would not have launched the rule making in 1977 if she thought it would produce a policy result different from the one with which the agency had started.

About the policy's potential impact—assuming there had been no election—I have two kinds of speculations. Even if one assumed that the carcinogen policy might not be successful as an exercise in generic resolution of recurrent issues, leading to subsequent summary disposition of individual cases, from the point of view of OSHA's administrator, it may still have been a useful exercise. Everybody involved in developing health standards within the agency would know what the agency's ground rules were, know what the administrator thought, and know how the people ultimately making decisions would proceed to behave.

There was a high level of disagreement among many OSHA officials over what the ultimate objectives of the agency ought to be and whether the carcinogen policy was worth pursuing. If the OSHA administrator finally produced a set of rules that reflects a commitment to carcinogen regulation and defined the terms under which it will be carried out, that may have achieved important bureaucratic objectives. But OSHA's more-important objective was to simplify the subsequent standard-setting process, and it seemed doubtful that was going to occur, even before the election.

First, OSHA cannot avoid hearings on the establishment of occupational-health standards. The range of issues that is involved in the decision whether, and at what level, to limit exposure is much broader than those that are preliminarily resolved by the cancer policy. So OSHA is unavoidably committed to holding hearings on all proposed health standards, even if the issues are framed by the cancer policy. In the rule-making context, any arguments or information that anybody wants to submit can come in, whether or not they are ostensibly excluded by the cancer policy. OSHA's instructions to its administrative law judge make that person essentially a custodian of the record, with no authority to rule on the admissibility of evidence. Accordingly, a participant can introduce a test that purports to demonstrate a no-effect level for a carcinogen, and it will become part of the administrative record.

OSHA will then be confronted with the question of whether it can say, "Our policy makes that evidence irrelevant; therefore, we will not read the study." If an agency has spent a considerable amount of time on establishing a standard for a particular chemical, the agency's lawyer is likely to advise the administrator that that piece of evidence should be treated on the merits. The agency may not have to spend the same amount of time as if there were no policy, but it had better look at the study and discuss it because a reviewing court will ask why it treated the study as unimportant. The lawyer who submitted the study will characterize it as supporting an exception to the general proposition established by the cancer policy.

If these suppositions are correct, the agency time and effort invested in treating irrelevant evidence in hearings that will inevitably take place are not going to be much less than it was spending prior to the adoption of the cancer policy, treating those same issues without any legislative guidance.

OSHA's effort to codify principles of scientific evaluation for regulatory purposes may not be manageable in these circumstances. First, the issues addressed and purportedly resolved by OSHA's cancer policy were far more numerous than those embraced in other generic rule makings. These range from questions about how one evaluates human studies and animal studies to mechanisms of carcinogenesis.

Second, in prior cases, agencies have dealt with a science that had come to stasis. By contrast, OSHA was attempting to define scientific parameters about which there remained wide dispute within the scientific community at large and certainly within the affected communities regulated by OSHA.

Third, OSHA was operating in a field, according to many, where future scientific findings promise considerable refinements in the ability to evaluate the potency of carcinogens, to discern their mechanisms of action, and perhaps to differentiate among them based on their potential risk for humans. The prospect of penetrating inquiry in the near term, which will make many of the conclusions of the carcinogen policy obsolete, is substantial. This will make it more likely that data submitted in subsequent proceedings will warrant full evaluation rather than be dismissed as foreclosed by outdated regulations.

Comment

J. William Haun

From the point of view of a scientifically trained person, my principal impression of the analysis of the genesis and flowering of the GCP is the relative absence of science as such and the overwhelming presence of scientists. Indeed this is a case history of the preeminence of the opinion of scientists over the objective analysis of data that can be called science.

The ad hoc committee's "Evaluation of Chemical Carcinogens" was a direct response to the 1969 report by the Food Protection Committee of the National Research Council-National Academy of Science. Few if any chemicals were readily detectable at levels below the toxicologically insignificant level of 0.1 parts per million—at least short of a major effort—and the pragmatists who tended to make up the Food Protection Committee said such an effort was not warranted when compared to other risks from the food supply.

In the aftermath of the Food Protection Committee, the environmental movement broke over the country like a wave. The first Earth Day, which fell in 1970, had a real impact on some scientists. Also in this period, someone from the International Center for Research on Cancer stated that 90 percent of all human cancers are of environmental origin, although environment was not defined.

A logical scenario, then, would have Dr. Saffiotti discussing these assertions regarding environmental carcinogens with his director, who brought it to the surgeon general, who responded in a logical way: convene an expert group to see if it can arrive at any better understanding of carcinogenic chemicals.

This, then, is a mechanism by which a group of scientists was formed and took the opportunity to put their combined opinions on the record. It would be truly exceptional if any scientific data were considered (other than as verbal statements) in such a committee, or if any useful record of the deliberations existed. It does not surprise me that no journal would publish such a record. It lacked any scientific qualifications.

It is really remarkable how Saffiotti and Schneiderman, working as a team, succeeded in implanting their simple idea in almost every proceeding dealing with carcinogens. Every agency in Washington was looking for a piece of the environmental action and this paper was a lawyer's dream—a source of expert testimony that was predictable and resistant to cross-examination.

Problems in the Ad Hoc Committee's Analysis

The whole concept of cancer testing reflected in the committee report is built around the exposure of inbred strains of animals that are susceptible to all kinds of health problems, including cancer, even if they are protected from all unusual exposure. Indeed it is reported that in some desirable strains, up to 40 percent of the animals will become cancerous even if not exposed to known carcinogens. The literature is filled with notes that wild strains, even guinea pigs, are too resistant to be used for testing.

Thus, while for scientific purposes this sharpening of the sensitivity of tests is needed for efficiency and minimal costs in laboratories, I have great difficulty in attaching more than suspicion to a positive result.

The Category I listing condemns the material tested before the public and unions and creates a potential crisis. This, I suspect, leads to the real problems addressed in the *Benzene* case.

The problems left by the committee's report can be summarized by one statement and four questions:

1. Congenitally ill mice are not people.
2. Does a positive test mean a real risk?
3. What is that risk?
4. Is it significant?
5. What can be done about it?

Appropriateness of Generic Resolution of Scientific Factual Questions in Carcinogen Regulation

For several years, a battle has raged between industrial scientists and policy makers on one hand and their government counterparts over the concept of the base data set: the minimum amount of data needed to evaluate the magnitude of risk resulting from marketing a chemical product. Most American scientists abhor the base-set concept, preferring a case-by-case determination as to appropriate data. This could well be the scientific approach, but one has to be understanding of a goverment agency that may deal with hundreds or thousands of compounds each year, with few trained individuals and facing arbitrariness as a charge at every turn.

In an ideal world, government scientists and industry scientists could meet as colleagues and define a set of data that would realistically define each compound's peculiar testing needs. The Europeans sometimes approach this ideal, the Japanese almost always.

In our litigious system, where criminal charges lurk for every error in judgment, even years after the fact, we probably need generic minimum data requirements just to ensure a standard of diligence and reasonable care.

The risk is that the base-data set can become a minimum, beyond which eager adminstrators must go to show their dedication, or a bureaucratic game that ends without much meaning.

There can be no doubt that every case is unique. There is equally no doubt that good judgment can reduce the number of problems to a manageable level.

Science-policy and transscientific issues arise often in the course of scientific work; however, in that context, they define the agenda for theory and experiment, with the thought that eventually they can be answered in a factual way. Such issues typically are working hypotheses within a group of workers.

I can tell you from experience that such assumptions can give rise to bloody internecine wars in the academic community.

The difference is this: the quiet wars of academe have modest stakes, like tenure or a postdoctoral fellowship that may suddenly disappear. When resolved by a Saffiotti committee and sanctified by the courts, however, such answers gain a spurious status as laws of science, and any challenge to them must deal with all the power of society.

The really basic science-policy and transscientific issues are few: how do we keep an open mind? What if someone came up with proof of a no-effect level? Who would publish the work? Who would believe it?

Thus, while the advocates push for rules to bind future administrations, industry tries to avoid them. It is an unequal contest once the decision to regulate is reached.

In a similar way, absence of data renders science meaningless, and in the atmosphere of socratic dialogue, the scientist must merely say, "I don't know and cannot know." Even if limited data are available, varying interpretations customarily lead to Professor McGarity's conflicting inferences.

The worst part of the quasi-science to be found in testimony on this issue is the almost reverent attention lay persons, particularly lawyers, will pay to the wildest possible speculation when cloaked in authority. Frequently those authorities have no real idea how a single fertilized mammalian egg differentiates into skin, brain, or liver cells, much less arranges those parts for functioning. Proof of the repeated outcome of this process is not hard to find, but knowledge is empirical, not conceptual.

In any area of work, an institution cannot decide anything. People decide, and an agency decision is only as right or wrong as the people are. However, agency management always has the advantage; the hearings are structured by them, the initial witnesses are invited by them.

Forging Consistent Interagency Cancer Policy

The goal of a consistent federal policy on carcinogens presents difficulty in several ways. First, such a position, once devised in the "furnace of public debate," can be a straitjacket, requiring courage to change it that may well be beyond the risk-aversion threshold of bureaucrats and politicians. Second, such a policy, if limited enough or broad enough to encompass work places, in-home environments, and the global environment, will not be of much use. Finally, I believe the public has become so cynical about the whole area of regulation that the long-term result of a consistent policy consistently applied will be absolute confusion leading to public ridicule and ignoring of even valid signals. Already, the rush to press with carcinogen "evidence" for coffee, tobacco, and saccharin is leading to disenchantment.

Some Concerns from a Scientist in Industry
Regarding Policy Formulation

In reading the records and other papers in connection with the matter, one is struck by the recurring notion that experimentation is difficult. Large-scale animal tests are dismissed as impractical. On the other hand, industry actions triggered by even one of these rule-making activities can be difficult, expensive, and time-consuming. In the *Benzene* case, industry costs of several billions were thought to be required. Cancellation of DDT cost many millions of dollars every year.

Is it any wonder that industry people keep asking for some measure of proof? If mice or rats or dogs are too expensive, then what about miles of pipe, millions of horsepower, and millions of engineering time to achieve some feasible control?

Many of the policy hearings are preordained. Evidence consists of statements of belief, from which selections are made on some basis, presumably because some statements of belief are more equal than others. There are many instances in the ad hoc committee report's preamble of OSHA's discounting the statements of an AIHC witness saying that such viewpoint derives from misunderstanding of the laws of nature. Some examples are found at 45FR5026, 5027, 5031, and 5032.

In fact, many, if not most, industrial appearances are made not with any hope of affecting agency action but of balancing the record for what is often regarded as inevitable litigation. This is a sad commentary on science but accounts for the continued hope for an objective, scientific body to replace the courts. I am doubtful that such a group could be effective.

Many people, then, see the GCP as an attempt to install permanently a set of judgments with which they may disagree in such a way as to foreclose any further attempts to modify them. These are not science but personal value judgments enshrined. The vast expenditure of time and effort that Professor McGarity correctly identifies as out of all proportion to the easily perceived administrative benefit is more readily explained in the political realm. In the Carter administration, an unprecedented number of dedicated activists with a zero-risk commitment were appointed to responsible office. This group of people, correctly reading this policy effort as a historic artifact sure to change, saw this (and other similar proceedings) as a one-time opportunity to embed these attitudes in the policy of government for all time, if all procedural graces were followed so as to preclude effective challenge in the courts. The effort may well have succeeded.

6

The Role of the National Academy of Sciences in Public Policy and Regulatory Decision Making

Clifford Grobstein

Nature of NAS and Its Mandate

The National Academy of Sciences (NAS) came into existence through an act of incorporation passed by Congress and signed by President Lincoln in 1863. Its mandate was to provide advice to the federal government on matters of science and technology.[1] Its formation, however, was in the lineage of existing academies in Europe that served both honorific and national purposes. The two roles of the NAS—honorific and adviser to government—persist to this day. The dual function is relevant to the strengths and weaknesses of the contemporary NAS as a contributor to public policy and regulatory decision making.

For more than a half-century, despite continuing effort of its officers, the NAS had indifferent success in gaining federal acceptance of its advisory role. It took the military emergency of World War I, with its increasing emphasis on technological warfare, to bring recognition that a relatively small group of scientists, no matter how eminent in their special fields, could not alone cope with the needs of government for practical technical advice. An initiative by NAS leaders, supported and implemented by President Wilson, established the National Research Council (NRC) in 1916 as a mechanism to recruit expertise beyond the select and limited membership of the academy itself. Initially designed to bring together scientists and engineers from academic institutions, industry, and government, the NRC evolved into the operating arm of the NAS in providing advice to the federal government.[2] This fundamental step, broadening participation in the advisory role under the NAS charter yet preserving the prestige and eminence of the honorific auspices, is the key to the current role of the academy, not only in regulatory policy but in national policy generally.

As science and technology have been increasing in impact upon our society, so too have regulatory processes. Regulation in any complex system stems from a need to integrate part processes into an effective whole. In a complex and dynamic society the objective and yardstick of the integration is the general welfare; however, it may be politically defined at a particular time. Now that science and technology have thoroughly permeated our society, regulation necessarily has a high scientific and technological content. Not surprisingly, therefore, the NAS-NRC—given its fundamental charter—has become a frequent if not formal participant in regulatory policy making and decision. By no means, however, is regulation the sole or even the primary concentration of the NAS-NRC.

Before focusing on the nature of NAS-NRC participation, a little more history will provide useful perspective. World War II generated a new pulse of awareness that science and technology are central to national strength and security. So clear and urgent had this message become in the early 1940s that administrators of science and governmental leaders judged it imperative to create new interactive mechanisms between them to meet the developing military emergency. The National Defense Research Committee and its successor Office of Scientific Research and Development were designed for wartime mobilization of science, cutting across the usual stream of academic, industrial, and federal effort. The NAS-NRC played only a supportive role within the wartime complex. For example, a committee on food and nutrition was formed to recommend minimum nutritional requirements in the event of wartime food shortages. The Food and Nutrition Board continues after forty years and recently published the ninth edition of *Recommended Dietary Allowances.* At the close of the war, the national momentum was continued through new peacetime, science-oriented federal agencies, among them the Atomic Energy Commission, the National Institutes of Health, and the National Science Foundation. The high priority of science and technology, established in wartime, spread ever more widely into the general affairs of the nation, with undiminished momentum, for almost a quarter century.

Postwar expansion and proliferation of federal activity occurred primarily outside of the NAS-NRC. Unlike the Soviet Academy of Sciences, for example, the NAS is not a research agency and has not become an operating arm of government. By choice and circumstance, the NAS remains quasi-governmental, acknowledging its federal charter and advisory mission but continuingly asserting its private and independent status. It is true that this legal and philosophical stance is somewhat ambiguous, particularly given the fact that NAS's almost sole client (and overwhelming source of income) is the federal government.

Thus, although not embedded in the federal structure, the NAS-NRC has important ties to it and has manifestly been shaped in recent years by federal needs and activities. This is to say that the academy did not withdraw from its advisory role into honorific ease in the face of the enormously heightened power of governmental science. Indeed, in recent years it has moved deliberately, albeit cautiously, into greater engagement with governmental policy issues falling within its adivsory charter. This has been reflected in expanded activity and changing organization both within the academy and the National Research Council.

Organization of the Academy Complex

At the academy level the NAS now has been joined by two partners, the National Academy of Engineering (NAE) and the Institute of Medicine (IOM), to form, together with the NRC, the "academy complex." Both NAE and IOM are focused more on the applications of science and technology than on science's inner dynamic. In terms of honorific functions, each unit is independent; election to membership is exclusively the concern of the unit itself.[3] In other ways, however, the three units operate as a corporate entity, though not entirely equal in their relationships. In the most-important matter with respect to the role of the complex in regulatory processes, each unit designates members of its council to the governing board of the National Research Council (NAS provides seven members, NAE four, and IOM two). This body, chaired by the president of the NAS, is responsible for initiating and approving studies and reports undertaken within all constituent subdivisions of the NRC. The NAS carries out very few studies independently of the NRC, and NAE has entirely merged its study and report activities into the NRC. The IOM, however, newest and smallest of the three and focused particularly on health-policy issues, has its own full-time president and carries on studies in similar fashion to the NRC. IOM reports, like all those produced within the NRC, are subject to corporate appraisal by a report review committee answerable to the president of the NAS. Thus the NAS, as the named recipient of the federal charter and the responsible financial agent, is first among equals in the corporate complex (NAS-NAE-IOM-NRC).

The NRC has also become increasingly complex over the years. It was reorganized in the early 1970s into eight major divisions, each with its own governing council. Four of these divisions are referred to as assemblies and are disciplinary in focus: mathematical and physical sciences, life sciences, behavioral and social sciences, and engineering sciences. Four others, referred to as commissions, are topical in focus: natural resources, human resources, sociotechnical systems, and international relations. Within these eight major divisions are a bewildering array of boards, standing and ad hoc committees, working groups, panels, and other groups. In 1978 some three hundred reports were issued by the NRC, with an estimated nine thousand scientists and over one thousand staff members involved in their preparation. The reports range over an astonishing range of subjects, some narrow and specialized, others broad and general in impact. Although many members of the three honorific bodies are among the participants in NRC activities, by no means a majority are, and they make up only a small fraction of the effort. Thus, the NRC's commissions and assemblies, predominantly not consisting of members of the honorific bodies, are the operating mechanisms by which scientific and technical advice is brought to bear upon public policy, including regulatory policy in a significant but by no means a preponderant number of cases.

The Academy Process of Study and Report

NRC activities are not only exceedingly diverse in their content but also in their modus operandi. The first step in most NRC studies is an external request (albeit sometimes solicited) from an executive agency or the Congress. Requests range from relatively short-term and specific activities to long-term and general ones. Tasks may call for simple data accumulation and analysis or evaluation of complex policy issues. As example, the standing Food and Nutrition Board of the NRC has for years been recommending dietary allowances for essential nutrients. Basically this is a data-analysis task, relied on by various public and private groups in setting nutritional standards. A recent summary statement by the board, however, generated controversy and criticism because it was interpreted to run counter to widely accepted medical advice concerning levels of dietary cholesterol in relation to cardiovascular disease.[4] The incident illustrated the increasing difficulty in sharply separating primarily scientific analysis from policy or frankly political impacts.

In fact, increasingly frequently, requests for new NRC activity arise out of policy debate, often in relation to regulatory issues. Moreover, the tendency is growing to involve the NRC in the most-contentious areas where all else has failed. The saccharin study requested by Congress several years ago is a case in point.[5] Other examples are studies in process on health impacts of environmental change and the role of diet and nutrition in the etiology of cancer.

Whatever the initiation, it is followed by informal delineation of the study objective and plan and then by formal contracting between NRC and the responsible agency. The negotiation, on the NRC side the responsibility of senior professional staff, is often delicate. The federal side is attempting to fulfill a mission but one that may not be adequately presented in legislative or executive language. The NRC side must have in mind that expert studies require considerable independence and that an adviser should not be bound or restricted by the advisee. The charter and tradition of NAS-NRC particularly preclude its functioning as a contractor for services prescribed in the usual Washington manner. Hence, the language of the contract, which becomes the formal charge for the study and report, must clearly convey the intended mission yet provide considerable flexibility in its execution. This is not always achieved, despite review by senior staff officers and one or more NRC advisory councils.

The third, sometimes overlappiing step is selection of appropriate experts to carry out the study and to prepare the report. The almost-universal mechanism is a committee with a designated chairperson. Eligibility for committee membership derives first from expertise, usually attested to by national stature in a relevant scientific or technical field. Most NAS-NRC studies require multiple expertise, with appropriate representation and balance of specialities. The chairperson may be designated early in the process and may participate in subsequent selections, or the chairperson may be designated later or last, not for particular expertise but in order to lend stature, credibility, experience, or other administrative advantage.

Selection of the committee members is both important and sensitive. The process is entirely internal, with no publicly formulated procedures or documentation. Responsible senior staff carry out or supervise confidential consultations with trusted advisers in accord with NRC guidelines. NRC officers review and endorse nominations. Final approval of nominees for all studies involves the NAS president or immediate staff. Of particular concern in the selection process in recent years have been questions of minority representation and of bias, whether stemming from conflict of interest or preconceived opinions. The possibility of bias is not only considered in the selection process but also is the subject of committee briefing during the initial meeting. All members are requested to file a form listing relevant public advocacy and conceivable conflicting activities or relationships. Each member is asked to make a brief oral sumarizing statement. The committee chairperson is required to report to NRC officials any serious conflicts that may jeopardize the objectivity or credibility of the subsequent report. Such a ritual clearly affords no guarantees but does sensitize participants to the issues and to the expectation of objectivity.

Still more difficult is the matter of preformed opinion. Expertise involves knowledge and knowledge generates opinion. The issue is not only whether such opinion is open to change as new facts are disclosed or assembled in new ways but whether parties to controversy will find the study process credible. Ideally selection should yield experts who are yet uncommitted on the immediate issues involved. Practically this is not easily achieved, and effort is made to balance evident biases in one direction with equivalent biases in another. Involved is some ambiguity about the nature of the study process, whether it is at least in part adversarial or whether it is entirely deliberative. The issues raised are complex and have not been either dispassionately studied or extensively aired.

An additional concern about the selection process relates to its timing in relation to formulation of the charge. Since an ad hoc committee is not appointed until the formal charge is fixed, often no contribution to the charge is made by those who will perform the study. Committees often find addressing their charge difficult or even infeasible in the time frame provided. Their options are to exceed the time frame or to apply their expertise to establishing priorities, clearly explaining their rationale in their report. Once again, the issues are complex and have not been explicitly addressed as a matter of record. Most committees reach ad hoc resolution of the issues, and some studies run into serious difficulties as a result.

With the formation of a committee, standing or ad hoc, considerable authority and responsibility are formally vested in it. The following discussion assumes an ad hoc status. Since the selection process is intended to yield an expert group of the highest stature, the committee clearly must be given a free hand to plan and execute its study and freely to reach its conclusions. On the other hand, it is clearly under several strictures. First, there is the defined mission stipulated in the contract that antedates the committee. Second, the contract was negotiated by staff, frequently by the senior staff officer assigned to the committee. Staff, therefore, are initially better informed than the committee as to the charge and may have understandings of it not fully reflected in the formal language. Third, the committee report must meet corporate scrutiny and criticism through an established complex report review procedure. This reflects the fact that the report, although actually the product of a committee, overall will bear the academy imprimatur as its entitlement to attention.

These matters are variously conveyed to the committee as it begins operations. The chairperson may have explored them preliminarily with staff, but committee briefing on them normally is an important agenda item at the first meeting. Typically, the chairperson and perhaps several other members have had previous committee experience and can sharpen the discussion. For many committee members, however, it is likely that definition of the charge, of their individual responsibility, and of the authority of the committee are not fully clear until later.

There is no way to generalize the subsequent course of the study. Its nature and objective, the time span, its policy sensitivity, the personalities involved—all are factors in determining its structure and content. Three critically important roles, however, may be distinguished: committee chairperson, staff director, and committee members. The relative roles of the three vary considerably with personality and circumstance. Using the analogy of a symphony orchestra, individual members may be thought of as first-desk players leading combined voices of staff and outside sources of information. The staff director functions as the concert manager, and the chairperson can be thought of as the conductor. A major point of the analogy is that all three roles are essential and may be adjusted one to another in various ways to yield a successful process. Another is that committee members and chairperson are uncompensated part-time volunteers with heavy responsibilities elsewhere, while staff are salaried for the task and have a substantial time commitment.

Within the budget assigned to the study (as contracted and administered by staff), committees have wide latitude in carrying out their responsibilities. They may hold public meetings (increasingly favored by NAS policy in recent years), set up technical conferences, assemble data through subcontracts, commission special studies and working papers, and otherwise consult with their peers. Their regular meetings (usually three to six per year) are occupied with planning, discussion of issues, outlining their report, assigning responsibility for writing, critiquing drafts, and, in the final stages, seeking a consensus on the general content and thrust of their recommendations. Typically, individual committee members of subcommittees write the sections of the report within their own expertise, and the chairperson or staff, or both, supply introductory and integrating material. Staff participation may vary from mechanical compilation and editing to actual drafting of major sections of the report for committee review and acceptance. As the report is written, the chairperson and staff director become increasingly prominent in shaping it, with one or the other taking chief initiative, depending upon circumstance.

In its final stages, often hectic if a due date is approaching, the report goes to review potentially at least at two levels. In some complex organizational structures within the NRC, there may be even more than two review levels. Review involves submission of the draft report to a set of previously uninvolved experts for critique. Reviewers at successive levels are invited to comment on technical adequacy and accuracy (the expertise of the authors), on clarity and appropriateness of presentation, on response to charge, on cogency of recommendations in terms of data presented, on degree of objectivity and freedom from bias, and other facets. Reviewers' comments are relayed to the committee and staff, who are expected to respond to criticism and suggestion but not necessarily to yield to it. In the event of persistent and severe disagreement between reviewers and authors, the matter may be referred for resolution to a senior staff officer of the sponsoring NRC unit or to the appropriate advisory council. It is not rare for this to happen but is rare for reports to be blocked from delivery or publication. There are occasional cases, some well publicized, where dissension persists despite all efforts at accommodation.

The highest level of review is the report review committee, made up of members of the NAS, NAE, or IOM. Since its inception in the early 1970s, at the initiative of the current NAS president, the committee has been chaired by the NAS vice-president. The committee does not directly review all reports, reserving the option to accept reviews at lower level where these reveal no serious problems. Where problems have appeared or where the report on preliminary perusal is judged sensitive for any reason, a panel of reviewers is drawn from members of the three honorific organizations. The reviews are coordinated by the committee chairperson or by a committee member designated by the chairperson. Criticisms and suggestions are communicated to the chairperson of the authoring committee, who responds to the report review committee chairperson or designee. Accommodation is the usual course. In the event of persistent disagreement—a rare occurrence—there is provision for final adjudication by the NAS president, who is ex officio chairperson of the NRC.

Following completion of review, all nonmilitary reports are delivered to sponsoring parties and become public documents. When of sufficient public interest, they are released to the press. Reports usually carry a summary of the principal content and recommendations. Those that are expected to be of unusual public interest may be accompanied by a press release and may even be the subject of a press conference. Such reports may also have a letter of transmittal from the academy president focusing attention on and interpreting particular aspects. In a small number of instances, the special handling of reports at this level has itself come under criticism and has engendered controversy—for example, when sensitive matters are injudiciously worded in a press release or reinterpreted in the transmittal letter.

In summary, the process of study and report used by the academy complex involves many persons in complex relationships. Central are groups of part-time, uncompensated experts (committees), assisted and to some degree guided by salaried professional staff. Activities proceed in a context of the mission set by sponsors and by the overall corporate standards and procedures set by the academy governing bodies and president. Roles of participants vary with circumstance and undergo change as the study proceeds. The process is too complex normally to be dominated by any one person but flexible enough to be affected at various points in various ways. Its major objective is to assemble and evaluate scientific and technical data and to relate these to specific practical concerns.

NRC Studies and Reports as Adjuncts to Regulation

The scientific contribution to policy and decision making, whether in regulation or other areas, has three conceivable components. The first is substantive, having to do with assembly and interpretation of relevant scientifically valid information. A second is transitional in the sense that it proceeds beyond the strictly substantive but is not truly decisional. The third component is the decision process itself, occurring in the complex context of the social arena with conflicting values and interests playing their roles in a structured political framework.

A general consensus has emerged in recent years that the first component is essential to much current policymaking and requires the participation of highly competent scientists. There is also consensus that decision making itself is not a matter of science and is not, therefore, the business of scientists qua scientists. There is uncertainty and controversy, among scientists and nonscientists alike, with respect to the second component: whether it exists and, if so, what role scientists can and should play.

Clearly the relative importance of the three components may vary from issue to issue. In a highly technical and sophisticated area, the decision may virtually fall out of the first component. In an area that has yet to be clearly formulated scientifically and technically, however, the first component may have little decisional impact but may nonetheless be an essential exercise to ensure complete analysis of the issue. In many issues, there is a transitional or intermediate component; this is the difficult area that needs to be addressed more decisively in relating science to policymaking.

Problems of the Data Base

Any scientific process includes assembly and evaluation of relevant data. To a research scientist, data are the grist for new questions and hypotheses, to be answered or tested by seeking still more data. Policy studies, however, differ from "normal" science. The questions are derived not from scientific data but from presented practical needs or problems. The task is to find and interpret whatever scientific data may be relevant, even though the data may not have been obtained for the purpose. Moreover, practical needs or problems usually do not fit into a single field of investigation or into one scientific discipline. Instead they cut across fields and disciplines, demanding a number of kinds of expertise. Two steps, nonetheless, must be carried out: assembly of the relevant data and evaluation of the data in relation to the presented questions.

The first step may be laborious but poses no serious conceptual difficulty for a properly chosen group of experts. The group can assemble the data from individual personal knowledge, from consultation with colleagues in their specialties, and from suitable search of the relevant literature. Academy studies occasionally have been criticized for omission of significant areas of specialized knowledge. The answer is continued careful effort to ensure comprehensiveness and specialty balance in constituting study groups.

Evaluation of the data with respect to the issue presents more-fundamental problems. Some or all of the data often are not decisive for the question at issue either because the data were not reliably obtained or because they were not obtained for the present purpose. Purpose very much influences design of data collection and applicability. For instance, different disciplines have differing objectives and produce differing data patterns bearing on the same phenomenon; epidemiology and biochemistry have different data sets bearing on colon cancer, for example. In the long run, the two sets of data are expected to be concordant; at a given time they may appear to be discrepant. Similarly, data addressing theory-oriented questions are not necessarily directly applicable to practice-oriented questions. Radiation effects on laboratory-cultured cells may illuminate the mechanism of action of radiation on living systems but not be helpful in estimating therapeutic dosage for human tumors. Questions raised by experiences in the complex world of real phenomena are unlikely to find precise answers in preexisting data because the data were not collected with the particular question or purpose in mind.

Mismatch of presented questions and immediately available data bases can have several consequences. First, with great frequency expert groups report a need for more research to improve the match. Second, any conclusions drawn from the existing data carry a degree of uncertainty. Third, experts in different areas may fall into disagreement on the relative importance to be attached to nonconcordant data from the different sources. Disagreement may be initiated by differing scientific perspectives, but inadequate data also encourage display of extrascientific predilections in interpretation. Fourth, outside interests may seize on those data and expert opinions that best fit their own purposes or maintain that, in the absence of expert consensus on the limited data, any action should be scaled down or postponed pending further studies. Beset by these problems, the expert group must face the question whether an incomplete and qualified scientific input to the decision process is better than none at all. To that degree they become involved in the decision process itself.

Dealing with Uncertainty

Public-policy deliberation is always fraught with uncertainty. Conflicting values, contention among interest groups, and, most especially, estimation and forecasting of future consequences all heighten the climate of uncertainty. Into this context scientists are expected to inject precise and reliable answers, not another source of uncertainty.

But in fact scientific statements themselves characteristically carry uncertainty; useful scientific measurements specify the uncertainty level as precisely as possible. Such measurements, whether statistical or absolute, are useful within their stated limits and can fulfill important purposes. Population time trends and geographic differentials in disease incidence carry uncertainty both statistically and in causal significance. Such data, even though carrying a degree of uncertainty may generate etiological hypotheses, however, that can be tested in the laboratory. The resulting experimental data may have quite high certainty with respect to rats or mice but yet considerable uncertainty in application to humans. Epidemiological and animal data therefore must be weighed jointly in relation to policy. Yet neither singly nor jointly are they necessarily decisive in choosing between policy A and B. More usually, they are relevant information to a political judgment that includes value and interest considerations.

This uncertainty of scientific statements can neither be wished nor legislated away; it reflects the status and nature of current knowledge. Greater certainty may be attained through greater knowledge but at a cost in time and money for additional research. That research may have to be addressed to the policy question itself, yielding information that has little value for other purposes. Such research is policy oriented.

Relating to the Policy Context

Difficulties with the data base are magnified by the fact that many expert groups confronted by policy-generated issues are unfamiliar with the policy context within which their effort will be judged and used. The natural habitat of many of the experts is in secluded laboratories, generally academic but also industrial, far from Washington. Their expert status derives from assiduous avoidance of the very habits of thought and ways of life that characterize governmental policymaking. Indeed, even seasoned Washington veterans often have difficulty forecasting the impact of a particular report or recommendation. Not surprisingly, given a less-than-adequate data base, the need to generate a consensus among diverse perspectives and relative unfamiliarity with the policy terrain, such expert reports may fail to hit the policy target. On the one hand, they may prove overly cautious, out of focus, and with less than hoped-for pertinence to the specific decisions confronted by the sponsoring agency. On the other hand, they may contain injudicious statements, made worse when reported out of context by the media, that damage academy prestige and raise questions as to the competence of its involved expertise.

Coping with Bias

Uncertainties of the data base and lack of policy sophistication can be further complicated by problems of actual or conceivable bias. Regulation is controversial and necessarily bears differentially on contending interests. Any so-called objective contribution to regulation is subject to suspicion, particularly if that contribution turns out to give advantage to one interest over another. In academy reports, bias could exist at two levels: individual and corporate. Some academy procedures are designed to mitigate individual bias. Critics suggest that these measures do not always eliminate the problem, although they concede that there has been favorable affect. The procedures for selecting expert commitees are at the heart of the matter. Does balance of biases lead to objectivity? Or is an orientation and perspective required that recognizes and subordinates bias as inappropriate to the professional task?

The matter of corporate bias is even more difficult. The NAS came into existence through congressional action. As with comparable academies in

Europe, creation of a U.S. national academy of science was seen as mutually advantageous to science and government. Science was expected to gain in recognition and thereby governmental patronage. Government, meanwhile, would gain access to reliable advice. Thus there is benefit to all. But does the relationship necessarily foster objectivity? Scientists are naturally eager to promote science, and the academy unashamedly does so with respect to federal scientific support and protection of the rights of scientists under attack. Such bias is overt and generally regarded as socially acceptable. But does it also take covert, and even unconscious, forms? Can an academy so heavily supported by federal funds be truly an independent adviser? Is there inevitable inclination to become the implement of governmental purpose? The question can be asked whether the academy caters to those federal agencies that regularly sponsor and fund its studies, incidentally supporting its not-inconsiderable overhead budget. Such questions come easily to mind in an atmosphere of vigorously contending advocacy. They deserve frank discussion and study, both within the academy complex and outside it. This is particularly the responsibility of those who believe that the academy role in the policy process is constructive overall and that strengthening it wherever possible is of major importance. A considerable improvement, if only in public image, might be made by an expanded nonfederal fiscal base, unfortunately not easily achieved.

Addressing the Audience

To minimize even the appearance of bias is essential to maintenance of high credibility. Without credibility, the role of any independent adviser is empty. Credibility, in turn, is a determinant of the effectiveness of an adviser but is not the whole story. An adviser influencing public policy must also be easily understood and must directly address the needs of the advisee. In terms of the academy charter, the advisee is the government and its agencies—executive, legislative, and perhaps even judicial. But in our society, the government is intended to be the agent of the governed; it is the public on whose behalf the government operates—or should. To function effectively as a high-level adviser to the federal government, the academy complex must ensure access to its processes, in suitable measure, to interested elements of the complex public audience. The term *access* is not intended to imply physical presence but rather availability for evaluation and use.

NRC reports vary widely in their intended target audience, and authors of reports may not always be clear either who the audience is or how best to address it. Agency scientists, agency managers, congressional staff, actual legislators and executive decision makers, the media, and citizens (and their various groups) have very different communication requirements. Special effort is required to be sure that no motivated and attentive groups are excluded from access. This means providing suitable public entree to the NRC advisory process. This task is not easy and has given rise to much discussion and controversy. The academy complex takes the position, for example, that it is not subject to sunshine requirements designed to open up regulatory processes to public scrutiny and understanding. Its unwillingness to be regarded as a federal agency is important and understandable. There seems less justification for insistence on confidentiality beyond that regarded as acceptable for standard governmental operations. Greater openness of NRC studies has been symbolized by recent emphasis on public meetings held by study committees to receive comments and advice from both scientific and lay public. While it is true that full deliberation may benefit from some shelter from excessive public exposure, excessive confidentiality may also be detrimental. What seems essential is that the study process be open to scrutiny once its conclusions are reached. In this way, suspicion of possible covert influence can be minimized.

Corporate Consensus and Individual Views

It is the incorporated academy that has the responsibility for providing advice. In fact, it would be impossible and probably not even useful to obtain an informed consensus of the entire academy membership on each of the many matters on which the academy advises. The NAS has about thirteen hundred members and about two-thirds that number in the other two combined honorific units. Many of these members have little interest in the study-and-report function of the academy. Those who do generally have expertise in only a small sector of the report output. The corporate function thus is met through the academy-supervised NRC. The tactic used is to form small working parties (committees) of suitable expertise extending beyond the academy membership.

Committees have considerable independence in carrying out their task; however, if a report deviates sharply from established institutional norms, it is subject to correction through the report-review procedure. This mechanism is intended to maintain corporate responsibility. Although difficulties and even various forms of abuse are conceivable, the mechanism seems reasonable and indispensable under the circumstances. However, pressure for corporate responsibility can go too far if it demands untrammeled consensus on all issues. Science itself works toward consensus about phenomena under study, but it does so over time and with full exposure of all contending views. Almost every innovative departure begins as a minority view. To pressure too hard for consensus, especially in areas dominated by uncertainty, can not only repress individual views but may lead to bland consensus that fails to reflect adequately the actual state of scientific opinion. There-fore, while looking toward consensus and maintaining corporate respon-sibilty, the academy process does well when it records disagreement and dis-senting opinion, both within authoring committees and between them and the review process. No academy of science can be or should seek to appear monolithic, and no public policy rooted in the assumption of final authority can well serve our kind of society.

Science in the Policy Mode

The issues so far discussed are derivative from the disarmingly simple act of incorporation, but circumstances of 1863 have vastly altered during the almost century and a quarter since. Science is no longer an almost-unnoticed petitioner for federal interest; rather it is widely acknowledged to be a ma-jor bulwark of the general welfare and has thoroughly permeated govern-mental agencies in the past half-century. Science external to the government has also proliferated and is a major beneficiary of federal support. The NAS has been transformed from an honorific group limited to fifty mem-bers, without home or staff, to a complex institution commanding the par-ticipation of thousands of scientists and supportive scientific and adminis-trative personnel.

The tasks undertaken have acquired a new character and importance. The first federal request to the infant academy was to advise on possible "uniformity of weights, measures, and coins, considered in relation to domestic and international commerce."[6] Other early requests related to protection of iron ship bottoms from seawater and to correction of the mag-netic deviation of compasses in such ships. In contrast, the 1979 report of the NRC describes current issues and studies bearing on risk assessment, human ability testing, public-policy making, national statistics, techno-logical decision making, diesel engines and the biomedical effects of their emissions, strengths and limitations of epidemiology, planetary explora-tion, the state of school science, China's science and technology, surface mining and reclamation, technology and innovation, energy conservation, pharmaceuticals for developing countries, ethical aspects of health-science policy, and health promotion and disease prevention.[7]

This list, only a sampler, indicates the breadth and depth of involve-ment, not only of the NAS but of science generally, in public-policy issues. It seems time to recognize that a third major focus of scientific effort has come into being. There have been interminable discussions of the validity of the distinction between basic and applied science. Continuous and over-lapping though they are, for certain purposes it is useful to recognize that research may be internally oriented (seeking new knowledge to strengthen the theory and logical structure of science) or externally oriented (seeking new knowledge to expand its use in meeting human needs and aspirations.) Applied, or externally oriented, research has been almost solely technological in thrust up to fairly recently—seeking better technical means to control materials and energy. We are witnessing now the early stages of deliberate application of science to policymaking, both better to inform it and improve its mechanisms. This focus of science may be referred to as policy oriented or as science in the policy mode, in distinction to science in the theoretical or technological modes. As with the earlier distinction between theory-oriented and technology-oriented science, policy-oriented science overlaps and is continuous with the other two focuses and should not be thought of as sharply delineated in kind. Nonetheless, there are important characteristics of the new focus that differ from the old and need their own attention.

Science related to regulatory processes is one example of policy-oriented science. Regulation requires accurate and objective information (data) and hence is dependent upon science. Biophysics and biochemistry, for example, have brought new precision to measurement of toxic chemicals and to tracing their metabolism. New techniques provide enhanced capability to detect and monitor toxigens, toxins, and their metabolites. These techniques are products of theory-oriented and technology-oriented research, representing advances in fundamental science and its technological application. A commercial compound like saccharin, for example, stems from organic synthesis in a basic laboratory, followed by industrial applied research and development to meet a need. The toxicity of saccharin was detected and examined by toxicologists over many years. When the substance became the subject of agitated policy debate, scientific attention grew, largely under federal and industrial sponsorship. Saccharin became the subject of policy- or regulation-motivated research, not only to expand understanding of its action but better to cope wih the policy issues associated with it. The latter issues include risk assessment, cost-benefit analysis, and efficacy of labeling. Recent studies of saccharin are a prime illustration of science in the policy mode.

The generality of the phenomenon is indicated by the establishment of the National Institute for Occupational Safety and Health (NIOSH) and the National Center for Toxicological Research, federal scientific agencies created to provide accurate information on materials primarily of policy interest. The expanded need for scientific analysis of policy issues also is well illustrated by the expanded and altered activities of the NAS. It is my impression that the legitimate scope of these activities necessarily goes beyond the simple assembly and interpretation of existing data, the first and essential scientific contribution to policymaking. Beyond this, scientific expertise is necessary to recognize the need for new data accumulation to anticipate emerging issues, to point to possible or probable implications of new courses of action of changes of circumstance, to interpret for various audiences the scientific and technical content of political issues, and to provide access to decision makers to the best and latest technical information. This is the content of the transitional component. It is the province of policy-centered and decision-oriented science, bridging into the decision process but stopping short of the decision itself. Such science in the policy mode must remain free of advocacy but must also be free of constraints that limit its effectiveness in substantively enriching decision arenas, with equal access to all contending parties. The practice of such science requires something different from the usual characteristics of either fundamental or technologically oriented applied science. Greater resolution of and attention to this emergent scientific area is a task for the immediate future.

Examining a Case History

The case reported here illustrates some difficulties of policy-oriented science but is not to be taken as prototypical of Academy activities. The impact of academy studies and reports has been examined but never comprehensively or with full access to all information.[8] I am inclined to credit, provisionally and for heuristic reasons, the view of Boffey and other critics that a small percentage of NAS studies and reports are of high quality and considerable impact, a few are of poor quality and little impact, and the remainder range widely both in quality and impact. Looking at the latest NAS saccharin report, my impression is that it falls in the third category.[9] Its major impact was to solidify the congressional block to FDA action on general distribution of saccharin while having as yet essentially no impact on the larger issues addressed.

A public furor occurred when the FDA announced its intention, based on a series of studies culminating in a Canadian report in which FDA had confidence, to limit sharply the general use of saccharin as a noncaloric sweetener. The combined evidence indicated that saccharin in high dosage induces bladder cancer in male rats. The finding was regarded as definitive in toxicological terms and therefore required FDA to take action under its general charge, as well as under the Delaney amendment.

Alarmed by vociferous public protest against what was seen by many as overzealous regulation, Congress took the unusual step of imposing an eighteenth-month moratorium on the proposed FDA action. The statute requested further that a study be made, preferably by the NAS, of the evidence for carcinogenicity of saccharin and the general problems in ensuring a safe national food supply. The first task was to be completed within twelve months of the date of enactment, the second within fifteen months. The NAS assigned the saccharin study to the Assembly of Life Sciences within NRC, and the broader policy study was assigned to the IOM. Each study was to be carried out by a committee of suitable experts, and the entire operation was to be coordinated by an overall steering committee. It was clear that the congressional mandate encouraged activity well beyond data collection and interpretation.

The saccharin committee went about its fairly straightforward technical task in a well-organized and efficient way. Examining the relevant literature, it retraced the path taken by several earlier NAS committees that had examined saccharin, looked particularly carefully at the new Canadian data, and examined still more recent studies published or in prospect. Its conclusions were that, beyond question, saccharin is a low-potency carcinogen for the rat bladder but that epidemiological data are equivocal in demonstrating effects on human populations. Members of the committee were of different mind as to the appropriate regulatory course under the circumstances, as indicated by several minority comments eventually expressed. By decision of the steering committee, however, a formal recommendation about the regulation of saccharin, clearly requested by the Congress, was deferred to the second, more-general report. The rationale for this decision was that saccharin was only the tip of the iceberg that warranted congressional attention. The main mass was the statute governing FDA and the regulatory procedures that had grown up around it.

While the saccharin committee was at work on its well-defined task, the IOM committee was attempting to come to grips with its less-manageable one. The task was potentially huge and the time extremely limited. Moreover, the IOM committee believed it difficult to address larger issues without knowing the conclusions of the saccharin committee. After initiating a number of background studies, the committee marked time with little consensus as to direction. This alarmed the steering committee, which felt threatened by approaching deadlines. A reorganization followed, blending steering-committee responsibilities with those of the policy committee. A special drafting committee, consisting of the chairpersons of the three committees and several other steering-committee members, assumed responsibility for completing the policy report in consultation with the several committees. It was agreed that the technical saccharin report would constitute the first part of single overall report, with the policy aspect as the second part.

The overall report sought to make clear that saccharin is a single case worthy of consideration but not intrinsically the most consequential that might receive attention. The complex operation of an increasingly technological food production and distribution system was outlined. Costs and benefits of regulating such a system to maintain realistic risk levels were discussed. The statutory basis for current regulation was analyzed and found to be excessively elaborate, legalistic rather than scientific in concept, and rigid in implementation. It was proposed that Congress should reconsider the basic statute and make changes to yield wider regulatory options for FDA, while assuring it heightened availability of scientific advice. The report suggested that under these circumstances, greater public access to FDA decision-making rationales would improve credibility of the agency and allow it to focus more efficiently on higher-priority objectives. In such a framework, neither Congress nor NAS would need to address questions as specific as the particular regulatory steps appropriate for saccharin. Such decisions would be well within the mandate given by Congress to the FDA.

The only part of this clearly policy-oriented message that got through was that saccharin was not a sufficient public danger to warrant a politically destabilizing confrontation among the various interests upon whom food regulatory policy bears. The food industry did not want to lose saccharin until a suitable substitute could be found. Consumer interests did not want to lose the security of the Delaney amendment until they were sure the FDA would not be undermined by opposing political pressures. The FDA itself was not sure it would be better off if its whole authority came under scrutiny. And Congress had lots of other issues of higher priority on its mind. So low-calorie foods and beverages continue as a major item in the national diet despite expressed NAC-NRC-IOM concern that heavy exposure to such items, particularly in prenatal and young children, may show higher tumor incidences detectable epidemiologically in the early 2000s.

The message has not gotten through for a combination of reasons, among which is ineffective science in the policy mode. In the saccharin case, Congress, in a panic, undermined FDA responsibility by imposing an item veto on the agency's entirely justified action, given its existing congressional mandate. Congress also asked NAS, as its highest source of scientific advice, for a definitive answer in twelve months (much less by the time negotiation was completed and the study underway) to a question about a relatively minor food component whose status had been doubtful for twenty years. NAS accepted the charge, although it had done studies and provided reports on saccharin three times in the preceding ten years. At the same time, Congress asked for a study of quite large scope to be carried out in fifteen months, presumably signaling its intention to take action in a broad context in a time frame of about that length. The NAS accepted that charge as well, assigning it to a different NAS component from the first. Recognizing the political linkage of the two studies, however, a cumbersome organizational linkage was provided that had to be modified during the course of the study. Despite improvised improvement of the organizational defect the more fundamental study of longer-term impact has disappeared from sight since the political pressure generated by the saccharin controversy dissipated. The congressional memory seemingly was short when the report requested some eighteen months earlier was delivered by NAS.

Concluding Remarks

One does not know how often the saccharin scenario is repeated nor how such scenarios may affect issues of high importance. Nor should one underestimate the complexity of the linkages in our ways of formulating policy. However, as our society moves into a new millennium that seems likely to witness the continuing fruition of two centuries of ever-more rapidly advancing science and technology, it cannot afford to have public policy made without assured lines of deliberative communication with expert technical resources. Such communication occurs at the present time in many complex ways at many social levels. But at the highest level, and possibly about some of the most-important issues, effective communication is by no means assured.

Interaction between the federal government and the academy complex, although now gratifyingly frequent and generally constructive, seems to occur in some significant cases on a catch-as-catch-can basis, without guarantee that the two parties understand each other as to objectives and their feasibility or as to the priorities to be assigned to various topics to be addressed. The matter is of sufficient importance to be the subject of a study that would examine the record to date, sketch probable future needs, and propose procedural guidelines that take into account the nature of the interacting parties and the unusual relationship between them. Were such a study carried out, one of its prime focuses would be the relation of the academy complex to federal regulatory processes. Better definition and still greater effeceveness in this area would alone justify the time and cost of the study.

The NAS has a unique status as an independent, congressionally chartered, and prestigious institution with a good record in providing advice on science and technology to the federal government, including advice on regulatory processes. Its status is simply and soundly stated in the congressional act of incorporation and needs no legislative modification or elabortation. The importance of the relationship has grown enormously in the present century and is likely to grow still more in the next. The relationship has been constructive for the two parties and for the national interest. There is legitimate question, however, whether the relationship might not be significantly improved and strengthened.

The time seems appropriate for a new look in depth at the present state, at needs for the future, and at the possible formulation of mutual guidelines to ensure that the interaction proceeds effectively and in accordance with appropriate priorities on the two sides. Such comprehensive consideration was undertaken early in academy history, and the relationship again came under scrutiny in relation to both world wars. The involvement of the academy in regulatory processes makes clear that its role is not only important in military emergency. Perhaps the present time, when there is a growing sense of emergency with respect to our civil status, is an appropriate backdrop for sober deliberation on the overall academy role in public policy.

Notes

1. The actual language was: "the Academy shall, whenever called upon by any department of the Government, investigate, examine, experiment, and report upon any subject of science or art." The initiators of the concept of a national academy also expected it to strengthen then pursuit of science, and the status of scientists, in a nation still seeking cultural identity and maturity. See Rexmond C. Cochrane, *The National Academy of Sciences: The First Hundred Years 1863-1963* (Washington, D.C.: National Academy of Sciences, 1978), chap. 3.

2. Ibid., pp. 8ff.

3. IOM membership is not entirely honorific. During the stipulated five-year membership term, candidates accept responsibility for participation in IOM activities. It is also the case that the annual slate of nominees for IOM membership is approved by the NAS council.

4. Food and Nutrition Board, National Research Council, *Toward Healthful Diets* (Washington, D.C.: National Academy of Sciences, 1980). [In June 1982, an NAS panel issued a new report that "stands in sharp contrast to the controversial dietary advice" of the 1980 report. *New York Times*, June 17, 1982—ed.]

5. Committee for a Study on Saccharin and Food Safety Policy, *Saccharin: Technical Assessment of Risks and Benefits*, Report No. 1 (Washington, D.C.: National Research Council, National Academy of Sciences, 1978); *Food Safety Policy, Scientific and Societal Considerations*, Report No. 2 (Washington, D.C.: Institute of Medicine, National Academy of Sciences, 1979).

6. Cochrane, see n. 1, pp. 80 ff.

7. National Academy of Sciences, *The National Research Council in 1979: Current Issues and Studies* (Washington, D.C., 1979); available from Office of Information, NAS, 2101 Constitution Ave., Washington, D.C., 20418.

8. Philip M. Boffey, *The Brain Bank of America* (New York: McGraw-Hill, 1975).

9. See n. 5.

Comment

Harold P. Green

Dr. Grobstein discusses the general role of the National Academy of Sciences in providing advice on science and technology to the government, but I find somewhat puzzling his effort to focus on the role of the academy in regulatory matters. In some respects, he seems to regard academy advice on regulatory issues as a rather special case, but in other respects he seems to regard it only as an extension of the academy's traditional function. As an example of the latter, he states that requests for NRC activity "arise out of policy debate—often in relation to regulatory activities" and that the chartered purpose of NAS is to provide advice on science and technology to the federal government, "including advice on regulatory processes." On the other hand, he implies that NAS activities relating to regulatory matters are somehow qualitatively different from activities not related to regulation. For example, he states, "Science related to regulatory processes is one example of policy-oriented science. Regulation requires accurate and objective information (data) and hence is dependent upon science." It is not clear whether he regards NAS activities relating to regulation as more policy oriented than other activities directed toward helping the government, particularly those who help the government decide how to spend money.

It seems clear that any time the government seeks academy advice on any question, it is for the purpose of using the advice in making a decision. In this sense, all NAS activities conducted at government request are policy oriented. Moreover, in a regulatory context or otherwise, the advice is not worth very much unless it is based on "accurate and objective information (data)." I am puzzled, therefore, by the precise nature of the distinction that Dr. Grobstein seeks to draw between NAS activities that are related to regulatory processes and those that are not.

Still, it is clear that there are important distinctions. I think two are of fundamental importance. First, in the nonregulatory mode, the decision maker is usually not constrained—or at least is less constrained—by statutory pronouncements. Once the facts are in hand, the decision maker has latitude to make what he or she considers to be the best decision. In the regulatory mode, however, the decision by the regulator must be made within the confines of a statute that is the source of the regulator's authority and power. When the facts are in hand, the decision maker's basic inquiry must be what the law requires on the basis of those facts. Second, in the regulatory mode, private interests have enforceable rights to have certain kinds of decisions made and to have decisions made through specified procedures. Although some private interests may have expectations that can be satisifed or defeated by the decision in the nonregulatory mode, they do not have any rights with respect to the nature of the decision or the manner in which it is made.

Regulatory decisions are made within the framework of language used in statutes and rules. Seemingly ordinary words with well-accepted meanings may have special meanings for regulatory purposes; terms with which scientists are thoroughly familiar such as *toxic, additive, safe,* or *risk* may have special statutory definitions.

It is important to recognize the limitations of scientific bodies in providing reliable inputs into public-policy decisions. For example, to use examples drawn from actual academy studies, no competence beyond science would be necessary for a committee to answer the question whether a particular chemical poses a carcinogenic hazard or risk to humans. On the other hand, scientific competence alone cannot answer the questions whether there is a particular kind of exposure to a chemical that constitutes a virtually safe level of exposure. To answer the latter question, one must know the meaning of *safe*, which may be defined in the statute, and of *virtually*. One NAS committee declined to answer such a question because, it correctly observed, "determination of an acceptable risk would be a societal judgment and not based on scientific facts." Other NAS committees have, however, undertaken to offer judgments on questions of that kind.

The fact that a regulatory decision involves questions of scientific fact does not mean that the findings of fact must, or even can better, be made by a committee of scientists. The ultimate decision is made by the agency head, who is a political appointee and is politically accountable, as much for the acceptability of the decision as for its intrinsic soundness in terms of scientific fact. The case of saccharin neatly illustrates this point. The FDA's contemplated restriction on saccharin usage was out of step with political reality. Congress intervened to substitute its political judgment for the FDA's technical judgment. Dr. Grobstein suggests that the saccharin tale illustrates a poorly functioning regulatory process and a deficiency in the role of science. In my view, it represents the way the process should work.

In our scheme of government regulatory agencies are creatures of the Congress, which, through delegation of congressional power, perform legislative functions. Most of us seem prepared not to expect the political process to give us acts of Congress that are based on scientific fact, rationality, and sound principle. When, however, it comes to regulation rather than legislation, we expect more-principled, scientifically valid, and correct decisions. Certainly heads of regulatory agencies need not be as concerned about politics as are legislators since they do not stand for reelection every two or six years. Still, agency heads are subject to comparable political pressures in terms of continuing tenure, reappointment, advancement, and persuading Congress to appropriate adequate funds. It is not surprising, therefore, that regulatory agencies frequently make scientifically dubious decisions in order to remain in consonance with political reality. When this is recognized, it follows that it is not all that important that the regulatory agency have accurate and objective information and that scientists inject precise and reliable answers into the regulatory process.

Regulation involves costs and benefits to society, and the activity regulated also involves costs and benefits to society. Although science can assist us considerably in identifying and quantifying costs, it is of little help in identifying and quantifying benefits. Benefit, like beauty, is in the eye of the beholder. Where costs and benefits are considered in the context of whether society, or components of it, should be asked to assume costs in exchange for perceived benefits, this consideration is essentially legislative and political, not scientific.

This is not to say that it is inappropriate for the academy to play an important role in making regulatory decisions or that it is incapable of making major, constructive contributions. The point is, rather, that if the advice (as opposed to statement of scientific fact) of the NAS is in fact taken seriously and is an important factor shaping policy decision, disproportionate weight is probably being given to the opinions of an elite scientific establishment.

In this respect, I found Dr. Grobstein's remarks about committee formation and operation of particular interest. He observes that eligibility for committee membership derives primarily from expertise in a relevant scientific or technical field. I am pleased to report that this limitation should not be taken too seriously, since I, who have no expertise in any scientific or technical field, have served from time to time on academy committees, along with an occasional social-science or humanities person. Having reported this good news, there is also some bad news. Particularly since I did not really understand the science, I usually went along with what I perceived to be the committee consensus.

Here there is a real opportunity for progress. Where science is in the policy mode, it would be quite useful to have more than token representation on the committee of persons who are expert in nonscientific or technical fields, including some that are not necessarily relevant. For example, the process would be enhanced by the occasional participation of a poet or musician. A healthy balance of experts and lay persons will provide some assurance that the right questions are asked (and answered) and will also help in having the committee's labors described in its report in the vocabulary and style of ordinary political discourse. This is a point of critical importance. Science can play a major role in public-policy formulation over the long run only if it learns to use lay language. Coping with a few lay members of academy committees would be great practice for exposing the committee's position in the political arena.

Second, it is important that the committee be composed of persons who can work together in harmony toward building consensus. At the same time, it is important that nuances of individual opinion be permitted, indeed encouraged, to surface. The chairperson of the committee should be alert to these nuances and should encourage their expression in both the meetings and the committee's report.

Personality is an important factor. The personality of the chairperson is of critical importance, but in every committee with which I have worked there is invariably one member or perhaps two who tend to dominate the discussion and set its course. Expression of nuances is particularly useful to offset such domination. Nevertheless, one wonders to what extent the value of an academy study depends upon the personalities comprising the committee. One wonders whether, for example, two separate NAS committees, similarly constituted with respect to disciplinary backgrounds of its members, working in parallel but in total isolation from each other, would come up with comparable conclusions.

Over the past year or so, I have been a member of a special academy committee constituted by the governing board of the NRC to conduct an internal review of the procedures and practices of academy committees engaged in studies involving risk assessment. The committee's report is consistent with my observations as to inconsistencies among committees as to basic approach; the narrowness of disciplines represented; the fact that the effort to achieve consensus operates to obscure important differences; and the failure to discuss uncertainty adequately.

7

NIH's Consensus-Development Program: Theory, Process, and Critique

Charles Upton Lowe

Statement of the Problem

Emile Gley, an enterprising French biologist, discovered the internal secretion process of the pancreas around 1900. For motives that can be attributed only to eccentricity, he sealed the account of his experiments in an envelope and deposited it with the French Society of Biology in 1905 with instructions that the packet be opened only at his request. When Canadian physiologists F.G. Banting and Charles Best announced their discovery of insulin in 1921, Gley, then a professor of physiology in Paris, finally instructed the society to open his packet and publish its contents.

Obviously, the behavior of Gley—causing a two-decade lag in development of a critical area of medicine—cannot be imagined as typical of past or present biomedical investigators. Scientists rarely delay publication of their completed work. Nevertheless, after results of useful, validated innovations are published, lags often occur between publication on the one hand and clinical awareness and application on the other. The converse can also hold true: an innovation already in use may be found to be ineffective or even harmful, yet removal of that innovation from clinical practice may be unnecessarily delayed. Further, medical practices and technologies have been widely adopted despite the lack of reliable information about their benefits and risks.

In their search for the best means to prevent or treat individual disease, both physicians and patients have long appreciated this constellation of problems. Both have always been simultaneously loath to lose the possible advantages of a new treatment while wary of utilizing devices or procedures that have not stood the test of time or that may later be shown to be ineffective or even harmful. Although the resulting conservatism is a hallmark of modern medical practice, it has only recently been defined as a key element in a major social problem and a problem that federal programs with responsibility for knowledge generation must address.

The extensive contributions of Dr. Susan Asch are hereby acknowledged, as is the assistance of Kathie Bowing.

First attempts at solution of this problem were aimed primarily at improvement in information-transfer mechanisms. The proliferation of continuing medical-education programs, increased distribution of regular bulletins from various health-related federal agencies, the geometric increase in speciality and subspeciality publications, and the appearance of information packages intended for the newer media modes, such as cassette tape lectures, are all examples of attempts of this kind. Further, attention to dissemination has continued to be the cornerstone of the approach of many federal agencies, including the National Institutes of Health (NIH). The National Library of Medicine and now the Hill Center are evidence of this institutional commitment to dissemination.

Indeed, if one approaches this problem from the standpoint of providing more-appropriate messages, to better-targeted audiences, through more-efficient or attractive communication channels, the solutions appear to be clear and have a beguiling simplicity. In reality, however, this approach is in no way simple. A major source of complexity is that any innovations must be imposed upon and utilize the preexisting system for dissemination of medical technology, a massive structure that has been built up over many years. It includes the physicians, nurses, technicians, volunteers, administrators, and patients in some 7,500 hospitals, 13,000 nursing homes, 379,000 medical practices, 140 medical schools, 1,075 research centers, 561 health professional associations, and 307 nonprofit voluntary organizations. It is not a system that can be easily circumvented or altered, inasmuch as many influential members of the medical community have a substantial professional investment in it as it now exists.

Simultaneously, the position of medicine as a social institution has changed radically, as have the positions of the potential recipients in their respective personal social systems. Physicians are no longer the omniscient healers or personal friends; patients are no longer passive recipients of health sources. Rather they are more informed about and more responsible for the quality of their own health care. Public participation in the allocation of resources has become an imperative even in decisions concerning support of research at the boundaries of current scientific thinking.

The difficulties in improving knowledge transfer within complex, entrenched, and impersonal institutions are compounded by the knowledge explosion that has recently taken place in bioscience and medicine. Over the course of time, the messages produced by the biomedical knowledge generators have proved to be enormous in number; they have, however, continued to be transmitted through very limited types of channels, usually through the classic academic article for professional publication or presentation. The response to this has been a vast proliferation of professional journals, conferences, continuing-education courses, and similar phenomena, while the old system of the seepage of small bits of knowledge through personal networks, founded through apprenticeship experiences, has broken down.

The steady increase in the number of biomedical serials over the past century is evidence. By 1980, there were about 9,000 biomedical serials published in the United States alone. The total worldwide figure was about 22,000 serials in the health sciences. When restricted to a defined subset of scholarly health-science literature, there were approximately 244,000 articles from 2,700 journals in 1980, about 40 percent published in the United States (Mehnert 1981). An additional explosive effect has resulted from an order-of-magnitude increase in the numerical data within articles due to automated laboratory instrumentation and analytic techniques. Thus, attempts at solution of the problem of knowledge transfer that provided more channels and vehicles of communication simply compound the existing dilemma of the medical practitioner and the public.

An Approach to the Problem: Diffusion Theory

Although a great deal of attention and effort has been expended upon the problem of dissemination of medical knowledge, equal attention often has not been paid to the steps of knowledge-transfer process preceding and following dissemination. The totality of this process, from knowledge conception to behavioral implementation, is implied by the term *diffusion of innovations* more recently described as knowledge transfer and technology transfer. It is a complex, multifaceted social process, which extends far beyond the simple dissemination of information. It has been the subject of scientific scrutiny for well over fifty years. Examination of the process in many contexts and under many different conditions has allowed the development of general theory, which can be reapplied in the analysis of many different substantive areas, including bioscience and medicine.

The theories developed have differed widely in the specific terms used in describing diffusion but can be roughly divided into two general patterns of model construction. The first type is largely descriptive in nature; the models are variations on a theme first advanced by Lasswell (1946). Communication is conceptualized as the problem of who says what, to whom, through what channels, and with what effect. The basic structural elements of the model derived from Lasswell's are the source (the producer of the knowledge to be transmitted), the message (the knowledge transmitted, in a particular form), the channel (the pathways over which the knowledge travels), the receiver (or potential user of the knowledge), and the effects (or impact of the knowledge on the receiver's knowledge set on her or his behavior).

The process in which these elements are involved is communication. When the message is a new idea or piece of knowledge, the process is termed *diffusion* (Robertson 1971). The process is usually represented in models as a series of points (the elements) connected by vector forces (the processes) in a step-flow form, as though one element produced the next in a linear fashion. Incorporated in later versions of this model are feedback loops, whereby changes in one element reflect back to, and presumably influence, earlier elements in the process (Rogers and Shoemaker 1971).

Building on this basic schema, theorists more recently have approached the topic of diffusion from a systems-analytic rather than structural-functional perspective, with the goal of developing a set of criteria for innovation. Essentially these efforts have consisted of identifying a set of dimensions along which the structural elements and linking processes of the original flow model vary. Once these dimensions have been set forth, propositions are constructed to explain the constellation of positions along these various dimensions that the elements must occupy in order to maximize the likelihood that innovations will diffuse and be adopted in a system (Glazer et al. 1976). This has produced a construct of diffusion that has height, depth, and length, with a network of vectors connecting the whole.

As a result of analyses of many different systems, a rich and somewhat confusing literature has arisen. Clearly many different constellations of positions of the elements on their various dimensions will influence diffusion and adoption of innovations; however, several common threads run throughout all current approaches to this problem, and any analysis of diffusion and innovation processes using state-of-the-art theory must recognize at least these basic points.

The first point, common to all current diffusion theories that they are concerned with, is the transfer and concomitant transformation of knowledge: its generation, its intersection with other pieces of knowledge, its framing as a transmittable message, its reflection of other attributes of its generator, its molding by the attributes of its channels of transmission, its conveyance to particular persons and its reflection of their attributes, its integration into knowledge set with resulting transformation of the original knowledge, its initial application by the recipients and final routinization of its use—all responding to the environment within which sources, messages, channels, recipients, and applications coexist. This represents an evolution from earlier theories that treated the physical technology (such as seed corn or drugs), rather than knowledge, as the innovations to be diffused.

The second point of commonality in more-recent formulations is the recognition that this is clearly an interactive, rather than a directive, process. That is, this process cannot be interpreted as a one-way flow, as the very early models seemed to imply. Instead knowledge transfer must be viewed as a system rather than as isolated unidirectional processes. In this, as in every other system, therefore, each element and process is simultaneously responsive to, and covariant with, all the other elements and processes composing the system. Change in any element or process may lead to responsive changes in many others sequentially or coequally. Since knowledge is itself one of the mutable elements in the system, the process has come to be recognized as one of knowledge transformation as well as transfer.

An important point implied by approaching diffusion from a systems standpoint and emphasizing the interactive rather than directive nature of the process is that the constituent processes are inherently exchanges. This means that for one element of the system to be affected by another, something of value must be exchanged. This thing is not necessarily a physical item, nor is the value necessarily economic. Rather, the tender may be prestige, power self-esteem, or other social goods. This point is often not stated in formal exchange-theory terminology but is nonetheless a nearly universal underlying theme (Levine and White 1961).

Recognition of this point allows us to appreciate and avoid a logical fallacy: the assumption that since the knowledge-transfer system has high social value, knowledge must therefore be one of the valued items involved in the individual exchanges within the system. The point is that participants in a knowledge-transfer system do not always gladly accept information because it is a valued item, nor do they always participate in the system because of an intrinsic need for information and understanding.

Another important point that has emerged in the development of a systems approach to this problem is the recognition that diffusion of innovations cannot be simply viewed as an interaction among individuals. The participants may be particular organizations as well, and the interactions studied may be between individuals within organizations, between organizations themselves, or between organizations and individuals (Kaluzny, Gentry, and Veney 1974; Hage and Dewar 1973).

A final point of systems and organization behavior, emphasized in all current theories of diffusion and drawn from the general body of theory, is that knowledge-handling systems are imbedded in matrices composed of many other social systems, all of which impinge upon its operation at many points (Katz and Kahn 1966; Aiken and Hage 1968).

In summary, the current theories of knowledge handling are essentially system approaches, which view knowledge transfer as complex phenomena best described as a large set of mutually dependent covarying elements, bound together by explicit interactions between the elements. Knowledge-handling systems are composed of, surrounded by, and interdigitated with other social systems, which affect the function of the system in many ways. The corollary is obvious; changes in knowledge-handling systems (or diffusion processes) can be effected by intervention at any point, but any changes made will have ramifications for the entire system, and quite possibly for contingent or constituent systems as well.

These points may seem to be obvious and simply a restatement of systems theory with knowledge as the defining variable of the system described; however, the major points described in this overview have often been broadly ignored in supposed applications of this perspective to practical problems of knowledge transfer. The bulk of federal programs in this area offer a ready target for examination.

Typically governmental agencies have taken a mass media or archival approach to knowledge transfer, which continues to posit a unilinear, noninteractive step-flow model of knowledge handling. Investigators write journal articles or send personal letters to intermediate recipients, conveying information, who abridge and filter information; these recipients then transmit the information by lectures, letters, or review articles to primary user-recipients. Although acknowledging the full sequence of steps involved in knowledge transfer, these approaches concentrate in application on the element of channel. Brief attention is sometimes given to the message and the recipients, but interventions involving the source and the applications are not considered; the argument advanced is that, for various reasons, these are beyond the scope of the possible feasible predictions, adjustments, or interventions available. These approaches tend to concentrate on the mechanical aspects of knowledge transmission, while the social aspects are largely ignored. They often equate knowledge and information, ignoring the interpretive dimension of knowledge and therefore treat the knowledge as immutable.

Another difficulty with these applied approaches is that they have not spoken to the possible interactions of elements in the process that are not in sequence in the linear step-flow model: the source and the recipient, or the message and the application. For example, the specificity of the message to be transmitted may depend upon the intended or anticipated type of application. If the intended application of the knowledge must be in the form of a specific procedure, then the message must contain very specific information in order to allow and encourage the intended application.

Finally, they have generally ignored the exchanges implied in the interaction of the system elements and have treated knowledge handling as a straight delivery system, moving information from a source to a recipient, through defined channels. Often no feedback loop is included; the applied approaches have certainly not considered the notion that this movement of facts must be powered by some exchange yielding social energy. Probably secondary to this omission, these approaches have concomitantly committed the logical fallacy warned against earlier: they have assumed that the potential recipients of the knowledge desire it and that facilitating its transfer is simply a matter of removing barriers and easing the natural passive flow of information.

Evolution of NIH's Consensus-Development Effort

The consequent bottlenecking of knowledge, inappropriate transfer of research results, and uneven access to advances in medical knowledge and technology has become increasingly apparent to practicing physicians and to the general public. Equally apparent is the inadequacy of government attempts to remedy the situation when these attempts concentrate only on improving the mechanisms for information transmission. In 1974, the Congress created the President's Biomedical Research Panel to investigate this problem among other related issues; in 1976 the panel reported to Congress, making a series of recommendations.

It stressed the need for more-effective transfer of biomedical research to the clinical practice of medicine. The panel observed that a major impediment to effective transfer was the often-conflicting, confusing, or unsusbstantiated interpretations of biomedical and clinical research. It identified the imperative for the establishment by government of a mechanism to ensure the translation and dissemination of knowledge to federal health agencies in particular and to the health-care delivery system in general (Murphy, President's Biomedical Research Panel 1976).

This report stimulated congressional hearings that focused on the need for a mechanism to facilitate biomedical-technology transfer. At that time, no focal point for such transfer existed within the federal system. Senator Edward Kennedy, the subcommittee chairman, voiced his strong support at the hearings for assigning that role to the Office of the Director, NIH. It seemed appropriate that the NIH assume this central role, considering its position as the nation's largest sponsor of biomedical research. The NIH sponsors 41 percent of all medical research and development in the United States and is responsible for two-thirds of all federal funds for health research (NIH 1978).

Establishment of the Office for Medical
Applications of Research

The Office for Medical Applications of Reasearch (OMAR) was officially established at the NIH in October 1977 to improve the translation of biomedical-research results into knowledge that can effectively be employed in the practice of medicine and public health. OMAR is intended to be the facilitator that will permit basic and, in particular, clinical research to be transferred more rapidly into health-care practice.

It was clear from past experience, however, that such facilitation must involve a great deal more than passive transfer of information. The panel had not only expressed the need but had emphasized the difference between translation and dissemination. Further, a superb institution, the National Library of Medicine, was already engaged in assembling, organizing, referencing, and distributing biomedical scientific information. There was no need to duplicate this function.

It was obvious, then, that the difficulty lay neither in the production of knowledge nor in the technical process of its indexing and distribution. Examined in terms of the classic models, the unexplored areas were the complex of relationships among the source, the messages, the recipients, and the applications, as well as the exchanges that formed the bases for these interactions.

The first problem for the NIH was to identify those components of the process to which its charge and expertise were applicable. Having done so, it then needed to devise a means to supplement, amplify, or build upon the existing diffuse, tedious, and haphazard system and to provide a crisp, rapid, and logically coherent formal program. A historical precedent for such an attempt is the slow but steady supplementation and replacement of common law by statute.

The Consensus-Development Program

The process that has evolved in response to these imperatives is the NIH consensus-development program. This program is supervised and coordinated by the Office for Medical Applications of Research in the Office of the Director. This unique program is an attempt to reproduce in microcosm, at one time and in one place, the process of knowledge evaluation, transfer, and transformation that ordinarily occurs within the context of the entire biomedical system and its contingent systems. Obviously, this could be undertaken only for selected topics; the task of condensing and filtering all new findings produced by biomedical research through one program would be monumental, unrealistic, and probably unnecessary. Instead the program attempts to address areas of biomedical knowledge presenting particular problems—for example, topics around which a brisk controversy revolves, application of research results that involve a major revision in very widely used procedures, or review of a procedure that shows high potential for possibly inappropriate application. Currently this reproduction of the whole societal process is embodied in a consensus conference, conducted as a public hearing, with a predetermined format. In its simplest form, the consensus conference follows this sequence. An NIH institute selects the technology for examination, establishes an internal planning committee, and identifies critical questions concerning the scientific validity of the technology. In conjunction with the OMAR staff, the institute selects a chair for the conference and begins to formulate the scientific program, topically arranged to answer the questions posed. Speakers, generally considered experts in their fields, are next recruited. Finally a consensus panel is established. This process can consume from six to nine months. The planning group is dissolved once the panel is constituted, and speakers may not be panelists. The chair is commonly included in the planning group and plays an important part in orchestrating the conference.

The panel consists of scientists, clinical specialists and generalists, interested nonmedical professionals, and representatives of consumer and special-interest health groups. Almost all panels contain one or more epidemiologists or biometricians.

The audience is largely composed of clinicians and investigators with a particular interest in the technology under review. Primary-care physicians, congressional staffs, interested lay persons, and representatives of a variety of public-interest groups also attend. The press is commonly present in significant numbers.

The conference, conducted as an open meeting, consumes two and a half days. For the first two, the speakers present the data necessary to answer the questions formulated in the planning stage. The panel and audience listen, question, and comment. On the evening of the second day, the panel convenes in executive session to formulate answers to the questions. This session is led by the chair of the panel and is held in private rooms where the panel is in essence sequestered. Food and drink are provided, and speed typists and duplicating facilities are available, under the direction of a professional logistics manager. The only other people present are the one or two institute program scientists and the OMAR staff members who have been instrumental in arranging the conference.

The chair may choose to have the panel address the questions as a committee of the whole or as separate task forces. In any case, the written statement must be based upon only the peer-reviewed data presented in open conference, except that it should and does reflect the judgment of the panel members on both the rigor and the practical applicability of these data. The answers to these questions become the consensus statement, which is distributed and read aloud to the other participants on the following day. The panel may then modify the statement in response to queries, comments, and challenges by the audience and speakers.

Final revisions and approval by the chair and panel are done by mail. The complete statement is then published in from one to six high-circulation medical journals, distributed to libraries, and mailed to more than 20,000 individuals and organizations, including continuing-medical-education directors, present and former conference participants, and others who have requested this or other statements. The statement contains the names and affiliations of the consensus panel. Recent versions include six to eight key references to the biomedical literature. The addition of these references has proven essential since the statement validates the technology but does not instruct in its application. The statement is not intended to direct the physician on how to practice medicine but rather to call attention to new procedures or modifications in old procedures, while providing assurance that these new or modified procedures appear to be safe and efficacious, in the light of all the relevant data. As it now stands, the issue is then closed and there is no provision for further revision or feedback.

An Evaluation

Application of Diffusion Theory to the Consensus Conference

Having identified the structure of a consensus conference, it now appears appropriate to relate the component parts to the theoretical elements of source, message, channel, recipient, and effect, as well as the terms used to describe processes linking them. This exercise should help to illuminate the novel position occupied by OMAR in the process of diffusion of biomedical applications.

In this setting, the sources of knowledge are the investigators funded by or recognized as expert by bureaus, institutes, and divisions (BIDs) of NIH. The BIDs identify knowledge that has emerged from research and is ripe for evaluation and apparently ready for transfer into use as practical medical applications. This becomes the technology subjected to consensus evaluation and validation. The same sources frame a set of central questions that facilitate evaluation of the consensus topic (the knowledge). OMAR participates in this formulation of questions as a representative of the potential recipients. This is the initial step in the transformation of the knowledge into a useful message. The message in this context is the final consensus statement, which constitutes an answer to the central questions.

Thus, in the early steps of the consensus process, the interactions between the source and the message, the source and the potential recipients, and the message and the potential recipients are reproduced, allowing the NIH and the biomedical community as a whole to structure and supervise the form and conduct of these interactions. This underlines the crucial role of the consensus-question construction because it is these questions that must produce and require a broad-based process of review and evaluation that significantly reduces the information overload in the knowledge-transfer system. Further, the questions also act as boundary-setting devices to ensure that the message transmitted does not exceed the charge and the expertise of the NIH.

The panel members are asked to evaluate the data presented and the scientific discussion that follows and from this information construct a new, useful, and hopefully succinct message. These experts and interested nonexperts on the panel are presumably acting as intermediaries in the knowledge-transfer system, although they may also be knowledge sources in some cases. They perform the key functions of knowledge evaluation, validation, and synthesis, which are the primary bottlenecks in the transfer process. The panel members cull through the mass of information on a particular topic and select those pieces that justify retention on the basis of their scientific verity and their applicability. They then identify the conclusions regarding safety and efficacy that logically can be drawn on the basis of those data that are germane, scientifically sound, and applicable. Finally, they certify, through their own repute and standing, that these conclusions and recommendations are valid and that, to the best of their knowledge, all the pertinent evidence available has been taken into account in constructing them.

The Critical Role of Validation

It is this process of validation that differentiates the knowledge-transformation mission of NIH from that of agencies whose task is simply knowledge dispersion. This function must be clearly separated from pure indexing of information. The necessity for validation of knowledge is not peculiar to medicine, but it is invariably produced by the interaction of medicine's essential conservatism with the constant increase in new knowledge.

Validation can be accomplished in several ways: one major means is authentication by primary and intermediate sources regarded as prestigious and expert. Validation of this type capitalizes on the ability and experience of NIH in mobilizing expertise and in providing the data necessary for the formulation or authoritative statements. The NIH attempts to provide message validation by authentication through constructing a representative panel. Panel members represent either those biomedical systems with which the NIH articulates or the individuals who ultimately will receive the knowledge contained in the consensus statement.

On an individual level, this approach is consistent with the well-documented psychological principle that people will most readily agree with the position of others if they perceive those others to be like themselves.

On an organizational level, the representation may be explicit rather than dependent on an implicit identification process. In addition, organizational representation may hinge on an implicit understanding that, in exchange for involvement in the NIH consensus process, special-interest organizations in the biomedical arena will refrain from conducting a duplicate or parallel exercise that has the potential for creating a competing, or even contradictory, message, thus confusing the recipient of the NIH message. Finally, representation on the panel also provides the opportunity for an organization (or individual) to state a minority opinion—a message within the message that the subject is not closed, that disagreement exists, and that more knowledge is needed to produce consensus.

Although identification by message recipients with the specific participants in the NIH process may confer one type of validity on the message produced, a second type of identification process may also be operative here: identification of the recipient with the cognitive style involved in the consensus process, particularly in the case of clinicians. The inductive style of logic is central to the learning process used in medical schools, and its adoption and constant use in clinical practice reinforces this mode of problem solving by physicians. It is precisely this style that is followed in the consensus process and that underlies the consensus statement. The consensus statement, therefore, should have intuitive appeal to practicing physicians on the basis of their identification with the cognitive process by which it is produced. To allow both representative and cognitive identification with the knowledge-transformation system to occur, the potential recipients of its products must be aware of the identity of the participants and the logical style of the process. The process, therefore, must be an entirely open, high-visibility phenomenon.

The last element in the diffusion schema is the effects. These are somewhat difficult to define in the context of the consensus program. Both the integration of knowledge into the recipients' general cognizance and the application of the knowledge in practice may be regarded as effects, a sense congruent with general diffusion theory. The direct encouragement of application by the knowledge recipients is, in the main, not within the mission of NIH, however, and is limited to the provision of the knowledge in a form accessible and specific enough to allow application. Thus NIH may develop means of enhancing knowlege, receipt, and cognitive integration but not knowledge implementation and utilization.

The theoretical separation is made more easily than the practical one. This dichotomy of effects presents a significant problem of measurement for program evaluation. If we are to develop outcome measures of program effectiveness, they must either concentrate on knowledge receipt and integration or must factor for the variables that intervene between knowledge integration and knowlege implementation.

The Need for a Formal Feedback Channel

There is at least one major disjunction in our current diffusion system, creating a barrier to measuring success in either way: the lack of a formal feedback channel from the wider constituency. This structural defect results in a lack of assurance that the message contained in the consensus statement is reaching the intended audience or that this audience considers the message valid and useful. Although we receive requests for information and comments on various conferences, these are not systematic. We estimate that as many as half the active practitioners in this country receive our message, but the fate of the message remains unknown.

If we measure effects, or impact, as changes in behavior or medical professionals regarding technology usage, consistent with consensus recommendations, the variables that intervene between knowledge and behavior must be considered. Obviously the consensus statement is but one of a multitude of information sources available to physicians in making professional decisions. Therefore the contribution of the consensus statement cannot be isolated and assessed as one factor. Rather it must be seen as one item in a complex matrix of factors that affect such decision making, such as the norms and values of the individual physicians and patients, economic and legal considerations, and other constraints imposed by the institutions and social subsets within which the practitioner and the patient function.

The existence of these and other factors that confound the adoption process may preclude utilizing adoption as the measure of the impact of the consensus program. Indeed, it is possible that the complexity of the adoption process precludes the use of any single evaluative scheme. Rather, it may be necessary to use multiple methods, each designed to accommodate a specific technology with the frame created by the individual decision maker's values and circumstances and the multiple uncontrolled variables that enter into the assessment.

Evaluation research strives to determine the highest correlation possible between change in a system and a given program intervention and can be applied to highly complex and dynamic systems. Faced with the problems posed by the analysis of such systems, evaluators and program administrators must seek creative solutions to formulate evaluation strategy. One solution is suggested by an analogy with practice in the law.

It is my understanding that there are distinct differences between judgments made and evidence required in addressing legal issues that are based on the principle of beyond a reasonable doubt, as in criminal cases, and those required (for civil cases or tort law) that use clear-and-convincing-evidence standards or the preponderance-of-the-weight-of-the-evidence standards. This difference in legal theory could be extrapolated to equivalent differences in evaluation methods.

In cases of the first type, cause and effect is clearly determined through one set of measurements of the phenomena. This is an admirable goal but seldom, if ever, attainable in scientific investigations of any kind.

A second method of proof, referred to as convergent validity (Campbell and Fiske 1959), is analogous to the preponderance-of-the-evidence standard in the law. This approach utilizes various measurements of the same phenomena made using different methods, which are then correlated. The more positive the correlation, the greater the increase in confidence that single component measurements reflect the program's effects accurately. For example, we might examine the number of citations of the consensus statement in other scientific papers and attempt to correlate this with a measure of behavioral change, such as increased use of a pharmaceutical product needed for the new procedure.

Conclusion

The function best performed by NIH is validation of new knowledge. This work may open the floodgate of acceptance where simple modification of methods for communication has failed to do so.

Through the application of diffusion theory, it has become clear why it must be the responsibility of the nation's principal source of support for biomedical investigation, the NIH, to validate the innovations it has sponsored. The consensus-development program has emerged as the response of the NIH to this perceived responsibility.

It has appeared necessary to acknowledge areas of uncertainty, gaps in feedback of information, and formal issues that militate against any confidence that the true impact of this program can ever be measured. The nature of the information system, the heterogeneity of the audience, and the formidable economic issues, both personal to the provider and consumers and institutional to hospitals, all contribute to confounding any analysis.

At best we have created a beacon, a lighthouse, upon which both practitioners and consumers can take bearings. A physician has the assurance that a recommended technology can be used with safety and effectiveness, and the patient a certain peace of mind that when subjected to a new procedure, the technology has been sieved through a fine-mesh screen that eliminates the dross.

We provide community truth as currently perceived and develop this truth through a process that taps the thinking of the most expert. Consensus has, to be sure, an ephemeral quality, but it seems to be the best we can offer at this time.

References

Aiken, M., and Hage, J. 1968. "Organizational Interdependence and Intraorganizational Structure." *American Sociological Review* 33:912-930.

Blalock, H.M., Jr., and Blalock, A. 1968. *Methodology in Social Research.* New York: McGraw-Hill.

Campbell, D., and Fiske, D. 1959. "Convergent and Discriminant Validation by the Multitrait-multimethod Matrix." *Psychological Bulletin* 56:81-105.

Glaser, E.; Abelsch, H.; McKee, M.; Watson, G.; Garrison, K.; and Lewin, M. 1976. *Putting Knowledge to Use: A Distillation of the Literature Regarding Knowledge Transfer and Change.* Los Angeles: Human Interaction Research Institute.

Hage, H., and Dewar, R. 1973. "Elite Values versus Organizational Structure in Predicting Innovation." *Administrative Science Quarterly* 18: 279-290.

Kaluzny, A.D.; Gentry, J.T.; and Veney, J.E., eds. 1974. *Innovation in Health-Care Organization.* Chapel Hill: University of North Carolina, Department of Health Administration.

Katz, D., and Kahn, R. 1966. *The Social Psychology of Organizations.* New York: Wiley.

Lasswell, H. 1946. In Smith, Bruce, et al. *Propaganda, Communication, and Public Opinion.* Princeton: Princeton University Press.

Levine, S., and White, P. 1961. "Exchange as a Conceptual Framework for the Study of Interorganizational Relationships." *Administrative Science Quarterly* 5:583-601.

Mehnert, R. 1981. Personal Communication. Bethesda, Md.: National Library of Medicine, NIH.

Murphy, F.D., Chairman. 1976. *Report of the President's Biomedical Research Panel.* DHEW Publishing No. (os) 76-500. Washington, D.C.: U.S. Government Printing Office.

National Academy of Sciences. Committee on Technology and Health Care. 1979. *Medical Technology and the Health Care System: A Study of the Diffusion of Equipment-Embodied Technology.* Washington, D.C.: National Academy of Engineering, Institute of Medicine, National Research Council, National Academy of Sciences.

National Institutes of Health. 1978. *Basic Data Relating to the National Institutes of Health.* (NIH) 78-1261. Washington, D.C.: U.S. Government Printing Office.

Robertson, T. 1971. *Diffusion—Innovation Behavior and Communication.* New York: Holt Rinehart and Winston.

Rogers, E., and Shoemaker, F.F. 1971. *Communication of Innovations: A Cross-Cultural Approach.* New York: Free Press.

Willems, J.S. 1979. The Relationship between the Diffusion of Medical Technology and the Organization and Economics of Health Care Delivery. In Wagner, J., ed., *Medical Technology.* DHEW pub. no. (PHS) 79-3254. Washington, D.C.: NCHSR.

Comment: On Public Acceptance of Regulatory Decisions Involving Technology-Based Health Risks

Kenneth H. Thompson

The type of creative thinking represented by the innovative program of knowledge transfer at the NIH is particularly welcome in an age when the public is more likely than before to question and challenge the policies governing the risks to which they are subjected, whether as patients, as workers, or as home owners and parents exposed to toxic wastes. As Dr. Lowe points out, the typical American is no longer a passive recipient of the prescriptions of authorities, whether those decision makers be physicians, regulators, or judges.

The activist, participatory, authority-challenging orientation of Americans is at once a manifestation of what is best in our civic culture and yet also poses severe tests of the capacity of our administrative system to resolve effectively technology-based policy issues, particularly those involving the health risks to which our citizens are subjected. Judicially mandated changes must be made in the risk-regulatory process systematically to tap the views of unorganized but affected individuals.

Evidence on Public Attitudes toward Risk

Evidence on the attitudes of the American public toward technology-based hazards to their health and the government's efforts to regulate these risks reveals a number of disturbing findings.

In the first place, little consensus exists regarding health risks. Different groups in society exhibit significantly diverse sets of attitudes toward health hazards. This lack of consensus on risk in America is often overlooked, since pollsters tend to report their findings in terms of the attitudes of the American people as a whole. Their findings, typically prepared for newspaper publication, are rushed to press with an emphasis on topicality rather than analysis.

An illustration of the great extent to which groups differ in their perceptions of and responses to risks can be seen through analysis of data from a recent Louis Harris survey, "Risk in a Complex Society" (Harris 1980). For this study, the Harris organization polled not only a sample of the

American public but tapped the attitudes of other key decision-making groups, such as corporate executives, congressmen and their key aides, and federal regulators. As figure 7-1 shows, attitudes of individuals converge or vary widely according to the social group they are in and to the type of risk. In this case, the attitudes of the general public and those of the corporate executives differ hardly at all with regard to whether financial and personal-safety risks had increased over time. But when it comes to the basic necessities of life, striking differences emerge. Majorities of the American people feel our food supply, water supply, household products, and the chemicals we use expose our society to more risks now than twenty years ago. The corporate executives polled took opposing views, with majorities perceiving less risk now than before.

A similar lack of consensus emerges between the two groups on the seriousness of health hazards. When given a choice between agreeing that American society is becoming overly sensitive to risk or accepting that we are becoming more aware of risk and taking realistic precautions, a majority of top corporate executives viewed American society as being too sensitive to risk, while more than three out of four Americans in the general public took the opposite position, viewing society as merely taking realistic precautions against the risks of which we are becoming aware.

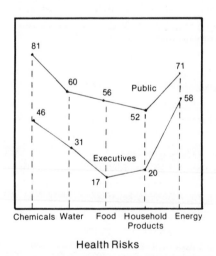 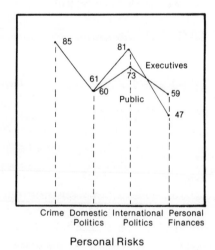

Source: Harris 1980.

Figure 7-1. Attitudes of Corporate Executive and American Public toward Changes in Personal and Health Risks: Percentage Saying There Is More Risk Now than Twenty Years Ago.

In general, evidence from survey research data shows that those Americans in relatively powerless and disadvantaged social positions view themselves as the most vulnerable to risk at the present time. Harris has found that the members of the American public who currently feel most vulnerable to risk include women; those aged sixty-five and over; those who lack a high-school diploma; the separated, divorced, and widowed; low-income persons earning $7,500 or less per year; and blacks and Hispanics. Another pollster, Gene Pokorny, has reported similar findings (Pokorny 1979). Those who are most likely to feel that the risks they take every day outweigh the benefits they derive tend to be blacks, people of low income, and those with low levels of education. Americans who feel that benefits outweigh risks in their lives are the whites, the younger, the college educated, suburban and rural residents, and the more affluent.

Exhibiting a pessimistic mood, less than a third of all Americans were able to say they felt the benefits they derived in their everyday lives outweighed the risks. Sixty-nine percent responded that they either suffered greater risk of harm than benefits, did not know, or felt the two were roughly equal. Such pessimism can hardly be viewed as a vote of confidence in the efficacy of our risk-regulatory mechanisms.

Little consensus exists among Americans in various walks of life about the degree to which they are exposed to hazards due to technology, the extent to which these hazards are increasing or decreasing over time, and whether the benefits of technology outweigh the hazards to which they are subjected in their lives. As one moves from positions of power and privilege in society to the strata of the powerless and disadvantaged, the sense of pessimism about risks and vulnerability to technologically based hazards increases.

Whether the stratification of attitudes toward risk is primarily a psychologically induced phenomenon or has its base in objective life-style circumstances cannot be determined at this time. On the one hand, differences in the objective circumstances of their lives may account for the different attitudes of top corporate executives and the general public toward risk in society. Generally corporate executives will have command of much greater financial resources than the general public, enabling them to control many more aspects of their lives and the concomitant risks. On the other hand, the control that executives exert in certain portions of their lives may spill over and influence their perceptions of the control they exert over their health risks, whether any basis in fact exists for this attitude.

The greater control subjectively experienced by corporate executives than that perceived by the general public is reflected in the breakdown of responses to the question: "How much control do you feel you have over the risks faced in daily living—complete control, a great deal of control, some control, or hardly any control at all?"

A majority of corporate executives indicated they had a high level of control over the risks they faced. In contrast, two out of three members of the general public said they had only some or hardly any control at all over the risks they faced. (See table 7-1.) This finding is highly significant, for a subjective sense of control over a situation is strongly related to risk taking or risk aversion.

Public Attitudes toward Risk Regulation

The evidence on the public's views toward government efforts to regulate risk is limited, but the picture that emerges is of a citizenry that views itself as relegated to the sidelines while powerful groups, dominated by lawyers, contest over high stakes within the administrative-law arena.

For example only a third of those recently polled (36 percent) believed the federal government gave much attention to the environmental views of individual citizens like themselves. Furthermore, less than half of the Americans sampled (44 percent) believe that the federal government provides either a great deal or even just some opportunity for citizens to express their views on environmental issues (Mitchell 1980).

These negative attitudes are backed up by the findings of a recent study of public attitudes toward federal regulation in a small, midwestern community. That report, the U.S. Regulatory Council's *Regulation: The View from Janesville, Wisconsin* (Danaceau 1980), while only an impressionistic analysis in a particular small city, does provide an indication of widespread citizen aversion to and alienation from the regulatory process.

The Janesville study suggests several sources of public dissatisfaction with the risk-regulatory process. In the first place, the political balance and responsiveness of the regulatory process appears to be questioned by the average citizen. Instead of feeling that their interests are being given fair representation, Americans tend to feel they are being ignored in favor of special interest. Furthermore, there is evidence to indicate Americans feel that the regulatory process is not responsive to their needs because it has been captured by attorneys wedded to an adversary tradition.

Table 7-1
Feelings toward Control over Risks

	Executives	General Public
Complete or a great deal of control	48%	32%
Some or hardly any control	41	67
It depends and not sure	1	2

Source: Harris 1980.

The American public is not only deeply divided over the health hazards it faces and suspicious of the risk-regulatory process. In addition, public actions indicate that where the health of their children and their property values are threatened, Americans may be willing to resort to direct and violent actions. A recent Environmental Protection Agency report on the siting of hazardous-waste facilities cites evidence of the use of threats and violence in connection with such controversies (EPA 1979).

It is a maxim of political science that political stability in a democratic society has as a necessary condition a modicum of public confidence in the fairness and efficiency of the government's mediating mechanisms. The evidence I have reviewed suggests that this requisite level of support may be seriously eroded.

Proposed Solutions

One response to the problem of making agency decision making in the field of risk regulation more politically responsive has been to call for more-explicit guidance to the regulatory agencies from elected officials. The judiciary in particular, uneasy over their roles, have called for more public involvement in risk regulation. For example, Judge David Bazelon recently argued that the electorate must be given a chance to have ultimate control over the allocation of risks and benefits it experiences but did not identify any specific manner in which this viewpoint is to be articulated (Bazelon 1981). Judge Howard Markey has called for greater involvement of elected officials in risk decision making:

> If our republican form of democracy means anything, it means that the people, through their representatives, shall make the basic decisions controlling their lives. The type and extent of the risks acceptable in their lives is perhaps the most basic of all those decisions. The power to make those final decisions should not be even indirectly vested in a few unelected bureaucrats, who have virtual life tenure in their jobs, under review by a few unelected judges who have a constitutional life tenure. [U.S. House of Representatives 1979]

At the conclusion of an analysis of the margin-of-safety approach to standard setting in the Clean Air Act, I too called for Congress to take greater responsibility for risk regulation (Thompson 1979). I am now convinced, however, that given the rewards in our political system for basing legislation on nothing more than pious but ambiguous shibboleths such as "cost-effective" (Solid Waste Disposal Act), "unreasonable risk" (Toxic Substances Control Act), and "adequate margin of safety" (Clean Air Act) coupled with the effective demise of the delegation doctrine, approaches other than relying on a congressional sense of political responsibility must be explored.

A spate of requirements calling for various forms of public participation have been featured in recent legislation. Increased public participation in the regulatory process has been sought through proposals requiring public access to agency information, the holding of public meetings and hearings, the development of advisory committees, and an office of public intervenor.

Such procedures to facilitate public participation have had limited success at best. Information demands under the Freedom of Information Act have come primarily from corporations. Public meetings, hearings, and advisory committees tend to represent the small, activist portion of the population, and just what interest the public intervenor represents is a question yet to be effectively answered. Finally, none of these techniques draw on the views of the unorganized but affected public.

The Sample Survey as a Mode of
Citizen Participation

A technique does exist for incorporating the view of the unorganized but affected public in the risk-regulatory process that has not been utilized on any systematic basis by government agencies: a sample survey of affected citizens.

The sample survey has a number of strengths in comparison with other forms of participation. Unlike most other participatory modes that incorporate the views of a few self-selected citizens, most with special interests to promote or defend, a sample survey self-consciously seeks out a representative group of citizens. As a consequence, the composite of views that a survey reports can be accepted with confidence as faithfully representing the attitudes of all components of society. Representiveness is not left to chance or self-selection but is obtained through the application of sampling methodology used to construct the sample.

Second, a well-designed and sufficiently lengthy interview can obtain the views of citizens in richness and detail far beyond the capability of referenda or interpretations of what the vote for one candidate over another can produce. Thus, the mandate from a survey is a much less ambiguous guide than those from elections or referenda.

Of course, it is possible to skew questions to achieve a predetermined outcome, but such problems can be met through the use by an agency of panels of technical experts on survey questionnaire and sample matrix construction. Since the wording of survey questions must be revealed and any bias in sampling can be detected through comparison of the demographic attributes of the sample actually drawn with other sources such as census data, problems of deliberate bias or distortion are likely to be few.

What is more likely to be a problem is a rejection of the use of surveys of affected publics by regulatory officials. After conducting a careful set of surveys on public attitudes toward environmental planning in recent years, Professor Milbrath found his results ignored by agency officials. He surmised that two factors were at work to block utilization of relevant survey findings. First, Milbrath has found that most bureaucrats are not familiar with the use of data from survey research. Second, and perhaps more fundamental, Milbrath concludes that agency officials are more accustomed to maps and statistics than to working with people (Milbrath 1980).

If it is true that regulators, more comfortable with the resolution of technological problems than political controversies, are resistant to incorporating the sampled views of the unorganized but affected public in the agency decision-making process, is there some political or legal lever that would encourage such incorporation?

In discussing the components of adequate process, Judge Bazelon implies what may serve as a basis for overcoming the reluctance of agency decision makers to sample the affected public. He suggests that agencies should open their decision-making processes to all relevant information and all affected participants in order to meet the demands of adequate process (Bazelon 1981). Thus it can be argued that agencies must obtain relevant information on the views of those whose lives are to be affected by their decisions in order to develop adequate process. In my view, such judicial innovation is required at the present time. Mandating the use of sample surveys in the resolution of science policy decisions as a necessary component of an adequate record is a promising approach to resensitizing bureaucratic authority to the will of the people.

Conclusion

Sample surveys have been used for a number of purposes ranging from political polling to studies of the health practices of the general public. Their potential has not been fully explored, however. For example, Dr. Lowe raises a problem where a well-constructed survey may possibly provide a solution. What he terms a major disjunction in the current diffusion system, lack of a formal feedback channel from the wider constituency, could be remedied through the use of systematic sampling of the intended audience of consensus statements. Since it has been shown that satisfying high response rates may be obtained from samples of practicing physicians, the fate of consensus-statement messages need not remain unknown (Shosteck and Fairweather 1979).

Neither must the attitudes of the American people concerning the health hazards to which they are subjected remain unknown. No more-effective means exists for receiving the point of view of unorganized members of the affected public than a well-designed sample survey.

Beside providing the regulatory agencies with a means of becoming more politically sensitive and responsive in their often-agonizing decisions over risks that they have a mandate to make, regular and objective polling of public attitudes can be conducive to political stability and aid in reaching consensus. A natural reaction in reading a survey question is to ask oneself, "How would I answer that question?" The very process of examining the diversity of responses to an objective survey can help defuse a volatile situation. Not only do individuals gain satisfaction from knowing that decision makers are seriously seeking out the views of citizens, but the very diversity of reported responses can lead to tempering the intensity of views of any single participant. Comparison of one's views with those of others can foster consensus, while knowledge that decision makers sought citizen views acts to legitimize the decisions actually reached.

Regular use of survey techniques to sample the attitudes of those affected by agency health-risk decisions, mandated by the judiciary as an essential component of an adequate record, could well be the next stage of democratic political development in this country—the necessary widening of public control to counterbalance the concentrated power of the bureaucracy and make it politically responsive.

References

Bazelon, D.L. 1981. "The Judiciary: What Role in Health Improvement?" *Science* 211:792-793.

Danaceau, P. 1980. *Regulation: The View from Janesville, Wisconsin, and a Regulator's Perspective.* Washington, D.C.: U.S. Regulatory Council, Executive Office of the President.

Environmental Protection Agency. Office of Water and Waste Management. 1979. *Siting of Hazardous Waste Management Facilities and Public Opposition.* Washington, D.C.: U.S. Government Printing Office. An environmental protection publication (SW-809) in the solid-waste management series.

Harris, L. 1980. *Risk in a Complex Society.* New York: Marsh and McLennan.

Milbrath, L. 1980. "Incorporating the Views of the Uninterested But Impacted Public in Environmental Planning." *Policy Studies Journal* 8:913-920.

Mitchell, R. 1980. *Public Opinion on Environmental Issues.* Washington, D.C.: U.S. Government Printing Office (329-221-6586).

Pokorny, G. 1979. "Living Dangerously . . . Sometimes." *Public Opinion* 2:10-13.

Shosteck, H., and Fairweather, W. 1979. "Physician Response Rates to Mail and Personal Interview Surveys." *Public Opinion Quarterly* 43: 206-217.

Thompson, K. 1979. "Margin of Safety as a Risk-Management Concept in Environmental Legislation." *Columbia Journal of Environmental Law* 6:1-29.

U.S. Congress. House. Committee on Science and Technology. 1980. *Risk/ Benefit Analysis in the Legislative Process, Committee Report No. 71, Hearings, July 24 and 25, 1979.* Washington, D.C.: U.S. Government Printing Office.

8

The Role of Advisory Committees in Resolving Regulatory Issues Involving Science and Technology: Experience from OSHA and the EPA

Nicholas A. Ashford

The use of advisory committees by regulatory agencies to help resolve issues involving science and technology has taken on increasing importance in the last few years. The advisory committees differ in their legal origins, their purposes, their composition, and the specific issues that they address.

In 1972, Congress expressed a concern that advisory committees not cross the line between advice and improper influence and strove to ensure advisory committee accountability through the passage of the Federal Advisory Committee Act (FACA). While Congress utilized FACA to embrace the advisory committee as a "frequently . . . useful and beneficial means of furnishing expert advice, ideas, and diverse opinions to the Federal Government," it nonetheless declared that "the need for many existing advisory committees has not been reviewed" and concluded that the creation and operation of advisory committees should be more strictly controlled. Accordingly the act contains specific findings that new advisory committees should be kept to a necessary minimum; that advisory committees should be terminated when they have served their purpose; that the establishment, operation, administration, and duration of advisory committees should be subject to uniform procedures; and that relevant information regarding advisory committees should be made available to the public.

In both the Carter and Reagan administrations, the executive branch has displayed a schizophrenic attitude toward advisory committees. Under former President Carter, proposals were encouraged for the increased use of panels or groups of experts to solve difficult regulatory questions, and, at the same time, a directive was issued not to create new advisory committees. Under the Heritage Foundation's blueprint for government reorganization in the Reagan administration, the existing advisory groups are seen as essential for the missions of the Environmental Protection Agency (EPA) but are criticized in the context of the Occupational Safety and Health Administration (OSHA). If advisory committees are seen as a means by which more-

165

informed regulatory decisions might be made, a love-hate relationship is inevitable if there is basic disagreement about the goals or the desirability of the agency missions that the committees serve.

The purposes of this chapter are to examine the use of advisory committees by OSHA and EPA in the context of regulating toxic substances in manufacturing and to offer suggestions for improved use of advisory committees by regulatory agencies. It addresses the multiple and sometimes conflicting purposes of advisory committees; their legal origin, constitution, and obligations; the experience of specific committees; and makes recommendations for improvement.

The Purposes of Advisory Committees

Advisory committees may satisfy one or more of the following purposes:

1. They bring needed scientific or technological expertise to the agency decision-making process.
2. They provide a mechanism for reaching a consensus on difficult-to-resolve scientific or technological issues.
3. They provide a mechanism for policy guidance when the factual resolution of scientific or technological issues is not possible in the traditional sense.
4. They provide a means of expanding the participation of interested parties in the regulatory decision-making process.

A committee of technical experts addressing the toxicity of carbon monoxide or alternative ventilation technologies might be constituted to meet the first purpose. Here, there may be little real disagreement on scientific or technical issues. The function served is to provide the agency with the latest and best information related to science and technology.

The extent to which the existing data from conflicting human studies indicate that saccharin is a human carcinogen is an issue that goes to the second purpose. The best scientific judgment may emerge from a group of technical experts, although there may be considerable disagreement among the experts.

Examples of issues that are not resolvable in a strictly technical sense include the problem of extrapolating animal data to humans for exposure to toxic substances; the existence of a finite threshold for carcinogens; the usefulness of short-term in vitro tests for assessing carcinogenicity; the reversibility of cell transformation induced by carcinogens; the distinction between benign and malignant tumors; the magnitude of the occupational and environmental health problems; and the prediction of technological innovation in response to a regulation. Here, the questions really revolve around policy issues rather than science. For example, in the absence of human evidence of cancer, how should occupational exposure to a substance, known to cause cancer in animals, be controlled?

The first two purposes appear to be concerned with fact finding, while the last two purposes focus more on a correct process for decision making. In the third purpose, if scientific or technological issues are not resolvable in the technical sense, proper representation of interested (affected) as well as knowledgeable parties on the advisory committee would appear to be necessary to ensure a fair process. The distinction between fact finding and fair process begins to blur where scientific judgment is subject to prejudices and bias or where difficult judgment calls (found in the second purpose) vary widely and there exist divergent, but not clearly incorrect, points of view. As the circuit-court reviews of the OSHA cases state, issues on the frontiers of scientific knowledge are not factual determinations in the usual sense. They are social-policy decisions, legislative rather than judicial in character. It is not always possible to obtain a committee with both expertise and balance, and pains must be taken to avoid a tyranny of the experts.

The last purpose of an advisory committee—providing an opportunity for participation—may be especially important. In addition to increasing the likelihood of a more-correct resolution of regulatory issues, participation serves a political purpose of fair representation and can provide a chance to avoid subsequent adversary interactions. It also serves to raise the consciousness of technical experts to views not previously encountered. For example, the former head of OSHA, Eula Bingham, is a toxicologist who first served as chairman of OSHA's ad hoc advisory committee on coke-oven emissions. Thus, advisory committees can serve as a mechanism for facilitating the entry of technical people into the regulatory agencies.

The drafting of the specific technical questions to be addressed by advisory committees may result in different degrees of confidence in the information and conclusions that emerge. If a panel of experts were asked to determine which control technologies could solve an emissions problem, more-objective results might be obtained than if the same panel were asked to determine the economic feasibility of the control options. The success of an advisory committee may also be different on questions of science as compared to questions of technology. Finally, asking an advisory committee to evaluate the performance of an existing regulatory program may lead to very different results than requesting recommendations for a revision of regulatory strategy. These various topical areas are characterized by different uncertainties and variations in social and political values.

In sum, the assessment of the usefulness of advisory committees depends on the topic addressed; the extent of expertise, paradigmatic bias, and prejudice of individual members; and balance of the committee and whether fact finding or policy guidance is sought. For the most part, agencies are not obliged to accept the conclusions of their advisory committees; they are required only to consider them. This treatment of technical issues by regulatory agencies has been confirmed by the reviewing courts and reflects the judicial recognition of the difference between questions of science and questions of science-regulatory policy. However, a technically strong and balanced committee can provide persuasive technical and political influence on an agency's decision-making process, unless the committee's activities are weakened by inadequate resources, inappropriate time limitations, or an administration that has already made up its mind.

An advisory committee may also be used by agencies to delay action by deferring to the committee's deliberation. A committee may also be used to rubber-stamp an agency's position or justify inactivity. It is hoped that this does not characterize most committees.

The Legal Framework for OSHA and EPA Advisory Committees

Advisory committees in general are subject to FACA, which provides guidelines and procedures imposed in addition to specific requirements from environmental legislation or specific charters. The most-significant requirements are for open meetings, detailed transcripts, a limited right of public participation, and the attendance of a federal government representative at advisory committee meetings.

In addition, sections 5(b)(2) and (c) require that the membership be "fairly balanced in terms of points of view represented and the functions to be performed" by the committee. A recent commentary on the operation of FACA concludes, "Doubt has existed . . . whether this means that various political, ethnic, geographic, educational, and societal points of view are to be represented, or that the members should have a balance of relevant training, experience and professional competence."[1]

In formulating an operational definition of balance for the purposes of meeting the requirements of FACA, three candidate criteria can be clearly identified: competence, discipline, and bias-allegiance.[2] Balance in the effectiveness of technical argument certainly requires equivalent competence or expertise among antagonists. On the other hand, experts as a group may need to be tempered by the participation of nonexpert members. Each discipline carries its own paradigmatic bias, and there may be a need to have both nonexperts and several disciplines (competently) represented on an advisory committee, the mixture depending on the questions to be addressed.

Finally, political, institutional, ethnic, or sexual bias needs to be adequately balanced. Most attention in addressing the fair-balance requirement seems to have been focused on bias-allegiance. Competence and discipline have not received the balancing effort they may deserve.

For the purpose of analysis here, advisory committees may be divided into several kinds:

1.   Permanent advisory committees created by statute to advise agencies on science, technology, or general policy issues.
2.   Quasi-permanent committees to aid agencies in general technical matters or policy issues. These committees are usually created administratively by charter and are subject to the two-year renewal requirement of section 14 of FACA.
3.   Ad hoc advisory committees to deal with a specific scientific or technical issue. These committees may be authorized specifically by statute or administratively.

This chapter examines four advisory committees, two each in OSHA and EPA.

Section 7(a) of the Occupational Safety and Health Act (OSH Act) establishes a mandatory, permanent, balanced advisory committee known as the National Advisory Committee on Occupational Safety and Health (NACOSH), to advise the secretaries of labor and of health and human services on general issues pertaining to the administration of the OSH Act. The committee has twelve members who are to be drawn from management, labor, the occupational-safety and health professions, and the public and who are to be selected "upon the basis of their experience and competence in the field of occupational safety and health." NACOSH is required to hold no fewer than two meetings during each calendar year.

In addition, the OSH Act makes provision for the creation of limited-lifetime, balanced, ad hoc advisory committees to consider specific subjects related to the setting of occupational standards. The authority for such committees is found in section 7(b) of the act, which empowers but does not require the secretary of labor to appoint special advisory committees "to assist him in his standard-setting functions under Section 6." Each of these committees is to have no more than fifteen members and is to be balanced equally between "persons qualified by experience and affiliation to present the viewpoint of the employers involved" and "persons similarly qualified to present the viewpoint of the workers involved." In addition, an ad hoc committee must include at least one representative of a state health and safety agency and may include other persons "who are qualified by knowledge and experience to make a useful contribution," so long as the number of such persons on the committee does not exceed the number of representatives of federal and state agencies.

The two types of OSHA advisory committees have both technical and nontechnical experts, and the members vary significantly in background and training.

The EPA originally established administratively the Science Advisory Board (SAB) in 1974. Subsequently the board was established statutorily by the Environmental Research, Development, and Demonstration Act of 1978. The board consists of five standing committees and an executive committee, who meet periodically with the EPA administrator "to provide advice . . . on the scientific and technical aspects of environmental problems and issues." The membership is to be "a body of independent scientists and engineers of sufficient size and diversity to provide a range of expertise required to assess the scientific and technical aspects of environmental issues." Additional committees may be drawn from the members. The board is not specifically required to be balanced in terms of institutional or political bias. Further, nonscientists or engineers do not appear to be welcome. Thus the board may not be truly balanced.

EPA's regulation of toxic substances is also assisted by an administratively created advisory committee, known as the Administrator's Toxic Substance Advisory Committee (ATSAC). This quasi-permanent, balanced committee focuses primarily on issues of policy rather than issues of science. According to its charter, ATSAC is to advise the EPA "on policy, technical and procedural matters relating to the environmental, economic, and social aspects" of implementing the Toxic Substances Control Act (TSCA) and to "consider and comment on proposals for rules and regulations." However, it is directed to "generally defer" to the SAB on scientific matters. The committee is composed of sixteen members who are to be drawn, "in appropriate balance," from three groups: manufacturers, processors, and users of chemical substances; environmental, health, and public-interest organizations; and other interested parties, "including, but not limited to, labor organizations, professional societies, and state and local interests." The committee is also authorized to form subcommittees to deal with specific issues. ATSAC itself is to hold from three to six meetings a year; the subcommittees are directed to meet "as needed." In sum, the committee is balanced, quasi-permanent, and policy oriented rather than focused on scientific issues.

In addition to scientific and technical competence being represented in the committees themselves, both ATSAC and NACOSH typically request outside experts to address them on technical issues, and education of the committees is a continuing process.

Analysis of the Role of Advisory Committees

Table 8-1 illustrates the differences among the relevant advisory committees for the area of toxic-substances control in the manufacturing context. OSHA's twelve-member permanent committee, NACOSH, is balanced and

Table 8-1

Characteristics of EPA and OSHA Advisory Committees

	OSHA	EPA		
Permanent	NACOSH		SAB	
Quasi-permanent				ATSAC
Ad hoc		Specific Standards		
Policy-oriented	X	X		X
Science and technology		X	X	
Balanced	X	X		X
Expert only			X	

policy oriented while its standard-setting, up-to-fifteen member advisory committees are short-lived, balanced, and concerned with both science-technology and policy issues related to a specific standard. Flexibility in the ability to address a technical issue arises from the ability to appoint separate advisory committees for different standards. Since each standards committee may also address policy issues and must recommend regulatory action, consistency of regulatory approaches among different committees may be lacking. Overall regulatory guidance is provided by the permanent advisory committee.

EPA's science advice comes from a permanent and large-membered SAB, which, while consisting of technical experts, is not balanced. Ability to address a variety of issues comes from its use of committees drawn from its large membership. Advice on regulatory policy issues in the toxic-substances area covered by the 1976 Toxic Substances Control Act (TSCA) comes from the balanced sixteen-member ATSAC, which generally must defer to the SAB on science issues. ATSAC has concentrated on monitoring the implementation of TSCA, which is still incomplete. It has addressed regulatory strategies for old and new chemicals, testing rules, the effects of regulation on innovation in the chemical industry, and other issues. Since no significant regulatory actions other than on PCBs have occurred, its effectiveness is yet to be tested. Yet analysis of its transcripts reveals intelligent, probing discussions of issues that closely parallel the kinds of discussions held by NACOSH, OSHA's permanent policy-advisory committee. One striking feature of ATSAC is the presence of several environmental lawyers, as well as scientists.

The SAB is concerned with science issues in all contexts of EPA activity. In a broad sense, its activities are to include the review of EPA programs and strategies, the review of the scientific basis of proposed criteria documents, standards, limitations, and regulations, and the recommendation of new standards and programs. EPA records for 1979 indicate that

SAB activities for that year focused mainly on analyses of the scientific bases of proposed standards, on evaluations of the health effects of particular toxins, and on general issues of evaluation methodology and environmental modeling. Its activities relevant to TSCA are described by EPA as follows:

> Analysis of the scientific data bases now in existence and new ones required for implementation of the Toxic Substances Control Act (TSCA) is the continuing activity of a permanent subcommittee. The subcommittee also is analyzing the potential of current and planned EPA research to provide necessary support for TSCA.

The ATSAC deferring of scientific issues to the SAB differs from the OSHA dual-committee approach because the science and policy issues in the EPA context appear to be much more separated.

NACOSH has been a major forum for discussing and clarifying controversial issues before unnecessary adversarial interactions occur. The idea of adopting a generic cancer policy was widely discussed by NACOSH long before OSHA decided to promulgate a formal rule. NACOSH was the intellectual testing ground, and a review of the transcripts reveals good discussions of all the difficult science-law questions. Reproductive hazards were also discussed with sophistication. The difficulty of assessing OSHA's effectiveness from existing disease and injury data is a frequently discussed subject. Research needs and opportunities are often addressed. Review of both NACOSH and ATSAC transcripts reveals that most controversy occurs regarding policy issues and not scientific questions, even where the science is uncertain. There has been a certain maturation in both NACOSH and ATSAC, which recognizes that uncertainty in science or technology is no excuse for not formulating an agency response, but parties differ widely on what that response should be.

The use of the standards-setting advisory committees by OSHA has been varied. A committee is not always—in fact, usually is not—appointed, since it is an elective mechanism for OSHA. Sometimes OSHA takes the committee's advice and bases its standard on the committee's recommendations (such as with coke-oven emissions), and sometimes it departs greatly and with vigorous opposition (such as the early experience with pesticide exposures). One possible explanation for underutilization of advisory committees in this context is the relative shortage of occupational-health experts compared with environmental-health scientists.

Looking at the question from a general perspective, advisory committees—both science and policy oriented—have the potential to contribute significantly to facilitating the decision-making process in regulatory agencies. Historically, their members have been knowledgeable and their deliberations generally valuable and instructive. They have handled the science and technology questions well; however, their less-than-frequent meetings or short assignments have left them relatively underutilized.

Recommendations for Improving the Effectiveness of Advisory Committees

The factors influencing the effectiveness of advisory committees in resolving regulatory issues involving science and technology are numerous. Frequent meetings, agency support in the form of financial and staff resources, and access to key agency personnel all contribute. Sufficient tenure of members on the committee, security from political removal, and an absence of conflict of interest are important. Committee independence and agency cooperation in defining agenda items are crucial. Expertise and fair balance in its broadest sense are necessary. Finally, public and press interest in the committee's work is necessary if advisory committees are to serve as an effective check on regulatory-agency activities.

Notes

1. Michael H. Cardozo, "The Federal Advisory Committee Act in Operation," *Administrative Law Review* 33 (1981):55.

2. These criteria are also discussed in an unpublished working paper prepared by a team of consultants to the Charles F. Kettering Foundation. See Charles F. Kettering Foundation, "Criteria for the Selection of Federal Advisory Committee Members" (Dayton, Ohio, August 20, 1981).

Comment: Channels of Communication between Various Subsets of the Public and a Regulatory Agency

Anna J. Harrison

The American Chemical Society accepts the premise that effective regulations are essential if human health and the environment are to be protected from the adverse effects of chemicals. It also makes the basic assumption that for a regulation to be effective, the regulation must have credibility with the general public, the technological community, and the scientific community. If credibility is not achieved with any of these, delaying tactics, litigation, and noncompliance are to be expected. To achieve a regulation that merits credibility with diverse subsets of the public requires effective communication among those who regulate, those who are served by the regulation, and those who bear the burden of regulation. Advisory committees are one mechanism but by no means the only mechanism of communication.

For a regulation to have credibility with the general public, of which the technological and scientific communities are subsets, both the protection provided by the regulation and the burden placed upon the public by the regulation must be reasonably compatible with the mores of society. The public creates the pressure to regulate (to protect); the public also creates the demand for goods and services. The pursuit of one frequently, perhaps always, jeopardizes the attainment of the other, and all regulations are manifestations of value judgments made by the administrator as the duly authorized surrogate of Congress.

For a regulation to have credibility with the technological community, performance standards must reflect the toxicity of the chemical and be within the reach of current technology. The magnitude of the adverse effects of a chemical on human health and the environment is a function of the toxicity of the chemical and of the exposure. Toxicity of a chemical is a property of the chemical and can be experimentally determined for a given species exposed through a specific route such as skin contact or inhalation or ingestion. The chronic toxicity of a chemical with respect to humans can be inferred only from studies with other species or from the interpretation of epidemiological studies. The strategy of regulation is the control of exposure through any combination of the mandatory restriction of use of the chemical, the mandatory restriction of the release of the chemical into the environment, of which the work place is a subunit, and the mandatory use of a specified warning label on the container of the product in commerce.

For a regulation to have credibility with the scientific community, the regulation must not be inconsistent with the current state of scientific knowledge. For a given regulatory question, relevant current knowledge includes the identification of that which has not been experimentally studied, the identification of that which has been studied, the assessment of the validity of these studies, the assessment of the uncertainties associated with reported experimental values, the identification of relevant models that have been proposed, and the analysis of the tests to which these models have been subjected.

To formulate an effective regulation, the agency must look to the scientific community to supplement its own literature search and assessment of that literature; to the technological community for information concerning current practices, planned technological changes, and an assessment of future capabilities; and to the public to learn what is acceptable to those who seek the protection of regulations and directly or indirectly bear to a significant degree the burden of regulations. It is important to recognize in any discussion of regulations that all of the above change continuously with time.

My involvement, on the part of the American Chemical Society, has been primarily with the implementation of the Toxic Substances Control Act (TSCA). This act is an extremely comprehensive piece of legislation that became effective on January 1, 1977. It delegates to the administrator of the Environmental Protection Agency (EPA) the responsibility and the authority to regulate the manufacture, processing, distribution, use, and disposal of all chemical substances not otherwise covered by another act. Much remains to be done before the act is fully implemented. At the time of writing, only two classes of compounds have been regulated under TSCA: polychlorinated biphenyls (PCBs) and fully halogenated chlorofluoroalkanes for use as the propellant in spray cans. The regulation of PCBs was mandated in the founding act.

The American Chemical Society (ACS) consists of some 120,000 individuals who have attained sufficient competence in chemistry or chemical engineering that they could be called chemists, although some prefer to be identified with closely related disciplines and professions. Approximately 65 percent of ACS members are employed by industry. Consequently, all ACS members are scientists, 65 percent have a close relation to industry, and all are members of the public. In its interaction with EPA, the ACS goal is to achieve reasonable regulations through nonadversarial processes. Its primary concern is that the goal of the legislation be achieved without unnecessarily impeding the extension of knowledge, the evolution of technology, and the delivery of goods and services of interest to the public and, in many cases, essential to the public welfare. For example, ACS supports regulations expressed in terms of performance standards, not in terms of mandated detailed methodologies and technologies. Performance standards encourage the evolution of experimental methodologies and technological processes.

ACS considers that it has among its members individuals with unique capabilities to assist an agency in assessing the current state of chemical knowledge and to identify areas of science amenable to study with current or developing methodologies and instrumentation. Also among its members are individuals with unique capabilities to assist an agency in assessing the current state of chemical technology and identifying areas of technology that, from a technical point of view, can be rapidly developed. It believes that it can best serve the cause of regulation by making the collective scientific and technological expertise of these individuals available to EPA through nonadversarial mechanisms.

ACS members as individuals should participate in the resolution of the value-issue problems inherent in regulation. In this they have exactly the same role as any other member of the public. Although it may be difficult to distinguish between informed scientific judgment and value judgments relating to personal commitments to the enhancement of the quality of life and the quality of the environment, it has become increasingly clear that ACS must continue to endeavor to make this distinction and to articulate the necessity to make the distinction. In TSCA, the primary criterion for rule making is unreasonable risk. Risk is dependent upon two parameters: the toxicity of the chemical and the level and duration of exposure. Both of these parameters can be assessed through quantitative measurements and modeling. The determination of reasonable or unreasonable risk is a value judgment based on a consideration of the other available options, the mores of society, and so on.

The EPA Science Advisory Board (SAB) and the administrator's Toxic Substances Advisory Committee (TSAC) discussed by Professor Ashford provide an interesting contrast. Both are advisory to the same individual, the administrator of EPA. The SAB is structured to provide counsel to the administrator on scientific and technological matters. The TSAC is structured to provide counsel on matters of values espoused by various subsets of the public. The SAB is the natural home of scientists and technologists in their role as specialists. The TSAC is the natural home of scientists and technologists only in their roles as members of the public. It is clear that small task forces within the framework of the SAB have been very effective in addressing well-defined scientific questions. Both the SAB and the TSAB report to Congress, however, so it is questionable whether either is a pure advisory unit. There is some evidence that their activities at times take on the characteristics of evaluation committees, and the relations with the administrator become adversarial in nature.

A number of interagency committees and international organizations are very significant resources. These include:

1. The Interagency Testing Committee (ITC): This is a permanent committee established by TSCA. It consists of the representatives of eight agencies and is charged with the selection of existing chemicals to be evaluated by EPA for priority testing. In making the periodic reviews necessary to make selections, tremendous quantities of information concerning acute and chronic toxicities, volumes of production, distribution, and disposal must be processed.
2. The Toxic Substances Strategy Committee (TSSC): This was a very large committee of representatives from various units of the executive branch of government established by the president in 1978 within the Council on Environmental Quality. The recommendations of this committee had a profound effect upon the determination of the strategies being utilized to implement TSCA.
3. The Organization for Economic Cooperation and Development (OECD): This organization has an active program in the protection of health and the environment from the adverse effects of chemicals. Its strategies have been developed to accommodate the philosophies and practices of its member nations. In some activities, such as the development of test standards, OECD is ahead of the U.S. agencies, and its documents are a valuable resource. Its strategies are also factors to be considered in the development of U.S. regulations that do not unnecessarily restrict the exchange of toxicity data and international trade.

Workshops and public meetings are essential mechanisms of communication. A recent experimental scoping workshop, carefully designed to be informal in structure and style, was a promising development in nonadversarial procedures. The workshop was called to review the two compounds and the two classes of compounds designated in the seventh report of the ITC for evaluation for priority testing. The participants were experts in the appropriate areas of toxicology invited by the agency and self-selected representatives of industry, labor, and public-interest groups. This meeting served to develop a cooperative approach to recognized problems and to delineate work that must be done by the agency.

The agency has provided the ACS draft copies of documents related to the implementation of TSCA in what seems to be the same time frame that these drafts are provided to the SAB and the TSAC. This allows the ACS to work informally with the agency to achieve a document free of errors and ambiguities. It also enables the society to suggest strategies that it believes to be more appropriate.

Considerations now in progress will probably lead to cooperative agreements between the agency and certain professional societies, including the ACS, for the annual review of test standards. The reports from the societies will then become part of the resources used by the agency in its annual review of test standards as required by the act.

The ACS is particularly gratified by these recent developments, which make it possible to interact with the agency before proposed actions are published in the *Federal Register*. Aberrations in scientific concepts and aberrations in the use of scientific terminology can be resolved in nonadversarial exchanges. With these confusions removed, it then becomes possible to address with confidence the merits of the proposed action.

More than four years of observations of the implementation of TSAC suggest that two quite different philosophical approaches are being whipsawed within the agency. One approach is to reduce the process of regulation to the traverse of a path prescribed by check lists. The other is to determine the appropriate action for each chemical through less prescribed processes. If this supposition is correct, an adversarial relation must exist within the agency. The ACS suspects that the legal component of the agency espouses the first approach, the scientific component the second. In a sense, the ACS is sympathetic to the interest in both approaches. If the formalized approach could be workable, the responsibilities of individuals in the agency would be diminished, and regulatory actions would be easier to defend. The compound-by-compound approach recognizes both the great complexity of factors involved in distinguishing between reasonable and unreasonable risk and the fragmentary nature of current knowledge. The position of the ACS is that one does not have either the knowledge or the wisdom to reduce the process of regulation to a formalized system without creating a structure so complex that its use at this time would place an unsustainable burden upon society. This point is brought up not to argue the merits of the two approaches but to point out that adversarial grouping within the agency may be inherent in the professional capabilities and interests of the staff.

9

The First FDA Public Board of Inquiry: The Aspartame Case

Vincent Brannigan

There are two different concepts of the science court. Scientists envision a proceeding where a group of scientists are given a question, they throw the lawyers out of the room, and then hash it out to conclusion. I called this the *science* court. The lawyers think of a proceeding with witnesses, questioning, and a verdict, except that the judges are scientists, aided by a legal adviser. I call this a science *court*. Emphatically, the Food and Drug Administration's (FDA) aspartame public board of inquiry (PBOI) was a *science* court.

Aspartame is an artifical sweetener composed entirely of two amino acids, aspartic acid and phenylalanine. It is a food additive under the Food, Drug and Cosmetics Act (FDCA), 21 USC 341; therefore the company proposing use of the additive (in this case, G.D. Searle and Co.) must prove that it is safe for use as a food additive.

In 1974 the FDA issued a regulation permitting the use of aspartame. Two parties filed objections and asked for a hearing: James Turner, a Washington attorney, and John Olney, a Washington University professor whose research included work on the amino acids in aspartame. These two parties were held to have raised a substantial objection and were entitled to a hearing.

The parties agreed to allow a PBOI to hear the case. A PBOI is constituted of a group of scientists answering scientific questions but functioning as a court, in place of an administrative law judge.

Doubts as to the authenticity of the data delayed the establishment of the PBOI until 1979. Three years were spent on evaluation of the data. The board was established in 1979 and held hearings on January 30, 31, and February 1, 1980. The decision was rendered on October 1, 1980. The board found sufficient doubt as to the safety of aspartame to prohibit it from use. All parties appealed to the FDA commissioner. On July 15, 1981, the commissioner reversed the board and approved aspartame.

The correspondence and other documents quoted in this study are all found in the aspartame case hearing docket, on file at the Office of Hearing Clerk, U.S. Food and Drug Administration, 5600 Fishers Lane, Rockville, Maryland. The following persons gave significant assistance in compiling this case report: Margaret Dayhoff, professor, Biophysics, Georgetown University; Ruth Dayhoff, pathologist, Veterans Administration; Valerie Ianieri, undergraduate student, Department of Nutrition, University of Maryland; Elizabeth Prather, chair, Department of Nutrition, University of Maryland.

The health questions in aspartame are not particularly complex. It was asserted as possibly causing mental retardation, brain damage, and brain tumor. Determining an answer to the question of safety is both complex and difficult, however. Food additives will not be approved unless there is reasonable evidence that they are safe for use, and the burden is on the manufacturer to prove that they are safe, rather than on the government or intervening party to prove that they are not.

Determining safety for aspartame is complicated by the following factors:

1. Aspartame is composed of two naturally occurring amino acids, aspartic acid and phenylalanine, both of which are a component of many ordinary foods. They are not synergistic in effect, so the action of each component is normally studied separately.
2. Aspartic acid and glatamic acid, the active component of monosodium glutamate (MSG), are essentially additive in toxic effect. MSG is generally recognized as safe. The FDCA requires the agency to consider any agent that adds to the effect of another food component. Determination of the safety of any particular level of aspartame is difficult unless the level of glatamic acid in the diet is known.
3. Phenylalanine is dangerous to those children who have phenylketenunia (PKU), a metabolic disorder that causes retardation if the child consumes phenylalanine. Most such children are identified at birth, but some, perhaps 25 percent, are not. The board was presented with the question of whether a risk to this very small group (about 200 per year) was a sufficient risk of injury to trigger the ban in the act. Since phenylalanine is common in all foods, the issue is the extra hazard posed by the small amount in aspartame.

Issue 1: Framing the Question to the PBOI

A PBOI is a consensual proceeding in which the parties waive their rights to an ordinary evidentiary hearing in favor of a PBOI. Since rules for the PBOI had not been promulgated, the parties in the aspartame case were able to negotiate the exact words of the charge to the PBOI. The following exchange took place:

> *Peter B. Hutt, FDA assistant general counsel, to Turner, 22 January, 1975:*
> In light of the objections filed by you and Dr. Olney, the Commissioner intends to frame the issues for the hearing as follows:
>
> 1. Whether approval of aspartame should be withdrawn because it causes or contributes to mental retardation or other brain damage.
> 2. What label warning statements are appropriate for aspartame if its approval is not withdrawn.

Turner to Hutt, 18 March, 1975
First of all, as I've pointed out to you in our discussions over the past few weeks, the way you indicated that the Commissioner intends to frame the issue is not acceptable. In its place I propose the framing of the issue as follows:

1. Whether approval of aspartame should be withdrawn because it poses a risk of contributing to mental retardation or other brain damage.
2. Whether the approval of aspartame should be withdrawn for any use in children's food in view of the similar risks and combined toxicity of glutamate and aspartame.
3. If approval of it is not withdrawn, what label warning statements are appropriate for aspartame in view of the similarity of risk and the combined toxicity of aspartame and glutamate.

Hutt to Turner, 21 March, 1975
Accordingly, the revised issues are as follows:

1. Whether aspartame poses a risk of contributing to mental retardation or other brain damage and, if so, whether approval of aspartame should be withdrawn for this reason on the ground that the available data and information fail to establish that the use of aspartame, under the conditions of use specified in the regulation, will be safe.
2. Whether aspartame and glutamate have a combined toxicity and, if so, whether approval of aspartame for any use in children's food should be withdrawn for this reason on the ground that the available data and information fail to establish that the use of aspartame, under the conditions of use specified in the regulation, will be safe.
3. Whether aspartame and glutamate have a combined toxicity and, if so, what label warning statements, if any, are appropriate if approval of aspartame is not withdrawn.

The final form, as it appeared in the *Federal Register* on June 1, 1979

1. The question has been raised whether the ingestion of aspartame, either alone or together with glutamate, poses a risk of contributing to mental retardation, brain damage, or undesirable effects on neuroendocrine regulatory systems. From available evidence, what can be concluded in relation to this question? The objecting parties believe that the ingestion of aspartame, either alone or together with glutamate, does pose a risk of contributing to these effects. The Bureau of Foods believes that the ingestion of aspartame, either alone or together with glutamate, does not pose a risk of contributing to these effects.
2. The question has been raised whether the ingestion of aspartame may induce brain neoplasms in the rat. From available evidence, what can be concluded in relation to this question? The objecting parties believe that available evidence suggest, without adequate ruling out, a possible association between aspartame ingestion and an increased incidence of brain neoplasms in the rat. The Bureau of Foods believes that available evidence does not show that ingestion of aspartame results in an increased incidence of brain neoplasms in the rat.

3. Based on answers to the above questions:
    a) Should aspartame be allowed for use in foods, or, instead, should
    approval of aspartame be withdrawn?
    b) If aspartame is allowed for use in foods, i.e., if its approval is not
    withdrawn, what conditions of use and labeling and label statements
    should be required, if any?

Clearly the parties had differing ideas about how the issue should be
framed. What is also clear is that they thought of the issues in traditional
legal terms. They asked the PBOI for a judgment—What shall be done?—
rather than an answer to the scientific question—What do we know about
aspartame? When the issues were finally printed in the *Federal Register*, the
difference is even clearer.

Questions 1 and 2 in the *Federal Register* notice are fundamentally different from question 3. They represent two types of questions. The first
type of question, questions 1 and 2, is one of fact or knowledge. What is the
true state of nature? Question 3 is one of options. Based on our knowledge,
what should we do? It would be incorrect to classify the first as scientific
and the second as legal or to call them questions of fact and of law. They
represent two entirely different functions, which are present in many views
of human endeavor. They can be referred to as a knowledge model and an
options model.

In the knowledge model, the attempt is to accept a statement as true or
false using as a structure the express requirements of a school of thought.
They may be more or less rigorous. One knows things in chemistry in a very
different way from psychology. There may be explicit uncertainties in existing knowledge. Traditionally, some such fields have been referred to as
disciplines. If a statement of fact is made, it must be made in accordance
with the standard of proof of the discipline. Scientific disciplines would
prefer to admit ignorance rather than make a false claim of knowledge.

In the options model, the actors are faced with a choice. Available
knowledge is marshaled; best estimates are added in; options are examined
and choices are made. Voting is an options model.

The same individual can function in both models. A university scientist
operates in the options model when deciding which research to conduct but
in the knowledge model when conducting the research. What is most important is that the standard for examination of the activities of such an individual is different in the two areas.

In an area such as medicine, the duality of the decision making is pro-
nounced. There are treatments available that we select as options, even
though our knowledge of how they work is limited.

It would be fair to generalize that in conducting research, scientists tend
to operate in a knowledge model. They answer questions rather than make
choices. Physicians most typically operate in an options model; they choose

among courses. The most important difference between the two models is their treatment of uncertainty in the knowledge model.

The aspartame PBOI was asked to operate in both the knowledge and options models. Questions 1 and 2 were in the knowledge model; they asked for a level of knowledge. But question 3 was in the options model; it required the board to choose a course of conduct. What was left uncertain was which option to choose if the knowledge proved uncertain. Obvious questions can be asked. Did the answers to questions 1 and 2 have to meet the standards of a specific discipline and if so, which one? Does the structure and makeup of the PBOI qualify it to make options decisions in the area of public health, and what rules decisions were to be used?

In the knowledge model, one can normally replicate the activities of a knowledge developer and confirm or deny any findings. If there are limitations on the certainty or quality of the knowledge developed, they are expected to be clearly stated. If a conclusion cannot be reached, that is stated, and that is the end of it. If a conclusion is reached, others can analyze it and determine whether the conclusion meets acceptable standards. If an error was made, the conclusion can normally be proved incorrect. One has the choice of not coming to a conclusion. In the options model, one must choose, despite the uncertainty.

It is a criticism of the options model that one can only observe the process of coming to a decision and determine whether the decision process meets acceptable standards. When we disagree with the conclusion, we do so on the basis that we have come to a different conclusion, not that we can prove that the other party came to the wrong conclusion.

Issue 2: Constituting the Board

The second issue dealt with the composition of the PBOI. The board was selected from lists prepared by each side. The choice of one member of the board, Dr. Vernon Young, was highly controversial. Sherwin Gardner, acting commissioner of Food and Drugs, said to Jennie Peterson, hearing clerk, on August 16, 1979:

> Dr. Young has indicated that he may, in the near future, be the recipient of grant support from the A.E. Staley Manufacturing Company for the purpose of conducting research to assess the nutritive value of soy protein concentrate and possibly the nutritional and metabolic significance of modified starches in human diets. A.E. Staley manufactures corn wet milling products, including corn sweeteners. I have concluded that this grant does not represent a conflict of interest because corn sweeteners would not be in direct competition with the low caloric artificial sweetener such as aspartame, but rather with products such as sugar. If any of the participants in this proceeding have any objection to the service of Dr. Young as

a Board member, they should be submitted to no later than seven days from the receipt of this announcement.

In a reply dated August 29, 1979, Dr. Olney objected to the inclusion of Dr. Young for two reasons: First, Young was from the MIT Department of Nutrition, as were Dr. Nauta, chairman of the PBOI, Dr. Miller, the FDA bureau director for food, and several Searle consultants. Dr. Young had written articles on nonaspartame substances in collaboration with Searle researchers. Olney alleged that this was a conflict of interest. Second, Olney considered Young's field, nutrition and metabolism, to be irrelevant to the question at issue, which he interpreted as a neuropathology question, not within Young's expertise. Consequently Gardner wrote to Olney on September 19, 1979, concerning the membership of the PBOI on aspartame and had reached the following conclusions:

1. Your objections to the composition of the Board are untimely. The relevant regulation, 21 CFR 13.10(b) (3), provides for the submission of objections to proposed members of a Board within 10 days after receipt of the names of nominees. The regulation does not provide for submission of objections after the Board has been selected. Therefore, the objections stated in your letter of August 29—after the selection of the Board—are out of line.
2. You had a full opportunity before the selection of the board to make the objections stated in your letter of August 29, 1979, and you failed to make them. In your letter of July 9, 1979, apart from a general disparagement of all of Searle's nominees, you did not object to Dr. Young, nor did you object to the selection of two members from MIT although that was an obvious possibility. Therefore, you waived your right to object to the selection of Dr. Young and to the selection of two Board members from MIT.
3. Dr. Young is qualified to serve on the Board. Since 1977, Dr. Young has been Professor of Nutritional Biochemistry in a distinguished Department of Food Science (MIT). He is a member of six prestigious professional societies and in some of them he has held high office. He is a member of the editorial board of two prestigious scientific publications (Journal of Nutrition and American Journal of Clinical Nutrition). Finally, Dr. Young had published an impressive array of scientific articles (122) in the area of amino acid and protein metabolism and in the nutritional problems of specific age groups (young and old).
4. The presence on the Board of two members from MIT does not constitute a conflict-of-interest, nor does it introduce any basis [sic] into the proceeding. Dr. Nauta and Dr. Young are both distinguished scientists of unimpeachable integrity. They have no association with the Bureau of Foods or with Searle. To our knowledge, they have not taken positions that would impair their ability to evaluate fairly and with an open mind the scientific evidence that will be presented to the Board. . . . They have colleagues who have expressed views on matters relevant to the hearing, and that some of those colleagues may testify before the Board, is not surprising: the community of scientists

with relevant expertise is a small one; the Department of Nutrition at MIT is a very distinguished one; and scientists rarely work in isolation. You have not presented any substantial reason for doubting that Dr. Nauta and Dr. Young will discharge their responsibilities in this matter fairly and objectively. Indeed, I am confident that they will.

Olney replied to Gardner on October 30, 1979:

In my letter of August 29, I clearly outlined serious problems of bias and conflict of interest created by your appointment of Dr. Young to the Panel. I further stated that this could be expected to render the Board dysfunctional in carrying out its responsibilities, especially considering the small size of the Board. In addition, since Dr. Young was selected preferentially ahead of much more relevantly qualified, duly nominated and available scientists, I charged that the Commissioner was guided by political bias rather than scientific considerations in selecting Dr. Young. I concluded that the appointment of Dr. Young places the Commissioner in violation of the apparent intent of the regulations governing panel selections.

In my letter of October 4, I made no statement that could reasonably be interpreted as a retraction, negation or modification of my protest; I merely took exception to the Commissioner's insinuation that I had intended to disparage the reputation of any scientists and I reiterated the point regarding Dr. Young's irrelevancy to the issues of the Board, my obvious purpose being to underscore the necessity for the Commissioner to employ more appropriate criteria in selecting new members for the expanded Panel. For the Commissioner to have misconstrued my October 4 letter as he did and use this as pretext for performing a 100% capitulation to the demands of G.D. Searle, strongly reinforces the pre-existing appearances that the Commissioner's actions are substantially biased in this matter.

The Commissioner's readiness to accept the G.D. Searle argument that panel expansion would involve undue delay is further evidence of the Commissioner's bias.

Two points seem apparent. First, it is absurd to solicit objections to an appointee, receive them, and then declare them out of time. Second, the rules clearly ask for responses to the candidates in terms of their individual qualifications. Olney objected to the board as a group, due to over-representation of MIT and the lack of certain fields of knowledge. The commissioner's statement that Olney should have objected to any possible panel is particularly absurd since under the decision rules (one from each panel of five plus one from either panel), two panels of five nominees produce one hundred different combinations. A better rule would be to name the panel and then ask for confidential assessments of the panel as constituted.

Bias and Conflict

Other than those technical complaints, Olney's protest raised a more-significant issue. Scientists often differ on fundamental concepts or practices, even within the same discipline. The law is long familiar with the concept of a school of medicine in negligence. In this case there are two problems: different disciplines and different schools of thought within some disciplines.

A school-of-thought problem is most likely to occur on the fringes of science, where issues are being tested with experimental evidence and no clear consensus exists in the field. The problem for the board was whether a difference in school of thought constitutes a bias impeding the decision maker.

There is also a problem of discipline. Some disciplines have axioms that are accepted as true by workers in the field. They then create structures dependent on those axioms. Scientific proof may be based solely on internal consistency with the axioms rather than external provability. This is particularly true in social sciences.

Judge Harold Leventhal said that a judge cannot tell whether the economist from the University of Chicago or Harvard University is correct. What is more to the point, neither can the economists. They may reject the axioms on which the other researcher's work is based. Although this problem might not occur regularly, it is particularly likely to occur when a question is given to scientists working on the fringe of human knowledge. It is therefore crucial that there be an understanding as to whether questions are knowledge or options questions.

In the options model, decision makers are asked to make a choice. Since they must make a choice, they must deal with both theories and evidence, possibly from a number of schools of thought and disciplines. Decision makers are a product of their own school of thought. The competition between schools of thought can be fierce. Since careers, grants, prizes, and the rest of the material rewards of science flow to those whose school of thought are accepted, the pressure on decision makers to reject all other schools of thought may be intense. Indeed they may even be completely convinced that the other schools of thought are simply wrong and discard their testimony in good faith.

The primary check on discipline and school of thought bias in a PBOI is in the framing of the question to the board, particularly by insisting on the knowledge model. In the knowledge model, a PBOI decision can be tested against the underlying discipline. One can compare the board's treatment of data with that normally accorded by the discipline. In the options model, there is no such test. There is no scientific method for making options choices in public policy. For example, if a panel of scientists were asked whether to gamble $20 billion on fusion power, there is no discipline that would allow them to evaluate an answer. The only check is on the bias of the panelists, but even that is an illusion, since the unbiased participant may be no more likely to come to a correct answer than a biased one. After all, those who are most strongly biased may be correct.

The problem is compounded when, as in this case, there is no general agreement on the nature of the dispute. Olney clearly believed the issue was one of neuropathology. He wanted to focus on the issue of what type of brain injury was caused by aspartame. The FDA commissioner believed the issue involved amino acid uptake by the brain. This is an issue of causation: whether aspartame would cause the injuries. Even if the individuals are unbiased in any classical sense, the naming of certain fields to the board clearly defines the question in terms of those fields. The concept of an expert board is useless unless there is agreement on what expertise is needed for the decision. If the commissioner was forced to define the question to the PBOI in the knowledge model, he would have to articulate the choice of fields in such a way as to make it part of the record.

If the question were phrased, "Does aspartame cause brain damage?" he could be forced to appoint those qualified to test brain damage. For example, if he is permitted to ask, "Is aspartame safe?" there is no control on the representation of fields on the board.

Diversity of Fields on the Board

The board as finally constituted was comprised of three scientists from three different fields. Lampert was a neuropathologist (a specialist in diseases of the brain), Nauta a neuroanatomist (a specialist in structure of the brain), and Young a nutritionist (a specialist in the body's ability to absorb amino acids). Olney wanted board members who were competent to determine whether aspartame could cause certain injuries. Searle Bureau of Foods wanted individuals who could determine whether animal tests showing injuries could be related to humans. The result was a board that had difficulties in acting collegially; instead, each member represented his own field.

Representation of Diverse Points of View

The board had two responses to the question of the need for diverse points of view. First, following the extensive discussions on the makeup of the PBOI, the board appointed two consultants to advise it on particular points. This allowed the board to secure evidence that was not proffered by a party and increased its expertise. It is probable that an expert board has a significant advantage over a lay judge, since it can identify with greater particularity what it does not know and secure consultants with appropriate credentials. Second, the FDA established rules for funding private parties, which allowed Olney to travel to Washington and to be assisted by counsel. The cost for his expert witnesses was also paid.

Issue 3: Limiting Evidence in the Proceeding

In 1975, before the PBOI was convened, certain questions were raised concerning the accuracy of the data submitted by Searle. The FDA suspended the proceeding and ordered a special independent observation of the data to be conducted by Universities Associated for Research and Education in Pathology (UAREP) group. Turner objected to the scope of the UAREP review and received in reply a letter, dated February 24, 1977, from Richard Merrill, then chief counsel to FDA:

> This letter responds to your letter of February 7, in which you stated that you were "unnerved" by my description of the parameters of the UAREP review.
> The express exclusion in the proposed contract of UAREP's consideration of "questions concerning the technical competence demonstrated in the planning and execution of the studies or the correctness and meaning of the conclusions to be drawn from the studies" should not be construed as indicating any lack of concern by FDA for these issues. Rather, it reflects our belief that FDA is itself capable of, and ultimately responsible for, judgments concerning the planning and execution of the studies based on analysis of the reports thereof and on UAREP's conclusions concerning their authenticity.
> No reason has been advanced by your letter or by anyone else why FDA cannot perform this function unaided by advice from UAREP. If you disagree with FDA's conclusions on these issues, the public board of inquiry on aspartame should provide a vehicle for a definitive resolution, at least for those studies about which you are most concerned.

The report was delivered on December 13, 1978, and on June 1, 1979, the notice of hearing on aspartame was filed. It contained the following statement on this point:

> FDA received the UAREP report on December 13, 1978 and has reviewed and evaluated it. The agency agrees with UAREP that the data submitted by G.D. Searle are authentic. The two parties who requested a hearing were informed of the results of the review of the data and that UAREP and FDA had concluded that the data are authentic.

Several different arbitrary terms were used in this letter. UAREP was to analyze the authenticity of the data, while FDA was to determine whether the planning and execution of the studies were correct and what scientific value the studies possessed.

The term *authenticity* is obviously a problem. If data were correct but incomplete or if research results were properly reported but proper procedure was not followed, were the data authentic? Was that for the UAREP or PBOI? Clearly any determination of lack of authenticity would have terminated the role of the PBOI. The letter from Merrill does not indicate the significance of an affirmative finding of authenticity, except to say that the ultimate conclusions of the FDA on planning, execution, and significance were to be resolved by the PBOI.

At the hearing, Turner attempted to question the validity of the data, but the board refused to consider the issue. Following the hearing, Turner made a direct appeal to the FDA commissioner to order a new hearing. It is clear from Turner's appeal and the board's decision that there was no agreement on the terms of the argument over the data. The decision said:

> The Board does not agree with Mr. Turner's statement that it has refused to hear evidence relating to scientific validity. Mr. Turner uses the term "scientific validity" to describe questions about the authenticity, reliability, and accuracy of the data submitted by Searle and relied on by the FDA in determining the safety of aspartame. Those questions were considered and resolved by the FDA and UAREP before convening this Board. Because it would be impossible for the Board to undertake a retrospective quality inspection of all the studies presented to it, the Board was not charged with making such an examination. The Board did not exclude evidence relating to the quality of appropriateness of the experimental design of the studies or the scientific conclusions that can validly be drawn from the studies. The Board believes that questions involving the proper interpretation of the data are, in fact, questions relating to scientific validity. Thus, although the board has decided that it should not repeat UAREP's authentication of the data, it has not decided to ignore questions concerning the scientific validity of the studies.
>
> The Board believes that its authority and responsibilities in this public proceeding are clearly delineated in the statement of issues published in the Federal Register of June 1, 1979 (44 Fed. Reg. 31716). Questions involving the authenticity, reliability, and accuracy of the data have already been resolved by FDA and UAREP. [PBOI decision at 11, 12]

Turner used the term *scientific validity* to include all research steps from planning the experiment, through execution, to scientific significance. The board preferred its own use of the term, which dealt with appropriateness of expert decision making but not whether the studies had been correctly reported.

Since proper execution of the studies was clearly a matter for FDA, the board erred when it rejected Turner's attempt to introduce evidence and denied his hearing on the data. It is clear that the source of confusion was the ambiguous statement of the FDA commissioner in the *Federal Register*. Several meanings could be given to the statement, "The data are authentic." It can refer to the evidentiary value of the data or to its scientific quality. As evidence, there are four choices:

1. It can be a conclusion that the fact at issue has been resolved by the competent decision maker, the commissioner in this case. This was the position taken by the Bureau of Foods in their appeal. The difficulty with such an approval is clear. It deprives the petitioner of his hearing on the authenticity of the data, guaranteed both by statute and by agreement. Turner obviously had not waived his right to contest the findings of the UAREP.
2. It can be a determination of relevance and materiality. This is a much more limited finding. It means that the data are sufficiently authentic to allow presentation to an ultimate fact finder.
3. It can be an acknowledgment that the FDA has no objection to the board's considering the evidence. This option is belied by the term *acceptance*.
4. It can be a statement of scientific quality, but here it is totally inadequate since it does not define the limits of the study.

The primary responsibility for the confusion must rest with the various commissioners of FDA. The limitations and prejudgments of evidence in a PBOI must be clearly and unambiguously stated. The commissioner had been alerted by Turner to the precise question at issue; he knew the board was proceeding in a scientific and not a legal framework, and he reviewed Turner's appeal immediately after the hearing. Yet no action was taken to avoid the possible waste of effort by all parties to the PBOI.

Issue 4: Conducting the Hearing

Since the hearing was designed to function in a scientific rather than a legal manner, several points are interesting.

Prehearing Activity

One of the prehearing requirements was to submit information to the board under 21 CFR 13.25. Olney's submission to the board provided an interesting response from Roger C. Thies, Searle's assistant general counsel:

> G.D. Searle & Co. has received a copy of a letter, dated July 30, 1979, from Dr. John Olney addressed to the Hearing Clerk purporting to enclose

material required by 21 CFR 13.25, which requires the disclosure of data and information by participants in a Board of Inquiry.

These materials consisted of a list of references that Dr. Olney states pertain to each of the issues to be considered by the Board of Inquiry as well as the statement that Dr. Olney intends to present additional "minor items of unpublished evidence from my own laboratory pertaining to glutamate or aspartate neurotoxicity." . . .

In addition, Dr. Olney has failed to submit the required signed statement that his submission complies with the requirements of 13.25. This omission is significant since Dr. Olney does not in any way indicate that he is enclosing all data, favorable or unfavorable to his position, which is in his files, nor has he stated whether he intends to rely on the views of any person other than himself.

Dr. Olney's letter is, on its face, only partial compliance with 13.25(a) (4), and ignores 13.25 (a) (2) (3) and (5). It is Searle's position that unless Dr. Olney submits forthwith *all* documents, favorable or unfavorable, in his files, relevant to this proceeding, including the unpublished evidence cited in his letter, and executes the signed statement required by 13.25 (a) (5), the waiver provision of section 21 CFR 13.25 (d) should be invoked against him.

In accordance with 21 CFR 13.25 (e), we are addressing these objections to the Chairman of the Public Board of Inquiry. However, since as of this date the Board has not yet been appointed, we also are requesting, by copy of this letter, that the Commissioner's office take prompt action to enforce the requirements of 21 CFR 13.25.

Such a response is clearly more legalistic that scientific. Olney's reply of August 13, 1979, is worth noting.

I have checked the 14 items from my list of references which Mr. Thies designates as incorrect citations and respectfully submit the following comments:

1-4 Correct as cited.
10 Correct except for misplacement of monosodium glutamate in title.
11 Change year from 1971 to 1972.
15 Change page from 310 to 319.
28 Correct except the third author's name omitted (Graves, I.P.).
70 Correct as cited.
87 Correct as cited.
93 Correct as cited.
97 Correct as cited.
102 Change page from 500 to 364.
103 Change second author's name "totticelli" to "Botticelli."
II-5 Change Phenylalanemia to Phenylalanimenia.
III-18 Change inclusive pages from 1037-1056 to 1037-1057. . . .

In my letter of July 30, 1979, I stated that I believed the materials I submitted complied with the requirements of 21 CFR 13.25. This belief was based on the fact that I did not receive any materials from the Bureau of Foods except a list of literature references, including items unavailable in my medical library. I believe that my original submission together with enclosures in this letter place me in full compliance with the requirements of 13.25, including the requirement of submitting all data in my files, whether favorable or unfavorable to my position. It should be mentioned that many of the references cited in my literature list are items which I do not have in my file, but rather would have to go to the Medical Library to xerox if I were asked to make copies available to other parties to the inquiry. Furthermore, many of the items are also included in the lists submitted either by Searle or the Bureau and therefore must be already available in the administrative record. Since I am a single private individual whose time is fully committed to other matters and who lacks funds to meet the expenses of the Board of Inquiry, I would interpret it as an undue burden on both my time and personal finances if I were required to furnish copies of all of the some 175 references cited in my literature list—almost all of which are public documents available to literate, intelligent individuals through Medical Library channels.

Presentation at the Hearing

The hearing was a model scientific debate. Each scientist made a presentation, followed by questions from other scientists. The issues were presented sharply.

Only two questions should be raised about the presentation:

1. The witnesses were not under oath. Oaths are not a requirement of an adjudicatory proceeding, but it is at least unusual to dispense with oaths without explanation.
2. More seriously, many of the witnesses presented their testimony by showing slides and commenting on them. The slides were not made part of the record at the hearing, making reconstruction and review of the hearing difficult, if not impossible.

Posthearing Activity

There was an unusual posthearing visit to Searle.

Nauta to All Participants in the Public Hearing, 16 April, 1980:

On March 28, 1980, two members of the Public Board of Inquiry, namely, Dr. Peter W. Lampert and myself, visited the research laboratories of G.D. Searle and Co. in Skokie, Illinois, as arranged previously by the Bureau of Foods, for the purpose of a personal viewing of the histological material bearing on the question whether the evidence indicates that aspartame contributes to the incidence of brain tumors in the rat.

G.D. Searle and Co., through the offices of Drs. Dodd and Sturtevant had placed the entire tumor-related case material at our disposal, as well as a private room and a double-head research microscope for simultaneous viewing of histological sections. We completed our examination of all tumor sections within the time of five hours. All mission-related discussions were among ourselves, but a laboratory staff member at our request supplied some technical information related to histological procedures and record keeping. During lunch with Dr. Sturtevant, no aspartame-related subjects were discussed. Our findings were most useful and will contribute significantly to the Board's deliberations.

Such a visit, unannounced, unwitnessed, unrecorded, is unheard of in ordinary adminstrative hearings. The rules of the board do not provide for such evidence. On the other hand, it is an act typical of a scientist. It meets the spirit of the proceeding but not the letter. Whatever Lampert and Nauta observed is not evidence of record, unless their observations, as expressed in the opinion, are evidence.

Issue 5: The Decision

The question of whether the ingestion of aspartame may induce brain neoplasms in rats was the most-controversial issue in determining the safety of aspartame. Two interesting issues were involved: (1) the propriety of combining two low-dose groups and two high-dose groups in test E 33/34 to produce a dose-effect relationship in rats and (2) the rate of spontaneous tumors in control groups in rat experiments.

The main concern of the issue of oncongenicity deals with the study of E 33/34, where a total of 320 rats received aspartame. Thirteen tumors were found by the board, reporting a 3.5 percent incidence of brain tumors. In group 1, rats were administered 1,000 milligrams (mg) per kilogram (kg) of body weight; four of eighty rats developed tumors. In group 2, the dose was 2,000 mg/kg; one of eighty rats developed tumors. In group 3, the dose was 4,000 mg/kg; five of eighty developed tumors. And in group 4, the dose was 6,000 to 8,000 mg/kg; four of eighty developed tumors.

Since the experimental groups were small in number of rats, the board combined the two low-dose and two high-dose groups when figuring the incidence of tumors. Thus, the incidence of 3.1 percent and 4.3 percent for the low- and high-dose groups, respectively, was calculated. This, in turn, suggested a dose-effect relationship.

The crux of the appeal with regard to E 33/34 lies with the practice of combining treated groups to yield a dose-effect relationship. The Bureau of Foods disagreed with the board's determination of a dose-response effect bias because it is based on selectively combined dosage groups. If a dose-effect relationship is shown to exist with aspartame, this is one criterion to determine the carcinogenicity of a substance. As various statistical tests are performed, the probability of finding a false statistical relationship increases.

Therefore, through decreasing the number of dose groups into high- and low-dose groups, the probability of determination of tumor incidence is increased.

The analysis of the data presented suggests a positive trend when studying the dose-tumor relationship. This means that as the dose increases, there is a significant increase in the incidence of tumors. The Bureau of Foods claimed that this determination is invalid because it is based on selectively combined dosage groups. This grouping is questionable because it is inconsistent with the original experimental protocol. By combining the two low-dose and two high-dose groups, the board calculated the higher incidence among the two new groups. This evaluation was one of the primary reasons for the adverse decision on the safety of aspartame. This type of postexperimental procedure of combining dosage groups may be scientifically unsound. Merely stating that there were small numbers of groups involved in the experiment, to justify the combining, may not be adequate justification for the procedure.

The usual practice of scientists is that the data should be analyzed as the study was originally designed. The five distinct groups were set up as distinct experimental elements comparing four treatment groups to one control group, and they should have been analyzed and discussed as such. If the original design were followed in the evaluation of the data, a dose-effect relationship could not justifiably be demonstrated. It would show 0.8 percent for the control group; 3.9 percent for group 1, 1.24 percent for group 2, 6.2 percent for group 3, and 1.26 percent for group 4. By manipulating the data, the board generated a dose-effect relationship between greater doses of aspartame and apparently increasing with respect to brain neoplasms (tumor incidence) in the rat. No scientific basis was provided for its action.

The second scientific appeal considered controversial concerns the data reported on the spontaneous tumor rate in control groups. In order to assess the oncogenic potential of a particular compound, it is important to compare the historical rate of spontaneous tumor occurrence of that found in the concurrent control animals of identical strains. The normal incidence of brain-tumor occurrence among the Sprague-Dawley (S-D) rat strain is difficult to determine. The reports that have been previously published were based on findings in rats that had been used in long-term studies designed to check the potential toxicity of a partial chemical compound. Other reports failed to state the protocol followed in brain examinations. Since many studies were not consistent, the board selected studies it felt most nearly normative as a basis for data collection. According to these data, the spontaneous central nervous system tumor incidence varied between 0.09 percent and 3.2 percent. Even these figures are not totally reliable, however, because the number of rats in one study was too small for valid determination, and the tumors in another study were noted after two years of age. Also tumor incidence in different groups of S-D rats from different commercial sources differs from group to group as much as it differs between the S-D and other rat strains.

If a statistically significant increase in the number of tumors is reported when the treated animals are compared to controls, then this is one determination that the agent is a carcinogen. The spontaneous incidence of tumors must be considered when determining carcinogenicity of studies.

These two decisions (to combine dosage groups in a study and to declare the control group abnormal and use another control group) are the essence of knowledge-model determination in a discipline. If they are acceptable, it is because the community of workers in that field finds it acceptable. Unfortunately, no support was given in the decision for these acts. The board was thus somewhat unscientific in its knowledge model deliberations.

It fared no better in the options model. One of the most interesting passages in the decision was the risk analysis.

> In attempting to assess the risk of focal (in particular, hypothalamic) brain damage connected with human aspartame consumption, the Board decided to adopt a 100 umol/dl concentration of GLU + ASP in the blood plasma as the critical level. This conservative assumption was made for reasons of caution: 100 umol/dl is the concentration at which a 50% occurrence of focal brain lesions has been reported for the infant mouse, the animal form generally thought to be most sensitive to the neurotoxic effects of glutamic and aspartic acid. [PBOI Decision at p. 35]

In other words, to the board the conservative level was the level where half of the test animals were injured. Clearly the board was in no position to label such a level conservative.

Issue 6: The Appeal to the Commissioner

The decision of the PBOI is accorded the status of the initial decision of an administrative law judge. Unfortunately, that is neither a guide for the board nor a limit on the commissioner's freedom. While the exact status of an initial decision of an administrative law judge is the subject of dispute, in the main it is a question of the commissioner's using the proper words. If an agency head states that he or she has reviewed the administrative law judge's findings and observations and has drawn a different conclusion from the evidence, in the main, the courts will support that action, even if the testimony is demeanor evidence directly within the observations of the administrative law judge.

The peculiar situation of the PBOI raises an important point: is the decision of the board evidence? Judicial decisions are not normally evidence in and of themselves, but a PBOI is composed of highly qualified experts who conduct a searching inquiry and then express their expert conclusions. These conclusions may be based on interpretation of the scientific evidence rather than accepted as concise scientific testimony. This is a crucial difference. The standard for review is fair evaluation of the entire record.

Three options are possible. The first is to treat the opinion of the PBOI precisely as an administrative law judge opinion. The commissioner can come to different conclusions, so long as these are supported by substantive evidence. Unfortunately, the entire rationale for convening a board of experts collapses if their opinion carries no more weight than that of an administrative law judge. In addition, they would be required to submit for review a proper legal record without the urgency or need to create such a record for their own decision and without the training to produce such a record.

A second possibility is to leave it to the discretion of the commissioner to accept the board's findings but permit the commissioner to accept the decision itself as substantial evidence, even if the underlying testimony of record is not adequate. This approach modifies the need for a classic administrative record. Acceptance of this alternative would allow the FDA to proceed with the aspartame case, even though the actual record is inadequate. The aspartame case would benefit from such a concept because of a peculiarity in the decision. No testimony was cited that would support the board's act in combining the E 33/34 study rats into larger groups. Therefore, there is no evidence in support of that decision unless the board's decision is not only part of the record but substantive evidence itself. The board is expert and is giving an expert opinion. Considering the scientific rather than legal nature of the PBOI, it is at least conceivable that the board's decision is as reliable evidence as that presented at the hearing. In addition, in this particular case, it is a limited form of evidence in the nature of impeachment rather substantive evidence.

Searle bore the burden of proof of aspartame safety. To meet its burden, it introduced study E 33/34 with an analysis indicating that it tended to demonstrate safety. The board reanalyzed the results, using its scientific expertise, and concluded that the study proved nothing. It would not meet scientific standards for proving the converse: that aspartame was dangerous. There would seem to be a policy argument in favor of allowing impeachment of scientific testimony by an expert board since it is equivalent to a finding of lack of credibility by an administrative law judge. Such a finding does not require opposing evidence.

Finally, it might be possible to treat the opinion as an entirely different type of initial decision. Make it conclusive, or at least give it the status of a jury finding, to be overturned only if no reasonable person could agree with the panel. This approval has the clear advantage of distinguishing a PBOI from an advisory committee. It has the disadvantage of requiring a clear, unequivocal charge to the PBOI, which might have to be framed after the evidence was presented. The concept is more like a science jury than a science court. Any choice from among these alternatives will emphasize some aspect of the decision process at the expense of others. There are two questions. The first is theoretical: how highly do we value scientific accuracy as opposed to procedural due process? The other is procedural: can we devise a mechanism that will carry out that balance?

Issue 7: The Record

The record in the aspartame proceeding can be distinguished in two ways. First, the office of the hearing clerk maintains a reasonably efficient, cumulative record of the entire proceeding. Second, it is impossible to determine what portion of the 162 volumes constitutes the hearing record.

What is the status of a document such as the letter of Dr. Brightman of NIH, one of the consultants to the board, to Nauta? Is it evidence?

> As I mentioned to you before the hearing was convened, my trust in Dr. John Olney has been gained at first hand. Some years ago I became interested in his work with another dicarboxylic acid, a-amino adipate. We followed his protocols and were able to corroborate his findings completely.
>
> Last week I called him to ask how the rest of the hearings had unfolded. I learned a number of unsettling things. He sent me a number of reprints concerning the effects of monosodium glutamate . . . , which reported that no consistent, morphological effects could be found. To summarize my doubts briefly, these investigators used immersion fixation rather than perfusion fixation of the CNS and paraffin embedding. The artifacts that invariably result from these methods would certainly tend to mask even unsubtle morphological changes produced by an administered agent. Secondly, there is no illustrative material for the reader to evaluate.
>
> I was appalled to learn that after years of dispute, the Bureau of Food and Drugs has not even attempted to repeat at least some of Olney's experiments. Even within the limits of personnel and budget that most of us must live, such an omission is shocking.
>
> Dr. Olney has also delved into the relationships between certain investigators, journal editors and manufacturers, as you have been informed. That some of the investigators get the bulk of their support from the manufacturers would make a careful, disinterested study by the Bureau absolutely mandatory. I am, therefore, left with a feeling of mistrust for these reports. As a citizen, I would like to see a complete ban on these unessential condiments until they have been proven, without doubt, to be harmless. The onus of proof is with the manufacturer and the eventual requirement of a warning label would strike me as an act of evasion on the part of the Bureau.

The problem of histological slides has already been noted. They were not available to a person reviewing the record of the proceedings. In a broader sense, it is obvious that no person or officer at FDA has the responsibility to supervise the preparation of a record.

A personal note can illustrate this point. As law clerk to the administrative law judge of the Consumer Products Safety Commission, I was responsible for ensuring that an appropriate, usable record was made and preserved. Several factors were involved:

1. The transcript was examined for errors, submitted to the parties, and corrected.
2. Exhibits were labeled and presented. During the testimony, a substantial effort was made to ensure that each exhibit being referred to was clearly identified in the transcript.
3. All factual findings were grouped together, and a clear distinction was made between them and argument and entered in the record.
4. Duplicate copies of the record were maintained in the office of the secretary in the administrative law judge's office.
5. When the record was closed, it was certified to the commission with a clear enumeration of what evidence was presented and used by the administrative law judge.

These steps would not interfere with the scientific value of the PBOI. They do not involve any legal rules of evidence or exclusion or require other legal consideration.

There is a broader concept of a record, however, which was never even mentioned in this proceeding. It concerns the concept of assembling the facts that will be needed by an ultimate decision maker. This ultimate decision maker may be a court or an administrator. The aspect that should distinguish a PBOI from a judge in a hearing should be an inquisitional frame of mind, a refusal to allow the parties to dictate the scope of the proceeding. In this case, the board had special consultants appointed who assisted it in the open hearing. For the most part, they acted as witnesses rather than commentators, but it was extremely important that they be present because they represented fields of expertise not present on the board.

Issue 8: The Commissioner's Decision

On July 15, 1981, the FDA commissioner made public a summary of his decision. His decision released aspartame for general public consumption. Several points are interesting.

1. The summary never mentions the Olney-Turner participation in the hearings or their status as parties to the proceeding.

2. The summary indicates that the commissioner considered evidence not of record in the hearing, as indicated in the following excerpts:

> I agree with the Bureau of Foods that the data presented at the hearing establish that there is a reasonable certainty that aspartame does not cause brain tumors in laboratory rats. This conclusion is confirmed by additional evidence submitted after the board issued its decision. [Summary decision, p. 8]

> This wider spectrum of reported spontaneous incidence rates is further supported by data submitted into the record by Searle and the Bureau of Foods after the board issued its decision. [Summary decision, p. 9]

> Finally, a third long-term study assessing aspartame's carcinogenic potential using a different strain of rat, concluded recently in Japan and submitted into the record after the Board issued its decision, also appears to be negative in terms of brain tumors. Although this study has not been critiqued by the hearing participants, the data on their face provide additional support for my conclusion on this issue. [Summary decision, p. 11]

This would seem to violate the Food and Drug Act, which requires the commissioner's order to be made on the record:

> The Secretary shall, after due notice, as promptly as possible hold such public hearing for the purpose of receiving evidence relevant and material to the issues raised by such objections. As soon as practicable after completion of the hearing, the Secretary shall by order act upon such objections and make such order public.

> Such order shall be based upon a fair evaluation of the entire record at such hearing, and shall include a statement setting forth in detail the findings and conclusions upon which the order is based.

3. Turner's appeal on the evidentiary issues is not mentioned.

4. Despite routine words of praise for the PBOI, it is clear from the summary decision that the commissioner attached no more weight to its findings than would do a lay administrative law judge.

Conclusions

The PBOI represents a significant possible improvement in adjudicatory decision making if:

1. The question to the board is phrased in a knowledge model.
2. The evidence to be used by the board is as reliable as that normally used by such scientists.
3. The board receives assistance in compiling a usable record for the commissioner on appeal.

4. The questions are answerable in the context of the fields represented by the board.
5. The board is provided with a clear description of the standards it is to use in accepting a proposition as proved, in particular whether the proof must meet disciplinary standards.
6. All parties are in agreement as to the weight to be attached to the board's decision.

In the main, the aspartame PBOI did not meet these standards.

Comment

Nancy L. Buc

In general, there appear to be two sets of circumstances where people start to talk about some sort of a science presence. One, and probably the more common, is where somebody does not like what the government is doing. Consider the nitrite situation. Research by a consultant to the Food and Drug Administration (FDA), Professor Newberne of the MIT nutrition department, led him to conclude that nitrites are a carcinogen. Nitrites are an extremely important component of hot dogs, and other products as well.

Professor Newberne, who by all reports is an extremely competent and well-respected scientist, all of a sudden is the source of enormous controversy, not all of which is rational or scientifically based.

There are calls for a science court by congressmen and senators, many of whom had never heard of a science court before the American Meat Institute explained to them what this was all about and what the FDA was doing.

In the context of all that, it turns out that there may have been problems with Dr. Newberne's assessment of his slides. FDA asked for help from Universities Associated for Research and Education in Pathology (UAREP) in reviewing the slides, and the group disagreed with Newberne, on the basis of a peer review of his slides, with his diagnoses of the tumors, and his judgments about his own data. FDA then essentially halted what would have been a rule-making process on nitrites.

One way to look at this is that a simple rule-making process, without a science court, worked. There were within the process mechanisms for asking questions that needed to be asked about the validity of the data, asking questions about whether these data supported a regulatory action. Those questions were asked and answered.

But in any event, that is one of the situations in which people want a science court—where they do not like what is going on. I think that is a pernicious situation. To decide whether you want a procedural device on the basis of whether you like what an agency is doing, for reasons that are utterly apart from whether you like its science or its law, seems to be a bad way to make public policy and to rewrite statutes. If that route is taken—as there is some indication that it might be—what will happen will be a series of additional procedural steps on an already-prolonged process—none of which have anything to do with principled decision making.

The other situation when a science presence is called for—when it is routinely used, though also without a court—is when people really do not know what to do. One that comes to mind is the chlorofluorocarbon situation with ozone. All of a sudden comes an assertion that the propellants in aerosols are going to wreck the ozone, and therefore, wreck humanity, since there will be no ozone. In that situation there was a felt need by all of the agencies that had any regulatory responsibility at all for somebody who knew about chlorofluorocarbons and ozone.

There are not many people with such a background because the issue apparently was relatively new. The National Academy of Sciences, fulfilling its traditional role, convened a panel, whose work apparently was generally accepted. There have not been a lot of attacks on that panel's scientific conclusions, either because nobody else knows any more about it than they do or because they were right. In any event, that issue flared up and died down, with the advice of some rather distinguished scientists who may not have been experts in those areas but whose scientific expertise was generally respected by a fairly wide community. That issue, like the one that Harold Peck discusses, raised the problem of who is an expert on a particular issue. It can be very hard to find somebody. What the National Academy of Sciences found for ozone was an interdisciplinary set of scientists who apparently transcended most people's objections.

In circumstances when the need is simply to know more, there are more than enough mechanisms available to get some scientists, or people who know, into the process. FDA uses them routinely.

One way is to hire such people directly. FDA's own staff consists of a number of scientists in a variety of disciplines. Thus, much of that basic scientific competence is already present at FDA.

FDA also routinely uses advisory committees of all sorts. They have worked on a variety of regular issues on new drug approvals and medical-device approvals, and they have also been called in for various types of crisis counseling, in situations like bendectin, a drug that is alleged to be a teratogen, and in situations like the ilozone-erythromycin estolate situation, where there were questions about whether the particular product caused more problems in children than had been originally anticipated. Advisory committees have been used in questions of intraocular lenses, which pose rather delicate questions both of statistical assessments and also of eye surgery kinds of assessments.

FDA already has access and can get access to almost anybody in the scientific community. By contrast, some of the concepts of the science court would require that its members be almost a sitting body; and one questions whether their competence will be as broad as would be necessary for what they would be called upon to do.

I would like to relate the cyclamate-saccharin-aspartame situation to Jerry Mashaw's model. These are all artificial sweeteners. Saccharin is the one that FDA proposed to ban, and Congress simply announced that that decision was not acceptable. Saccharin stayed on the market.

Cyclamates had been on the market for years until 1969 and the cyclamates uproar. Cyclamates are off the market; Abbott did considerable additional research and moved to relicense cyclamates, in a procedural situation much like the aspartame situation. FDA then issued a rather lengthy final decision, saying that cyclamates could not be approved under the same standard that will have to be applied to aspartame. Abbott immediately said that the decision was terrible science but chose not to appeal.

Assume for a minute that aspartame will be approved. Then we will have a situation in which aspartame is on the market lawfully; saccharin has been moved to be taken off but is still on the market lawfully; and cyclamates are not on the market. The scientific consensus seems to be that saccharin is probably a slightly stronger carcinogen than cyclamates. If that is so, then the stronger carcinogen is on the market and the weaker one is off because in one situation somebody was able to get the Congress to keep one on the market, and the other one not.

Aspartame by definition is either not a carcinogen or such a weak one that it falls below cyclamates on the scale if it is approved.

Now the question that should be asked is whether it makes any difference that there was a PBOI involved in aspartame in terms of how these decisions are made. The answer is probably not. Professor Brannigan is right in suggesting that the PBOI has created an utter mess. The questions about whether their own views are evidence, their viewing of the slides, not putting anybody under oath, not having a record, not even citing one single source in the record in their opinion is a source of rather considerable aggravation to the lawyers who are then going to have to make something out of it that certainly will be reviewed by a court, since there are parties apparently willing to sue on either side.

In that context, I would like to make a suggestion as to why the board was instructed the way it was by the commissioner, in the question of what to do with Turner's motion about authenticity. This interlocutory appeal came to the commissioner; and I think the right way to view it is as an interlocutory appeal problem. What does one do when the trial judge does not do what one of the litigants wants him to do, and he files an interlocutory appeal? There are several choices, and this is true of any appellate judge in that situation, which is what the commissioner is. The appeal can be sent back to the trial judge, or the judge can take the appeal.

In essence, the commissioner told the PBOI to make its judgment and then the agency would take it when it came back up. The issue is not at all settled as to what Turner's rights were, or should have been, or are, or will be, with respect to the Searle data. The issue will be appealed, and somebody will have to deal with it. Similarly, many of the other matters for which the board had such disdain, such as regular legal procedure, will have to be dealt with on appeal to the commissioner.

Finally, and probably most important, somebody has to do the mating of the scientific judgment to the statute. And that comes down to why I think the PBOI and other science courts are going to pose such a problem in the long run. The board almost intuited the statutory standard. In a way, they said, "Well, look, we really do not know, and it is not a good thing to let things out on the market that we don't know about. It would be better to make them prove that it is safe. So we will say no." That is almost precisely what Congress did in setting the statutory standard. In that sense, maybe they reached the right result, although I predict that it will come out the other way.

But the board did not do it for the right reasons, and I think that is important because the decision to license aspartame is not only a scientific decision. After deciding what the science has to say, the decision must be made as to the proper procedure. Vince Brannigan has outlined a whole host of problems with the procedure that was used, some of which may be actionable.

The next question is what standard Congress wants used here. That standard must be applied to what is known about the science. In the case of aspartame, the decision does not include economic or other kinds of cost-benefit factors, but it could in other contexts at FDA. It does not include policy factors. It does not include how FDA is going to explain its decision in such a way as to command public confidence that it knows what it is doing and that there is a difference between aspartame and cyclamates. That is something that judges do, but it is not much discussed. Unless FDA can explain why it distinguishes between aspartame and cyclamates, the public's confidence in its ability to govern will be suspect.

That, at bottom, is the issue. We are talking about governing. The government cannot be informed solely by science, although it cannot govern without science. That, for me, is what the issue comes down to: there are so many more kinds of questions that must be raised, so many more kinds of structures that must be dealt with, so many more issues that ought to go into the business of governing, that a PBOI winds up as too small a piece of what the total process ought to be about.

Comment

Harold M. Peck

The questions presented to the board were similar to questions that are continually posed to toxicologists in the course of their investigations. Perhaps definitions of toxicology and the activities of a toxicologist are in order. Toxicology is the study of the adverse effects of chemicals on living organisms. It is a multidisciplinary area in that in the intact animal, it includes clinical observations, biochemistry, hematology, pathology, reproduction and teratology, genetics, oncology, and so forth. It includes the several biological disciplines since the effects of a chemical, or drug, on the entire body are determined.

A toxicologist, and here I include the pathologist experienced in toxicology studies, evaluates the data observed from the toxicology studies and includes all other available biological data (pharmacology, efficacy, and so forth) and any necessary physical and chemical characteristics to make a determination of the safety of that chemical for its proposed use. The toxicologist continually makes decisions during all of these studies and may recommend that the development of a chemical be discontinued if she or he determines that the probable risk would be too great.

The decisions made by the toxicologist may be in the form of recommendations. These recommendations are seriously considered by superiors since the toxicologist's experience uniquely qualifies him or her for this action. The toxicologist who is making such decisions should have had years of experience as an evaluator of data from toxicology studies.

It has often been stated that the toxicologist should not take part in risk assessment. I disagree with this concept but do agree that that person's recommendations or decisions may become a part of the political process that is governed by existing regulations and sometimes by emotion as well as science.

If an advisory group or a public board of inquiry is concerned with questions involving toxicology, a scientist widely experienced in the toxicology discipline should be included in the group. The aspartame public board of inquiry as appointed was well qualified to make determinations of the relationship of aspartame dose to blood levels and safety with regard to individuals with phenylketonuria and to the acute pathology of the brain. The same decisions would have been made by a qualified toxicologist. The board, however, did not have a member qualified by experience to evaluate the incidence of brain tumors in rats in the two-year studies. Combining dose groups and elimination of one study with a relatively high incidence of brain tumors in the control group of rats for statistical analysis testifies to this.

207

In view of the relatively small difference between the incidence of brain tumors in the control and treated rats, a toxicologist would have examined and considered the range of brain-tumor incidence in similar-sized groups of control rats of the same strain. Such considerations would have resulted in a conclusion that aspartame did not induce brain tumors.

I examined the control historical data from rats used in studies not related to aspartame from our laboratory. (We use the same strain of rats as in the Searle aspartame studies.) In twenty-two groups of fifty male and fifty female control rats, the incidence of brain tumors varied from 0 percent to 5 percent. In four groups of rats, the incidence was 3 percent and in six groups 0 percent. Two identical control groups were used in each experiment, and in one case one control group had an incidence of 0 percent, whereas the other control group had an incidence of 3 percent. The incidence of 5 percent was in a study of 128 weeks; the other studies lasted 104 weeks. This result indicates that the older rats are more likely to have a higher incidence of brain tumors simply because they live longer. The range of tumor incidence is highly variable, and careful evaluation must be made of any slight increase of tumors in treated animals compared to control animals. The National Cancer Institute also uses historical controls to prove or disprove a relationship of tumors to treatment when the differences are sufficiently small to question any apparent statistical difference.

Because of the variable incidence of tumors in similar groups of control rats, it is not appropriate to determine the overall incidence of many groups of rats. It is more important to determine the low- and high-incidence rates among groups of control rats and then to determine if the incidence in the experiment under question falls within the range. If so, then a tumor incidence in treated rats within the normal range would be considered as unrelated to treatment even though the control animals had an unexpectedly low incidence. If the incidence in the treated rats was higher than the highest incidence in historical control animals, statistical anlaysis could be applied to determine if the difference was meaningful.

Preferably the historical data should be obtained from the laboratory in which the experiment in question was done. There is more assurance that the same procedures were used and the rats would have been obtained from the same colony. Historical data from literature sources should be used only when insufficient historical data have been accumulated by a laboratory.

In any case, the PBOI erred in not examining historical control data from the laboratory in which the aspartame studies were done. The historical data from the literature could be unreliable in providing adequate information relative to incidence of tumors in control animals.

The PBOI also erred in eliminating the aspartame study, which incorporated in utero exposure and in which the incidence of brain tumors in the control group was 3.5 percent. This incidence would not be considered bizarre by a toxicologist acquainted with variation in tumor incidence among groups of rats. Indeed the board should have considered the incidence in the control rats of the acceptable study to be low and should have recognized the variability of incidence of brain tumors based on the findings in the two control groups. In utero exposure of animals to a chemical is considered useful particularly in the case of aspartame where a fetus would be exposed if the mother were to consume aspartame in her daily diet. It is thought also that in utero exposure may provide an earlier indication of a carcinogenic property of a chemical and is generally recommended by the Bureau of Foods.

There appeared to be disagreement with regard to conflict of interest and bias of the prospective appointees to the PBOI. The members that were selected were from academia, and the conflict-of-interest problem was generally solved by selecting individuals with rather narrow fields of expertise. The conflict-of-interest problem may have prevented the appointment of a toxicologist to the board, although such a scientist was certainly desirable, if not necessary, since problems of toxicology were involved.

The selection of a toxicologist without conflict of interest would be very difficult since most of the qualified toxicologists are in government employ or are directly or indirectly employed by industry. Few academic toxicologists have had the opportunity to obtain experience in long-term toxicology studies, which was the point of concern in the aspartame discussions. In my opinion, conflict of interest and bias are defined too conservatively. Any toxicologist who does work for the pharmaceutical industry could be accused of having a conflict of interest since many drugs contain sweetening agents. If the conflict-of-interest definition is not modified, few, if any, qualified toxicologists could be appointed to a board of inquiry.

In the future the definitions of conflict of interest and bias should be examined very carefully and narrowed to mean scientific experimentation with the chemical under discussion or close association with the disagreeing parties.

The board of inquiry was in error in not obtaining a toxicologist as a consultant when the question, which was clearly a toxicologic question, was under discussion since the composition of the board did not include expertise in the areas of toxicology. Two members of the board were well qualified to examine the tissues to arrive at a decision that the appropriate diagnoses were made of the brain lesions but were not qualified to determine whether these lesions were related to treatment because of lack of experience in long-term studies.

The unwillingness of Turner and Olney to accept the decisions by the Food and Drug Administration (FDA) and the Universities Associated for Research and Education in Pathology group with regard to the authenticity and validity of the Searle data is interesting. The FDA is charged by implication by Congress with the responsibility of determining that studies on chemicals regulated by them are both authentic and valid. (It would be interesting to know if Searle consulted with the Bureau of Foods on the design of the long-term studies.) Once the FDA has made the decision, it would seem that there should be no reasonable objection by the disagreeing parties relative to the validity of the data being examined.

In conclusion, a major error in selecting the members of the PBOI was in not including a toxicologist (or toxicologic pathologist) who would be qualified to provide a scientific analysis of the incidence of brain tumors in the long-term studies in rats. If it was not possible to appoint a toxicologist, the board should have requested the services of a qualified toxicologist as a consultant.

Since, as Professor Brannigan stated, the public board of inquiry was a *science* board, the conflict-of-interest requirement should not have been so conservative as to eliminate participation by qualified scientists. Such conservatism serves no useful purpose and tends to limit truly scientific discussion and rational decisions.

Part III
Working Together: Lawyers, Scientists, Judges, Engineers

10 The Cognitive Style of Lawyers and Scientists

Peter G.W. Keen

This chapter explores differences in modes of thinking in specialized jobs that seem directly relevant to the interactions among scientists, lawyers, and professors and to the introduction of scientific evidence and expertise in the legal process.

The term *cognitive style* refers to the distinctive habits and strategies individuals rely on in complex analysis and decision making. Specialized tasks often require equally specialized ways of thinking. Judges seem most concerned with concrete facts, scientists with concepts and methods, and administrators with structure. Cognitive-style theory predicts that choice of occupation and effectiveness of performance in a job are correlated with the match between its implicit information-processing demands and the individual's style. Similarly, problems in coordination and communication between, say, judges and scientists partly reflect their differences in cognitive style. What is relevant, obvious, or fact to one may not be to the other. One person's logical analysis may be unacceptable or incomprehensible to the other.

The concept of cognitive style is well established in psychology. Kogan (1976:1) summarizes the assumption underlying the different models and labels used by researchers:

> There are individual differences in styles of perceiving, remembering, thinking and judging, and these individual variations, if not directly part of the personality, are at the very least intimately associated with variant non-cognitive dimensions of personality.

There are several models of cognitive style. This analysis focuses on a simple one, which derives from Jungian theory of psychological type (Jung 1923) and which uses the Myers-Briggs Type Indicator (MBTI) as a measure of style. The aim here is to make a case for looking at the whole issue of the relationship between science and law in terms of the personality and cognitive traits of the people involved, as well as the substantive problems of regulation and procedures.

The basic hypothesis is that there are marked differences between judges and scientists, especially in their concept of fact, and between lawyers and judges, on the one hand, and many professionals involving the social sciences in how they view evidence. These differences in cognitive

213

style make mutual understanding and even mutual respect difficult. More importantly, the scientist's or psychologist's mode of explanation may be significantly impeded, from each viewpoint, by many aspects of the legal process.

Judges tend to view fact in terms of concrete, discrete data, and scientists in terms of concept, relationships, and likelihood. Lawyers, judges, and scientists are all highly sequential and methodological in their reasoning. People in the helping professions, such as counseling and teaching, place more emphasis on values and viewpoint in their explanations.

This analysis presents data from a variety of sources on cognitive style and specialized occupations. There are as yet no systematic studies of judges and lawyers in this context. As a result, the arguments here raise rather than resolve questions. That said, it seems clear that there are marked specializations in mode of thinking among specialized professions. Those differences have been shown to relate to key aspects of personal and interpersonal behavior, communication, and decision making. Some data suggest that state judges are very different in style from scientists. If these basic arguments are sound, they seem to point to four potential directions of effort to improve the quality of the dialogue between scientists and the legal profession:

1. The lawyer must act as a translator or information broker between the scientist and the judge. That may often be done informally. If there is a fundamental problem of mutual understanding between many judges and most scientists, some brokerage role is essential. Judges cannot be expected to alter their effective fact-dominated, structured mode of evaluation. In a sense, they set the rules for the exchange of information, within the prescribed procedures and rules of evidence. The scientists may not be able to change their mode of explanation; even if they try, they are not likely to be clear or convincing. A formal translator is essential, one who understands both the legal and scientific mind without being an expert in both fields.

2. Participants in the judicial process may need to recognize that a key issue in assessing scientific explanations is to focus not on conclusions but on assumptions. In the view of judges, facts are facts; facts are not conditional on ideas or axiom. Scientists, by contrast, take the notion of axioms for granted; given the assumptions, the facts often follow. The real argument in science, the real source of uncertainty, is axioms. Scientists may disagree, given the same facts, if their unspoken assumptions differ.

3. Some mode of dialogue must be found that allows scientists room to breathe, to allow them to make their explanations in their own terms and at their own pace. Cognitive-style research draws attention to the ways social scientists explain themselves, the way engineers answer questions, and the way scientists work through a problem. The legal rules of procedure do not

allow the scientist thirty minutes to think. Psychologists, in particular, seem to need a chance to use their own mode of explanation. I have found in interviews with state judges that they are often irritated by the seeming inability of psychologists to make any coherent explanation or even to answer simple questions. Expert witnesses from the social sciences (including psychology) generally complain that the process is one of interrogation in which they cannot complete a thought. All they would like is ten minutes in which they can answer in their way. The concept of a science court seems to provide a potential mechanism for allowing them to do so.

4. Judges and lawyers must learn that accepting uncertainty is the issue for science. Facts do not speak for themselves, nor can uncertainty necessarily be eliminated by more facts. While a particular judge may not share the scientist's concept-focused, probabilistic currency of thought, he or she needs to recognize that it is valid in its context. The scientist must similarly respect the judge's rule-focused, fact-based mode of thinking as valid in its context. Perhaps the major value and purpose of cognitive-style research is to highlight for us that there are intelligences, not a simple intelligence.

Most areas of psychological theory and measures are contentious (and strongly dependent on axioms). Cognitive-style research is part of personality theory and as such fundamentally incompatible with a behaviorist approach. Keen and Bronsema (1981) discuss the validity of various cognitive-style measures and of the Myers-Briggs type indicator in particular. Nisbett and Temoshok (1976) present a strong argument against particular cognitive-style models, and Shouksmith (1970) the case for the cognitive-style approach. The central concern here is to establish that the psychology of individual differences in cognitive behavior may be a fruitful area for studying mutual understanding between the legal and scientific professions. Which cognitive-style theory of measures is most applicable is of secondary concern.

Decision-Making Methods and Assumptions:
Judges and Managers

The ideas presented here grew out of earlier research on the cognitive styles of managers and management scientists, an area where problems in mutual understanding seem to be a main cause of difficulties in implementing analytic models (Churchman and Schainblatt 1965; Huysmans 1970; McKenney and Keen 1974; Grayson 1973).

The focus on judges was stimulated by the experience a colleague and I had at the Stanford Business School in 1977. We went to the National Judicial College in Reno, Nevada, to teach for two days in part of a course on decision-making techniques. The main focus was on behavioral decision theory, a widely accepted method for handling problems involving uncertainty. There was one session on cognitive style.

The course was not the orderly process of brilliant exposition and enthusiastic acceptance the teachers expected. The judges by and large entirely rejected every aspect of the material: concepts, techniques, and recommendations. The assumptions and methods of analysis that business decision makers take for granted struck them as absurd. For example, executives often resolve uncertainty by including probability. If a project offers a 20 percent chance of making sales of $300,000, 35 percent of $400,000, 25 percent of $450,000, and 20 percent of $500,000, decision theory calculates an expected value: $(0.2 \times 300,000) + (0.35 \times 400,000) + (0.25 \times 450,000) + (0.2 \times 500,000) = (60,000 + 100,000 + 140,000 + 100,000) = \$400,000$. The normative approach underlying decision theory is to select the alternative that maximizes expected value. The classroom discussion quickly showed that the judges rejected this technique, which relies on quantifying probabilities to deal with uncertainty. In situations involving doubt, their own responsibility is to determine the facts and eliminate uncertainty. Their reasoning is rule based, not probabilistic. For several classroom examples used, their analysis reached entirely different conclusions from the teachers; both sides insisted theirs was correct.

One case problem in particular revealed the wide gap between the decision theorists' and the judges' view of the world. It involved a contested will. There were three legal issues: competence of the deceased, coercion, and fraud. The judges had watched an enactment of the trial. They disagreed as to the veracity of key witnesses and in the verdict. Their votes fall into a normal distribution, the bell-shaped curve that is the basis for statistical inference. The judges' assessment of one witness's credibility was as shown in table 10-1. To the decision theorist, this indicates uncertainty. The problem can be modeled as a decision tree (see figure 10-1).

Table 10-1
Judges' Assessment of One Witness's Credibility

1	2	3	4	5	6	7
Completely Untruthful		Somewhat Untruthful		Fairly Truthful		Completely Truthful
				x		
				x		
			x	x		
			x	x	x	
		x	x	x	x	
			x	x	x	x
	x	x	x	x	x	x

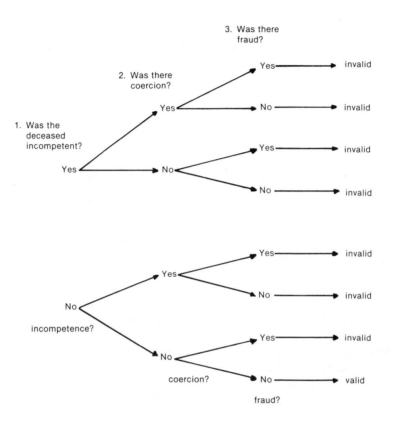

Figure 10-1. Decision Tree for Contested-Will Case

The decision maker needs to assign subjective probabilities, estimates of likelihood of each branch point. For example, the judge might estimate that there is a 60 percent chance of incompetence, a 90 percent chance of coercion, and a 30 percent chance of fraud. The joint probability of there being incompetence and coercion and fraud is $0.6 \times 0.9 \times 0.3 = 0.16$, equivalent to sixteen chances out of one hundred.

The judges in this situation disagreed. Either there is fraud or there is not. The values are 0 or 1, not 0.3 or some other assessment. Their conflicting votes do not indicate uncertainty.

The teachers counterattacked with the illustration of the decision makers' not having enough facts available but feeling that it is very slightly less likely that there was fraud than not, and the same with the issue of coercion and incompetence. The subjective probabilities are 0.49 for yes, there is fraud, and 0.51 for no on each branch of the tree. The likelihood that the will is valid (neither incompetence, fraud, norcoercion) is 0.51 × 0.51 × 0.51 = 0.13, or just over one in ten.

The judge's rule-based approach involves making a yes-no choice. The weight of the evidence is, however slightly, in favor of the will's being valid, on each of the three issues (51 percent − 49 percent) and the decision is:

1. Incompetence? No. (1)
2. Coercion? No. (1)
3. Fraud? No. (1)

A one in ten chance becomes certainty under this approach.

The teachers admitted that there were some valid reasons for using the judges' approach, especially since the analytic strategy is explicitly subjective. Regardless of this, it seems fair to state that the difference and the intensity of feeling on both sides reflect fundamental differences in thinking; the judges' strategy is suited not to handling uncertainty but to cutting through it decisively; and a decision theorist would still be horrified by the judges' assessment.

The reasons for the impasse seemed clear from the judges' scores on a cognitive-style measure, the MBTI. These differed markedly from those for a variety of business and technical groups about which I had earlier collected data. One scale on the MBTI (there are four independent scales) captures the extent to which an individual prefers to use sensing (S) as against intuition (N) in dealing with information. Those preferring to use sensing (Ss) prefer to deal with known facts rather than possibilities and relationships. Table 10-2 lists key characteristics of both types, taken from Myers (1962).

In scientific, technical, and intellectual fields, Ns dominate. The judges are markedly difficult to categorize. In four separate surveys, conducted between 1977 and 1980 at the National Judicial College, 115 state judges enrolled in courses on decision-making techniques completed the MBTI; 58 percent were Ss and 42 percent were Ns. The contrasts with almost all of the professions shown in table 10-3 are clear. To a large extent, the N style is a skill in thinking things up and the S one of getting things done. The S is a decision maker and heavily attentive to detailed facts; accountants, bankers, senior executives, and judges tend to be Ss. The N may be too aware of caveats, alternatives, and ideas to be as decisive.

Ss are attached to jobs involving attention to detail, facts, administration, and concreteness. Ns like ideas, possibilities, and theory. In intellectual fields, Ns dominate. Of high-school pupils in a college-preparatory cur-

Table 10-2

Cognitive-Style Differences between Sensing and Intuitive Types

Sensing Types	Intuitive Types
Dislike new problems unless there are standard ways to solve them	Like solving new problems
Like an established routine	Dislike doing the same thing over and over again
Enjoy using skills already learned more than learning new ones	Enjoy learning a new skill more than using it
Work more steadily, with realistic idea of how long it will take	Work in burst of energy powered by enthusiasm, with slack periods in between
Most usually work all the way through to reach a conclusion	Put two and two together quickly
Are impatient when the details get complicated	Are patient with complicated situations
Are patient with routine details	Are impatient with routine details
Rarely trust inspirations and do not usually get inspired	Follow their inspirations, good or bad
Seldom make errors of fact	Often get their facts a bit wrong
Tend to be good at precise work	Dislike taking time for precision

Source: Myers 1962:80a.

riculum, 42 percent are N; for noncollege preparatory students, only 14 percent are Ns; 83 percent of National Merit finalists are Ns (Myers 1962).

Since the initial classes at the National Judicial College in 1977, I have followed up the clue it offered as to the differences among lawyers, judges, and scientists that seem likely to affect mutual understanding and communication substantially. It is only a clue. Cognitive style, or rather cognitive specialization, is obviously only one determinant of individual behavior. Moreover, the rules of the legal process constrain much of that behavior, regardless of cognitive style. Nevertheless the clue is valuable. The data gathered so far and reported here indicate that the cognitive-style issue may be central, not peripheral, to any efforts to improve the ways in which scientific knowledge is used in the judicial process.

The Myers-Briggs Type Indicator

There are many models of cognitive style and even more measures. Almost all are flawed by major problems of validity: conceptual, construct, conver-

Table 10-3
MBTI Distribution of Ss versus Ns for Occupational Specialties

	Percent S	Percent N	Sample Size
Technical fields			
Engineering undergraduates	35	65	2,188
Engineering graduates	33	67	1,196
Scientific fields			
Science graduates	17	83	705
Research scientists	0	100	30
Intellectual fields			
Creative writers	12	88	17
Rhodes scholars	7	93	71
Creative architects	0	100	40
Mathematicians	3	97	28
Business			
Functional areas			
Accountants	87	13	na
Bank employees	71	29	na
Sales, customer relations	92	8	na
Managerial level or training			
Wharton undergraduates	72	28	488
MBAs (combined Wharton,			
Stanford, Harvard samples)	32	68	604
Middle managers	27	73	206
Senior executives	55	45	119
Owner-managers of small firms	86	14	150
Law			
Graduate law students	41	59	2,248
State judges	58	42	112

Sources: Center for Applications of Psychological Type 1980; Keen and Bronsema 1981; Myers 1980; deWaele 1978; McCaulley 1976; Mackinnon 1962; Wade 1981; Hoy 1979.

gent, discriminant, predictive and nomological (these are Bagozzi's categories of validity (1980)); the first two and the last one raise issues of theory and the others of statistical methodology.

Failure to resolve these complex issues has limited the quality and credibility of cognitive-style research (Taylor and Benbasat 1980; Keen and Bronsema 1981). They are not discussed in detail in this chapter because the concern here is with applying the concepts of cognitive style to the context of lawyers and scientists. (Appendix 10-A summarizes key conceptual and technical issues.) The MBTI (Myers 1962) is a simple, well-constructed, and well-supported instrument that many consider by far the most-valid measure of style. It is the basis for most of the ideas and empirical data reported here.

The MBTI was designed in the 1940s and has been refined and validated continuously since then. It is based on the Jungian theory of psychological type. It views mental functioning as dependent on the way people prefer to use their minds, in terms of the way they perceive data and the way they make judgments.

> *Perception* is here understood to include the processes of becoming aware—of things or people or occurrences or ideas. Judgment is understood to include the processes of coming to conclusions about what has been perceived. [Myers 1962:1]

Perception, by definition, determines what people see in a situation, and their judgment determines what they decide to do about it. These two distinctions correspond closely to concepts of cognitive style. McKenney and Keen (1974), for instance, distinguish between problem solving and data gathering. Keen (1973) after applying and analyzing twelve tests, concluded that the MBTI successfully captured his categories of cognitive style. Mason and Mitroff (1973), in an influential article on the relationship between information and individual differences in thinking, recommend the MBTI. Since then, it has increasingly been accepted as a conceptually valid instrument for measuring cognitive style. For a long time, it has been established as methodologically sound and is backed by many detailed studies of occupations, intellectual fields, and career paths. It has thus become the most widely used measure of cognitive style (Keen and Bronsema 1981).

The MBTI consists of 126 forced-choice questions. An example follows:

1. When you go somewhere for the day, would you rather:
   a. plan what you will do and when?
   b. just go?
2. Which word in each pair appeals to you more?
   a. literal
   b. figurative

The results are reported in terms of four independent dimensions (see table 10-4). Two relate to perception or data gathering: extraversion-introversion (EI) and sensing-intuition (SN). The other two refer to judgment or problem solving: thinking-feeling (TF) and judging-perceiving (JP).

The specific labels are somewhat misleading. Extraversion-introversion does not have the popular meaning of gregariousness or shyness but derives from Jung. Similarly, intuition is different from intuitive problem solving (Keen 1973). In general, it is more useful to refer to the scales as EI, SN, and so on and not focus on the labels.

The MBTI classifies a subject as either an E or an I, an S or an N, and so on. This classification indicates the type. The strength of the individual's preference for E versus I and so on is indicated by a number between 1 and

Table 10-4
MBTI Categories

1. Extraversion—introversion (E/I):
   E: Relates more easily to the outer world of people and things
   I: Relates more easily to the inner world of ideas
2. Sensing—intuition (S/N):
   S: Preference for known facts; reliance on concrete data and experience
   N: Looking for possibilities and relationship; focus on concepts and theory
3. Thinking—feeling (T/F):
   T: Judgments based on impersonal analysis and logic
   F: Judgments based on feelings and personal values
4. Judging—perceiving (J/P):
   J: Living in a planned, decided, orderly way, wanting to regulate life and control it
   P: Living in a flexible way, wanting to understand life and adapt to it

about 60 (it varies for each scale). Scores of 15 or less are regarded as indicating only a mild preference. Those above 30 show that the individual is a strong A or B. For example, the result

E   17

N   31

T   1

J   51

indicates this individual is an ENTJ (there are sixteen such categories) with a fairly strong preference for extraversion and intuition and a very strong one for judging. The other score is too low to indicate a marked preference; however,

the letter is considered the most important part of the score, as indicating which of the opposite sides of his nature the person prefers to use, and, presumably, has developed—or can develop—to a higher degree. [Myers 1962:3]

The MBTI is genuinely free of value judgments. If anything, it is a little too positive in ascribing virtues to each type. For example, this is Myers's summary of the ISTJ (common among judges), INTP (common among scientists), and INFP (rare among either but common with those in the liberal arts or counseling):

ISTJ
Serious, quiet, earn success by concentration and thoroughness. Practical, orderly, matter-of-fact, logical, realistic and dependable. See to it that

everything is well organized. Take responsibility. Make up their own minds as to what should be accomplished and work toward it steadily, regardless of protests or distractions.

INTP
Quiet, reserved, brilliant in exams, especially in theoretical or scientific subjects. Logical to the point of hair-splitting. Usually interested mainly in ideas, with little liking for parties or small talk. Need to have sharply defined interests. Tend to choose careers where some strong interest can be used and useful.

INFP
Full of enthusiasms and loyalties, but seldom talk of these until they know you well. Care about learning, ideas, language, and independent projects of their own. Tend to undertake too much, then somehow get it done. Friendly, but often too absorbed in what they are doing to be sociable. Little concerned with possessions or physical surroundings. (Myers 1976)

The lack of value judgments is of central importance for cognitive style, which is a theory of individual differences. Intelligent quotient (IQ) measures imply value; an IQ of 125 is better than one of 95. An N is not better than an S. The MBTI and related cognitive-style research stress the effectiveness of each style in the right context (Keen 1974). The strengths of the categories in work situations (Myers 1962) are:

E: ease with environment.

I: depth and concentration.

S: realism and observation, thoroughness and respect for detail.

N: insight, ingenuity, grasp of the complicated.

T: realism, analysis, logic, critical faculty.

F: enthusiasm, sympathetic understanding of people, persuasiveness.

J: organization.

P: adaptability.

Cognitive Style and Occupational Specialization

Table 10-3 compares professions and intellectual fields along three of the four MBTI dimensions. (The E/I scale has not been found to discriminate significantly or to relate as directly to cognitive style.) There are several problems in testing significant levels:

1. There is an absence of adequate population norms.
2. The MBTI scales have been explicitly developed as dichotom out (see appendix 10-A) and not as a spectrum, so that absolute scores are less meaningful than the letters.
3. Many authors do not report scores, only, as in table 10-5, the relative frequency of Ss versus Ns, and so on.

Keen and Bronsema (1981) use simple chi-square statistics, using MBA students who are representative of educated managers, the focus of that study.

For this chapter, the logical base populations are lawyers and judges, but since two available samples are from second-hand (law students) and small (judges) samples, as well as being only a subset of the two professions, there is no effort to test the significance level using either as the base for comparison. This task will be done when larger, more-systematic samples have been collected.

Table 10-5 indicates clear differences among specialties. They relate more to differences of perception of information (S/N scale) than to its use in problem solving and decision making (T/F and J/P):

1. Intellectual fields contain a preponderance of Ns; in scientific and technical areas, they are generally close to 90 percent.
2. Fields in which attention to detail and concrete action are key attract Ss. The judges are 55 percent Ss, which contrasts very strongly with every sample in the technical, scientific, and intellectual categories.
3. Technical specialists are mainly Ts with few Fs. The worlds of analysis, business, and structured thinking contain on the average 70 percent Ts. The Fs are found in the intellectual fields and the service professions (counseling, education, and health related).
4. Individuals whose work involves close contact with others tend to be Ss and Fs, sales and customer relations being the clearest example.

In general, those in the legal field, lawyers and judges are Ts, as are the scientists. The limited but replicated samples of state judges are mainly Ss. The theoretical and empirical work on cognitive style using the MBTI demonstrates that this degree difference from technical and scientific specialists is associated with equally marked differences in behavior.

Much of the MBTI work on occupational differences has focused on medicine. It has provided some striking results that suggest that examining the legal profession in the same way may highlight the range of specialized jobs and specialized thinking in a field that is often viewed as relatively undifferentiated. Table 10-6 indicates, for example, how cognitive-style differences lead people in medicine to concentrate on particular specialties.

Table 10-5
MBTI Types across Occupational Fields

	N	Percent S/N	p	Percent T/F	p	Percent J/P	p
Baseline figures							
Base population data	75,745	52-48		37-63		54-46	
Combined MBA samples	604	32-68		71-29		60-40	
Technical fields							
Engineering undergraduates	2,188	35-65	**	67-33	***	35-65	***
Engineering graduates	1,196	33-67		68-32	*	64-36	**
Data-processing professionals	122	41-59	*	74-26		81-19	***
Office automation specialists	217	34-66		77-23		74-26	***
Industrial management scientists	26	38-62		73-27		77-23	
Bell Laboratories supervisors	24	43-57		71-29		60-40	
Scientific fields							
Science students	705	17-83	***	69-31		49-51	***
Research scientists	30	0-100	***	77-23		60-40	
Intellectual fields							
Creative writers	17	12-88		35-65	**	27-73	**
Rhodes scholars	71	7-93	***	45-55	***	37-63	***
Theology	n/a	18-82		28-72		n/a	
Creative architects	40	0-100	***	50-50	**	40-60	**
Mathematicians	28	3-97	**	68-32		n/a	
Business							
Functional areas							
Accountants	n/a	87-13		73-27		n/a	
Bank employees	n/a	71-29		65-35		n/a	
Sales and customer relations	n/a	92-8		11-89		n/a	
Bank managers	42	70-30	***	55-45	*	52-48	
Marketing managers	23	43-57		83-17		83-17	*
Management consulting	79	35-65		78-22		72-28	*
Managerial level or training							
Wharton undergraduates	488	72-28	***	69-31		43-57	**
Middle managers	206	27-73		77-23		46-54	***
Senior executives	119	55-45	***	72-28		83-17	***
Owner-managers of small firms	150	86-14	***	81-19	**	75-25	***
Service professions							
Health related	n/a	49-51		20-80		n/a	
Education	n/a	55-45		19-81		n/a	
Counseling	n/a	15-85		15-85		n/a	
Academics							
Business school faculty	42	28-72		75-25		54-46	
Academic management scientists	23	15-85		69-31		58-42	
College teachers	60	27-73		45-55	***	n/a	
Law							
Graduate law students	2,248	41-59	***	73-27	*	57-43	**
State judges	112	58-42	***	66-34		78-22	***

Source: Keen and Bronsema 1981.

Note: *p* shows significance level comparing this group on this scale with combined MBA sample, which is used as indicator of general management MBTI profile.

$$* = p\ 0.05$$
$$** = p\ 0.01$$
$$*** = p\ 0.001$$

(chi-square statistic, 1 *df*)

The italicized figure shows which category contains majority of this group; for example, for % S/N, 35-65 means 35% S, 65% N; Ns dominant.

The base population of 75, 745 is the MBTI data bank built by the center for the Application of Psychological Type, University of Florida, 1970-1971.

The data comes from a longitudinal study of 4,000 medical students and their careers over a twenty-year period from the (1950s through the 1970s) (Myers 1980).

The degree of differentiation within a broad field may be a key issue. The mode of thinking of most pediatricians and its consequent implications for decision making, inference, and handling of people are markedly different from neurologists (SF: concrete, pragmatic, and feeling versus NT: conceptual, analytic, and dispassionate). They both are doctors. Preliminary surveys of lawyers suggest that patent lawyers and trial lawyers,

Table 10-6
Cognitive Style and Medical Specialities

Sensing Types			
With Thinking		*With Feeling*	
ISTJ		ISFJ	
Pathology	1.74	Anaesthesiology	1.76
Obstetrics, gynecology	1.46	ISFP	
Psychiatry	.44	Anaesthesiology	1.84
ISTP		General practice	1.40
Anaesthesiology	2.05	ESFP	
Psychiatry	.39	Obstetrics, gynecology	1.44
Pathology	.33	Medical faculty	.43
ESTP		Psychiatry	.33
Surgery	1.38	ESFJ	
Psychiatry	.25	Pediatrics	1.51
ESTJ		Psychiatry	.16
General practice	1.46		
Internal medicine	.68		
Psychiatry	.36		

Intuitives			
INFJ		INTJ	
Internal medicine	1.42	Neurology	2.75
INFP		Research	2.72
Psychiatry	2.04	Pathology	1.99
ENFP		Internal medicine	1.44
Psychiatry	1.52	INTP	
General practice	.73	Neurology	2.35
ENFJ		Research	1.98
Medical faculty	1.69	Psychiatry	1.84
		Pathology	1.78
		Obstetrics, gynecology	.44
		ENTP	
		General practice	.70
		ENTJ	
		Internal medicine	1.35

Source: Myers 1980:168.

Note: The figures shown are the actual frequency of this cognitive style compared with the expected frequency.

for example, are equally distinctive. Given the substantial difference between judges and scientists in terms of the SN scale on the MBTI, their mutual understanding will be low. The lawyer may be a necessary intermediary. It makes a difference if he or she is closer to the judge's or scientist's style (see figure 10-2).

A recent finding in a study of cognitive-style differences among managers is both surprising and relevant to the legal field (Keen and Bronsema 1981). It is hidden in table 10-3. Large-scale surveys of MBAs at major universities and middle managers in large organizations consistently show that Ns predominate. Ss are more frequent at lower levels. Top managers, however, include many Ss. The explanation for this unexpected result seems to be that the Ns' style is well suited to handling complexity; it is the thinking-up skill. Managers have to coordinate a range of functions: planning, forecasting, analysis, and control.

A large organization includes many professional and academic disciplines: economists, computer scientists, human-resource planners, lawyers, and even historians. Integrating their activities requires the Ns' willingness to play with concepts and use theoretical frameworks. Someone, however, has to eliminate, not add, to this complexity and uncertainty. The Ss' skill is getting things done, demanding the facts and only the facts. Ss hold that "matters inferred are not as reliable as matters explicitly stated" (Myers 1962).

The top executive's profile is very close to the judge's. And just as the executives are in general different from the middle managers, the state judges are not representative of the lawyers. (See table 10-7.)

Thus, not only is there specialization within broad fields but across levels. Self-selection presumably accounts for both. The similarity between

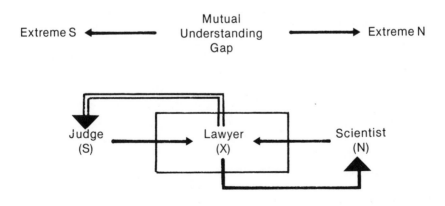

Figure 10-2. Lawyer as Intermediary

Table 10-7
MBTI Profiles of Selected Professions

	S	N	T	F	J	P
Top executives	58	42	66	34	78	22
Judges	55	45	72	28	83	17
State judges	41	59	66	34	78	22
Lawyers	58	42	73	27	57	43

Source: Keen and Bronsema 1981.

judges and executives highlights the fact that they are indeed decision makers. The strengths of the executive-judge are the obverse of their limitations.

Mutual Understanding

Mutual understanding is a major topic in studies of effective implementation of analytic models and computer-based information systems. The basic assumption in this tradition is Grayson's (1973): "Managers and management scientists are operating in two separate cultures. . . . Effective cooperation—even communication—between the two is just about minimal."

One issue in this chapter is whether cognitive style accounts for the problem and whether *lawyers,* or *judges,* and *scientists* can be substituted for *managers and management scientists.*

A number of methodologically sound studies make conclusions about the impact of cognitive style on preference for and use of information and on their interaction with other people.

1. Churchman and Schainblatt (1965), who first used the term *mutual understanding* and linked it to cognitive style, showed convincingly in a group problem-solving experiment that people will simply ignore information in a format that is not consistent with their own style. Huysmans (1970) similarly showed that "analytics" (who correspond to Ts) and "heuristics" (Fs) differed in their acceptance of an operations-research proposal, depending on its format. Analytics preferred a complete and explicit recommendation with full supporting evidence, while heuristics preferred a general, integrative report aimed at getting the main idea across without supporting formulas.

2. Keen (1973) found that cognitive specialists differ strongly in their choice of problems, in their strategy for solving them, and in their mode of explanation. Systematic subjects (Ts) tended to be very concerned with getting into a problem by defining how they would solve it. The Fs used a more trial-and-error approach and were less conscious of their methods. Both

styles were very effective on the problems they chose and ineffective on the ones at which the others excelled. The Fs' reasoning was not at all structured, and they justified their solutions on the basis of feelings and a sense of rightness.

3. Ghani (1980) showed that Ts and Fs on the MBTI differ in their preference for and performance using tabular (T's choice) and graphical information (F's).

4. Slocum (1978) found that change agents, (consultants and internal staff responsible for implementation) used different information and strategies (see table 10-8).

5. Mitroff and Kilman (1975) used stories to elicit individuals' concepts of the ideal organization to work in. For type ST, the emphasis in the stories is on factual details, physical features of work, impersonal organizational control, certainty, and specificity. For type NT, the emphasis was on broad global issues and theories of organization; also they were impersonally idealistic. The stories of the NFs revealed a global outlook, one that was generally personal and humanistic; they believed that organizations should serve humanity. The emphasis in the stories by the SF type was on facts and precision and human relations. The values were individual, not global.

Other general conclusions, derived from a range of studies using the MBTI, can be made. (No attributions are made here, since the conclusions draw on a wealth of references.) For example, in getting along with others in group problem solving, the emphasis of each style can be identified. In presenting sound ideas, S emphasizes facts, N emphasizes possibilities, T emphasizes logic and principles, and F emphasizes the human angle.

In responding to ideas, T emphasizes the impersonal and critical, and F emphasizes values and harmony.

In contributing to the discussion, S emphasizes getting things done, and N emphasizes thinking things up.

In making mistakes in handling others, S says, "It won't work," N says, "Let's not worry about details now," T says, "You're wrong," and F says, "Let Fred have his way."

Regarding perceptions of each other, the words people use to describe themselves and the words others use to describe them are amusingly dif-

Table 10-8
Information and Strategies of Change Agents

Type	Preferred Information	Preferred Strategy
ST	Task	Behavior modification
SF	People	Transactional analysis
NT	Organizational structure	Survey feedback
NF	People	Confronting meeting

ferent (see table 10-9). Given that judges tend to be STs, scientists NTs, and psychiatrists NFs, the implications of this list for the use of expert witnesses seem dramatic.

The findings summarized are evocative. A final point is worth making. A study of 375 married couples found that "there was significantly more similarity than difference between husband and wife on each of the four preferences. . . . The most frequent similarity was on SN, which suggests that seeing things the same way . . . does more to make a man and woman understand each other than a shared performance on EI or TF or JP" (Myers and Myers 1980). The issue of lawyers' using scientific evidence and expert witnesses (or vice-versa) explicitly centers around the importance of seeing things the same way.

Lawyers and Scientists

The lawyer's and the scientist's worlds are very different.[a] The word *fact* dominates in legal circles. The judge's job is to determine the facts. The lawyer's question is, What are the facts? They see facts in S terms (MBTI) as concrete, objective, and precise. Scientists rely on facts, too, but their facts are data, signs, observations, and referents that are meaningful only in relation to some organizing scheme. They are means to some end, not an end in themselves. Their facts are not the concrete, independent, pragmatic entities of the S.

The conversations of judges and lawyers equate facts with evidence. Scientists' concepts of evidence, and hence truth, are marked by inference and uncertainty. A given datum—fact—suggests or supports a particular hypothesis. It is not at all inconsistent for scientists to equivocate, disagree, or make their conclusions conditional.

The SN dimension of the MBTI corresponds directly to the extremes of fact versus concept and legal versus scientific evidence. The following illustrations indicate how quickly and completely the extremes can come to misunderstanding and conflict.

Asked which types of witnesses they find most difficult to deal with, several S judges identified psychiatrists as evasive, unclear, rarely able to say anything without beating about the bush, and consistently not addressing the question. The cognitive-style sessions at the Judicial College alerted

---

[a]The discussion in this section is based on a range of formal and informal sources: (1) field notes on interviews with lawyers and judges; (2) transcripts of a brief experiment in which lawyers and scientists tried, and largely failed, to work together on a problem involving the design of a multiuse ocean platform; (3) the experiences and perceptions of social scientists, political scientists, and economists in school finance cases (McDermott 1976, Lehne 1978, Keen and Clark 1978); and (4) MBTI data (Myers 1962, 1976; Keen 1973). Where relevant, the source for statements or hypotheses will be shown in the discussion.

Table 10-9
Self-Perception and Perception of Others

	How We See Ourselves	How Others See Us
T	analytical	cold
	organized	rigid
	systematic	nitpicking
	precise	indecisive
F	spontaneous	impulsive
	persuasive	manipulative
	sensitive	vindictive
	perceptive	melodramatic
S	competitive	unimaginative
	objective	opportunistic
	resourceful	cold-blooded
	realistic	domineering
N	idealistic	naive
	serious	dogmatic
	imaginative	pompous
	charismatic	devious

them to the possibility that the psychiatrists were explaining themselves as clearly as they could; they had no concrete facts, only concept-based facts and they shaped a variety of observations and ideas into a coherent whole, guided perhaps by theory.

In a second illustration, lawyers were unwilling to give direct answers to an ocean engineer's general question. The engineer was interested in building a multiuse platform and wanted to know "what legal issues I should think about." The lawyer responded, "Give me a specific case. I can't answer that. . . . Is it going to be inside the three-mile limit?" The engineer did not know: "I want to have some idea of the things I need to take into account before I decide to build it." The lawyer countered, "You have to be more definite." The structured fact-based thinking of the lawyers conflicted with the structured concept-based style of the engineers.

A final example of where cognitive style may have had substantial impact on a judicial process comes from the field of school-finance reform. A coalition of social scientists, lawyers, economists, and educators successfully challenged the finding of public educators in California in the case of *Serrano* v. *Priest* (96 Cal. 2d 487 (1971)). They lost in Texas *San Antonio Independent School District et al.* v. *Rodriguez et al.* (411 U.S. 1 (1973)), but over the past decade, state after state has accepted the view that the quality of a child's education should not depend on the wealth of his or her parents or neighbors.

McDermott, the lawyer for the plaintiff in *Serrano,* complains of the difficulty of getting social-science research into the judicial process (1976).

The key issue is how to define and measure equity. Since there are at least fifteen known measures (Berne 1977), this is no easy task. To complicate matters, there is a debate in social-science research over which measures of equity are the most suitable. It is not clear that any one measure is the right one. This uncertainty about equity does not sit well in the legal world of fact and evidence. The *Serrano* judge defined equity in his own manner as a range of spending per pupil that must not deviate by more than $120 from the high to the low end of the spectrum, a solution considered far too simplistic by the social scientists.

The social-scientists' debate concerning the definition of equity focuses on theory and uncertainty. The legal debate emphasizes fact and certainty. The dilemma is that the better the research becomes, the less acceptable or assimilable it is by the courts. Measuring equity in terms of overall range as the *Serrano* judge had ordered is simplistic when viewed from the social scientists' perspective, but it is rooted in concrete fact. Statistical measures of equity, which the social scientists use, are conditional and conceptual by definition.

Although McDermott does not ascribe the problem of getting good social-science research into the courts to cognitive style, his whole argument parallels the discussion here. Generally the courts are not responsive to what is clearly the N-ness of social science. Their S-ness forces the scientists into a mode of explanation that is overnarrow to them. The issue of the cognitive style of scientists and the legal field is in effect one of valid explanation. The gap McDermott identifies is wide.

State judges are far more distinctive in their cognitive style than lawyers seem to be. The judges are predominantly Ss and very structured in their thinking (indicated by the J/P scale). The lawyers as a group seem broader (see table 10-10).

The range of skills and tasks involved in the lawyers' jobs is obviously far less specialized than in those of the judges. Since judges are ex-lawyers, they obviously reflect a relatively specialized subset within the overall field.

Miller studied 2,248 law students from seven prominent universities and tracked the dropout rate (Myers 1976). We can define cognitive fit as the degree of match between the individual and the implicit information-processing demands of the job. The closer the fit, the more likely it is the in-

Table 10-10
Selected Profiles for Lawyers and Judges

	S	N	T	F	J	P
Lawyers	41	59	73	27	57	43
Judges	55	45	63	37	76	24

dividual will do well and feel comfortable. The mode of thinking the job involves is natural to him or her. We can expect that dropouts by and large do not feel comfortable.

Miller's results support this view. The dropouts showed no significant relation to college grades or admission-test scores but a clear correlation with cognitive style. The dropout rate for TJs is half that for FPs. Interestingly, there is no apparent difference between the Ss and Ns. Although facts are key to the judges' job and their preferred mode of thinking, there is room for ideas in the lawyers' mode. Of course, lawyers who are at the S end of the scale would seem more likely to become judges. Myers comments that the SN dimension seems to have most influence on occupational choice since it largely determines what will interest people. Within an occupation, it seems to influence what specialization is selected.

As a whole, the lawyers are more flexible than the judges. The JP scale captures need for structure and orderliness. Judges score higher on the J scale than almost any other group (table 10-13). Js like their work to be "organized, systematic and foreseeable." They "tend to see the power to decide as an enjoyable feature of the job. . . . Ps often find a routine decision as a burden and would rather *see* their way to a solution than deliver a crisp choice between alternatives" (Myers 1976).

The lawyers in Miller's sample are far more flexible than the judges, but the dropout rate for the Ps is almost double that for the Js (see table 10-11) (Myers 1980).

More significantly, the lawyers differ from both scientists and others involved in intellectual fields along the J/P dimension. There is a consistent pattern across occupations. Research, creative, and helping fields attract Ps; administrative, technical, and business jobs attract Js (table 10-5).

The JP dimension on the MBTI has been less studied in detail than the SN or TF scales (characteristics of Js and Ps are shown in table 10-12) (Myers 1980). Interviews with lawyers, judges, and technical specialists suggest it may be particularly relevant to the legal process, which is highly structured and based on rules of procedures for marshaling of arguments and even of courtroom behavior.

Judges who are strong Js put a premium on good administration, according to my own analyses of unpublished interviews. Lawyers who appear

Table 10-11
J and P Scales for Dropouts

	N	MBTI Scale	Dropouts	Percentage
J	1,281	57	160	1.2
P	967	43	214	2.2

Table 10-12
Job Characteristics of Js and Ps

Judging Types	Perceptive Types
Work best when they can plan their work and follow the plan	Adapt well to changing situations
Like to get things settled and finished	Do not mind leaving things open for alterations
May decide things too quickly	May have trouble making decisions
May dislike to interrupt the project they are on for a more-urgent one	May start too many projects and have difficulty in finishing them
May not notice new things that need to be done	May postpone unpleasant jobs
Want only the essentials needed to begin their work	Want to know all about a new job
Tend to be satisfied once they reach a judgment on a thing, situation, or person	Tend to be curious and welcome new light on a thing, situation, or person

Source: Myers 1976, p. 164. Reprinted with permission.

before them know they will not tolerate sloppiness or delay. Their court is well run. They like to maintain tidiness and tight schedules. They were able to identify the types of lawyers they had problems with and to whom they needed to provide occasional indirect help to make them more orderly. They described some of the problems they encountered with witnesses who present themselves poorly or seem disorganized.

Keen and Bronsema (1981) found limited evidence that practitioners are more likely to be Js than are academic and professionals. De Waele's small samples of management scientists (1978) support this argument, though only at the 0.10 significance level (see table 10-13).

My interviews suggest that the academic-practitioners distinction may hold for lawyers too. An individual's need for structure may not be satisfied

Table 10-13
Selected Profiles of Management Scientists

	E	I	S	N	T	F	J	P
Academics	31	69	15	85	69	31	58	42
Industry	35	65	38	62	73	27	72	23

in the university environment, which is open-ended, ambiguous, and lacking in clarity of organization. Similarly, in helping professions, flexibility and adaptability are needed, given the variety of situations involved and the need for responsive adjustment to others. Complex, illustrated fields of study may similarly attract those who enjoy variety and can adjust to ambiguity. Fields requiring disciplined procedures will deter them.

In comparing lawyers with scientists, it is important to recognize that these are both broad fields. The example of medical specialties is relevant. Larger samples of cognitive-style measures of lawyers are needed before firm conclusions can be reliably drawn. However, the following assertions seem reasonably well supported by existing data:

1. Most lawyers are closer in style to the scientists than are most judges.
2. The gap between the scientists and judges is so substantial that it amounts to two separate cultures.
3. The legal profession as a whole is more decisive and structured in its thinking than are most creative scientists (and than the helping professions in medicine and psychology).
4. The legal profession may be intolerant of and impede the academic researchers' less-decisive, more-adaptive mode of work and, hence, of expertise.
5. There is an obvious potential barrier to mutual understanding between lawyers and scientists, especially since the rules for debate and determination of valid fact and opinion are more comfortable for the judge than for the scientific expert.

Some final, minor examples are worth including. They are peripheral to the main argument, but suggestive in their implications. In interviews with judges, I was particularly interested in the outliers, those whose cognitive style is markedly different from the dominant one. For example, an NFP is rare among judges (5 out of 115 in the surveys). They do not like to handle facts in the same way as their peers (N), focus more on personal values than logic and legal analysis (F), and lack order and precision (P). They must surely bring some unusual skill that makes them legitimate in and comfortable with their work. Three of the five NFPs commented that they were noted for their willingness to handle child-custody cases. Here, facts, logic, and decisiveness are less effective than the NFP's cognitive style ideal. (In similar interviews with Bell Labs, the outliers were almost all in nontechnical functions, such as personnel or marketing. Their turnover was high, and they felt they were not valued by the dominant culture of NTHs and not listened to (Keen and Bronsema 1981).

The final point is that the best witness from an STJ judge's point of view may well be a police officer. The profiles of 270 urban police are very similar to the judge's. Eighty percent are S, 67 percent T, and 66 percent J. "They deal with one concrete situation after another where words are not as important as decisions and actions" (Myers 1976). The scientists deal with one abstract situation after another where decisions and final conclusions are not as important as open-mindedness and suspension of judgment.

Implications of Cognitive Style for the Use of Scientific Expertise

The differences in cognitive style among lawyers, judges, scientists, and other specialized fields are marked. They explain at most, however, only part of the problem involved in ensuring that courts have access to the best scientific evidence available and that such evidence is properly presented, interpreted, and used. Institutional, legislative, and statutory issues may be far more constraining in their impact than cognitive style.

Grayson's comment on managers and management scientists seems just as applicable to the law and many of the sciences: "The verb 'to think' is conjugated "I think clearly, 'you sometimes get muddled,' and 'he or she is stupid'" (Grayson 1973). The most marked feature of the experiment in which ocean engineers and lawyers tried to work on a common task is the extent to which each becomes frustrated by the inability of the other to understand the obvious. They end up talking down, irritated and treating the other like a child. I have found this response to be common. Obviously intelligent, highly qualified specialists implicitly view problems of communication as due to stupidity, not legitimate differences in mode of explanation and understanding. The main value of the cognitive-style paradigm may be to alert specialists to the degree of difference involved and to the legitimacy of other specialists' styles.

The arguments I have presented here require systematic data collection to permit a valid and rigorous test of several key hypotheses:

1. Lawyers, judges, and scientists show systematic differences in cognitive style from each other and some marked systematic differences within their own area; for example, it is expected that appellate judges are more likely to be Ns than those on the lower courts and that lawyers involved in antitrust, patent, and tax cases will also be Ns.
2. These differences will influence the effectiveness of communication; the degree of cooperation, understanding of questions, perception of veracity, expertise, and clarity of explanation will correlate directly with compatibility of cognitive style as well as the degree of scientific knowledge successfully introduced into the court proceedings.

3. Scientists will report difficulties in getting judges and lawyers to understand the issues of uncertainty they view as key. In turn, they will be criticized for their relative inability to stick to facts.

Assuming these hypothese are correct, these differences in cognitive style pose some practical, difficult problems:

1. Can most lawyers and most scientists really work together?
2. Can strong Ss who are judges feel comfortable with or be able to evaluate the evidence of a first-rate N or the opinions of an F?
3. Can judges accept that the conditional statements of experts and their disagreements may not be resolved by an appeal to fact? The conclusions experts reach are often heavily dependent on untestable assumptions and axioms. For the S, the currency of ideas is concrete facts; concepts are counterfeit. It is the reverse for many of the best and most-respected scientific thinkers. For social scientists, concrete, objective facts are data to be filtered, aggregated, and given meaning through probabilistic and statistical techniques and conceptual models.

Some of these problems may be resolvable:

1. Formal or informal mechanisms can be designed to allow the scientist to explain more fully assumptions rather than conclusions.
2. More attention can be paid to the lawyer's role as an information broker and translator, from the scientist's to the judge's framework and vice-versa; this function is currently done instinctively and informally by many lawyers.
3. The scientists can be provided more room and less pressure from the judge, to explain where facts are not complete or meaningful.

The concept of a science court meets most of these aims; however, if my analysis is correct, a critical strategic issue is to get all parties to understand the extent to which this is an issue of mutual understanding rather than truth, correct reasoning, or objective fact. Mutual understanding begins with mutual respect.

Appendix 10-A: Background Note on Underlying Theory for Cognitive-Style Models

Keen and Bronsema (1981) discuss the overall validity of cognitive-style models and the MBTI in particular, using six categories derived from Bagozzi (1981): concept, construct, convergent, discriminant, predictive, and nomological validity. Most cognitive-style models are unidimensional and bipolar; examples are field dependence-independence (Witkin 1964), cognitive simplicity-complexity (Bieri 1961), and convergent-divergent (Hudson 1966). Such models tend to be value laden and veridical (performance rather than behavior based).

The conceptual validity of cognitive-style models in general rests on the validity of social-cognitive theories of personality and intelligence. Mischel's book, *Personality and Assessment* (1968), is recommended as an introduction to the overall issue of the links between personality and intellect and to relate questions of measurement. Allport's *Pattern and Growth in Personality* (1965) is a classic presentation of the concept of personality. The MBTI rests on Jungian theory.

Construct, convergent, discriminant, and predictive validity are central determinants of the psychometric reliability of a measure. Most cognitive-style measures fall short in most of these areas. (See Keen and Bronsema 1981; Nisbett and Temoshok 1976; Taggart and Robey 1979; and Taylor and Benbasat 1980 for criticisms.) The MBTI is well established on all counts (Keen and Bronsema 1981) and is backed up by longitudinal and cross-sectional empirical studies.

Some of the criticisms in this chapter are that the MBTI is "a dubious indicator of cognitive style." Critics comment on the test methods (paper and pencil tests) in particular as simplistic for capturing important personality traits. Many of the objections are unanswerable. There is indeed a growing body of criticism, not only of personality tests such as the MBTI, but of utility theory, regression-based techniques, behaviorist assumptions, intelligence tests, and others. To criticize the MBTI's test items as simplistic is no more reasonable, and no less so, than saying that econometric analysis is invalid because it simplistically assumes a linear explanation of complex social, political, and economic phenomena. An adjuration of simple questions with one phrase invalidates the old tradition of psychological testing, including the California F-Scale, Minnesota Multiphase Personality Inventory, and Strong Vocational Interest Blank. The construction of a psychological instrument is a complex procedure that requires careful standardization, cross-correlations, rigorous statistical dissection, and criterion

development. The MBTI is generally viewed as among the more-reliable instruments in terms of psychometric validity; Stricker and Ross (1964) are
the main dissenters. Anastasi (1968:455) comments:

> With few exceptions, split-half reliabilities computed in samples of high
> school and college students (N = 26 to 100) fall in the upper .70s and
> .80s. The manual summarizes a considerable body of data contributing
> to the construct validation of the scores. The criteria employed in this
> research include scores on other personality inventories, grades and
> other indices of academic achievement, instructors' ratings of college
> students, turnover in several types of jobs, and evidence of distinguished
> creative achievement. The data reveal a number of significant relation-
> ships in the expected directions.

A selection of test items from the MBTI is a red herring, especially if the
critic does not consider what is done with the answers to the test questions
and how the MBTI was constructed, validated and scored.

I do not claim to demonstrate a clear difference in cognitive style between lawyers and scientists. The chain of argument is as follows:

1. Cognitive style is a conceptually valid concept of the nature of specialization in thinking and of the link between cognition and personality.
2. The MBTI is a valid measure of style (construct, convergent, discriminant).
3. Cognitive style as measured by the MBTI has been shown, consistently
   and reliably, to relate to choice of occupation, problem solving and
   decision making, communication, and group and organizational processes (predictive and nomological) validity.
4. There is reason to believe that the legal profession differs significantly
   along one (lawyers) or two (state judges) dimensions of cognitive style.
   This is the starting point for a systematic study, with adequate sample
   sizes and controls to permit reliable conclusion and generalization.
   Such a study is underway.
5. If there are differences in cognitive styles between judges and scientists,
   the problem of mutual explanation, communication, and evidence is a
   fundamental one, not a technical regulatory or procedural one.

Critics who essentially dislike argument 1 will reasonably assume argument 2 must be incorrect. An earlier draft of this chapter did not include
some figures on sample size and statistical significance; these have been added
to the version published here. I found criticisms of the earlier draft to be
puzzling and useful at the same time in forcing my own attention to
sharpening the objectives of the work.

The MBTI is a valid measure of cognitive style, the data presented
meaningful, and the case the chapter makes well worth consideration.

References

Allport, G.W. 1965. *Pattern and Growth in Personality*. New York: Holt, Rinehart and Winston.

Anastasi, A. 1968. *Psychological Testing*. 3d ed. New York: Macmillan.

Bagozzi, R.P. 1980. *Causal Models in Marketing*. New York: Wiley.

Berne, R. 1977. *Equity and Public Education: Conceptual Issues of Measurement*. Working Paper No. 4. New York: Graduate School of Public Administration, New York University.

Bieri, J. 1961. "Complexity-Simplicity as a Personality Variable in Cognitive and Preferential Behavior." In *Functions of Varied Experience*, edited by D.W. Fiske and S.R. Maddi. Homewood, Ill.: Dorsey.

Buros, O., ed. 1970. *Mental Measurement Yearbook*. Highland Park, N.J.: Gryphon Press.

Churchman, C.W., and Schainblatt, A.H. 1965. "The Research and the Manager: A Dialectic of Implementation." *Management Science* 2:B-69-87.

deWaele, M. 1978. "Managerial Style and the Design of Decision Aids." Ph.D. dissertation, University of California.

Ghani, J.A. 1980. "The Effects of Information Representation and Modification on Decision Performance." Ph.D. dissertation, University of Pennsylvania.

Grayson, C.J. 1973. "Management Science and Business Practice." *Harvard Business Review* 51:41-48.

Hoy, F. 1979. "Perceptions of Entrepreneurs—Implications for Consulting." Paper presented to the Third National Conference, Myers-Briggs Type Indicator, Philadelphia, October.

Hudson, L. 1966. *Contrary Imaginations*. London: Methuen.

Huysmans, J.H.B.M. 1970. *The Implementation of Operations Research*. New York: Wiley-Interscience.

Jung, K. 1923. *Psychological Types*. London: Routledge and Kegan Paul.

Keen, P.G.W. 1973. "The Implications of Cognitive Style for Individual Decision Making." D.B.A. dissertation, Harvard University.

Keen, P.G.W. 1977. "Cognitive Style and Career Specialization." In *Organization Careers: Some New Perspectives*, edited by J. Van Maanen. New York: Wiley.

Keen, P.G.W., and Bronsema, G. 1981. "Cognitive Style Research: A Perspective for Integration." *Proceedings of the Second International Conference on Information Systems*. Cambridge, Mass.: Center for Informations Systems Research, Sloan School of Management, Massachusetts Institute of Technology.

Keen, P.G.W., and Clark, D. 1978. *Simulations for School Finance: A Survey and Assessment*. New York: Ford Foundation research report.

Kogan, N. 1976. *Cognitive Styles in Infancy and Early Childhood.* New York: Wiley.

Lake, D.G.; Miles, M.B.; and Earle, R.B. 1973. *Measuring Human Behavior.* New York: Teachers College Press.

Lehne, R. 1978. *The Quest for Justice: The Politics of School Finance Reform.* New York: Longmans.

McCaulley, M.H. 1976. "Personality Variables: Model Profiles That Characterize Various Fields of Science." In *Birth of New Ways to Raise a Scientifically Literate Society: Research That May Help.* Symposium presented at the meeting of the American Association for the Advancement of Science, Boston, February.

McCaulley, M.H. 1977. *The Myers Longitudinal Medical Study.* Monograph II, Contract No. 231-76-0051, Health Resources Administration, DHEW. Gainesville, Fla.: Center for Applications of Psychological Type.

McCaulley, M.H., and Natter, F.L. 1974. "Psychological (Myers-Briggs) Type Differences in Education." In *The Governor's Task Force on Disruptive Youth: Phase II Report,* edited by M.H. Natter and F.L. Rollin. Tallahassee, Fla.: Office of the Governor.

McDermott, J.E. 1976. The Cost-Quality Debate in School Finance Litigation. In *Indeterminancy in Education,* edited by J.E. McDermott. Berkeley: McCutchan.

McKenney, J.L., and Keen, P.G.W. 1974. "How Managers' Minds Work." *Harvard Business Review* 52:79-90.

MacKinnon, D.W. 1962. "The Nature and Nurture of Creative Talent." *American Psychologist* 17:484-495.

Mason, R.O., and Mitroff, I.I. 1973. "A Program for Research on Management Information Systems." *Management Science* 19:475-487.

Mischel, W. 1968. *Personality and Assessment.* New York: Wiley.

Mitroff, I.I., and Kilmann, R.H. 1976. "Stories Managers Tell: A New Tool for Organizational Problem Solving." *Management Review* 64:19-28.

Mitroff, I.I., and Kilmann, R.H. 1976. "On Organization Stories: An Approach to the Design and Analysis of Organization through Myths and Stories." In *The Management of Organization Design,* edited by R.H. Kilmann, L.R. Pondy, and D.P. Slevin, vol. 1. Amsterdam: Elsevier.

Myers, I.B. 1962. *The Myers-Briggs Type Indicator Manual.* Palo Alto, Calif.: Consulting Psychologists Press.

Myers, I.B. 1976. *Introduction to Type.* 2d ed. Gainesville, Fla.: Center for Applications of Psychological Type.

Myers, I.B., and Myers, P.B. 1980. *Gifts Differing.* Palo Alto, Calif.: Consulting Psychologists Press.

Nisbett, R.E., and Temoshok, L. 1976. "Is There an 'External' Cognitive Style?" *Journal of Personality and Social Psychology* 33:36-47.

Shouksmith, G. 1970. *Intelligence, Creativity and Cognitive Style.* New York: Wiley.

Slocum, J.W., Jr. 1978. "Does Cognitive Style Affect Diagnosis and Invention Strategies of Change Agents?" *Group and Organization Studies* 3:199-210.

Stricker, L.J., and Ross, J. 1962. "A Description and Evaluation of the Myers-Briggs Type Indicator." *Educational Testing Service, Research Bulletin,* pp. 62-69.

Stricker, L.J., and Ross, J. 1964. "Some Correlates of a Jungian Personality Inventory." *Psychological Reports* 14:623-643.

Taggart, W., and Robey, D. 1979. "Minds and Managers: On the Dual Nature of Human Information Processing and Management." Unpublished paper. Florida International University.

Taylor, R.N., and Benbasat, I. 1980. "A Critique of Cognitive Styles, Theory and Research." *Proceedings of the First International Conference on Information Systems.* Cambridge, Mass.

Wade, P.F. 1981. "Some Factors Affecting Problem Solving and Effectiveness in Business, A Study of Management Consultants." Ph.D. dissertation, McGill University.

Witkin, H.A. 1964. "Origins of Cognitive Style." In *Cognition Theory, Research, Promise,* edited by M. Scheerer. New York: Harper and Row.

Witkin, H.A., and Goodenough, D.R. 1977. "Field Dependence and Interpersonal Behavior." *Psychological Bulletin* 84:661-689.

Witkin, H.A.; Moore, C.A.; Goodenough, D.R.; and Cox, P.W. 1977. "Field-dependent and Field-independent Cognitive Styles and Their Educational Implications." *Review of Educational Research* 47:1-64.

Comment

Milton R. Wessel

An article in the *Harvard Law Record* states:

> In a legal or regulatory dispute, the testimony of a balanced, objective scientist who scrupulously qualifies his statements to guard against over-interpretation, is likely to be almost useless to either side. Scientists with strong biases (known in advance to be most likely to suit the interests of the client) are much more likely to be sought out, if they have the requisite respectability and qualifications.[1]

Professor Keen has explained how differences in cognitive style make it difficult for judges, lawyers, and scientists to understand and work with each other. The difficulty may be even more serious than Professor Keen describes because existing dispute-resolution mechanisms do not always permit the participants to follow their own styles. Frequently they adopt the styles of others. The scientist, trained in the scientific method, becomes instead an advocate and an adversary; the judge, accustomed to applying the law to the facts, becomes a policymaker, a legislator, and a politician.

Confusion of Roles

The retention of scientists to support a litigant's position is an all-too-common feature of socioscientific litigation and its battle of experts. Indeed, adversary science and the adversary scientist have become objects for public ridicule and joke.

The remodeling of the judge into a legislator and the lawyer into a lobbyist is a more-recent development, and not so well understood. Increasingly in recent years, however, especially since enactment of the National Environmental Policy Act of 1969 (NEPA), the courts, administrative tribunals, and other dispute-resolution mechanisms have been called on to deal with risk-benefit controversies. These are disputes whose resolutions require the sensitive balancing of a vast number of positive and negative consequences of a proposed course of action or inaction. They are thus essentially legislative or political controversies, not judicial disputes in which relatively fixed rules are applied to facts.

A recent well-publicized case, *Berkey Photo Inc.* v. *Eastman Kodak Co.*, illustrates how problems can arise when the roles of scientist and lawyer are confused.[2] *Berkey* was a federal antitrust litigation. Plaintiff charged unlawful monopolization. Defendant claimed that its market position was the product of competence and excellence rather than unlawful conduct. Until the standard of conduct for monopoly cases is defined more precisely, this kind of controversy calls for risk-benefit balancing. Almost anything and everything is relevant; almost anything and everything goes.

Kodak retained a leading economist as its key expert witness. He had served as a member of the President's Council of Economic Advisers and as chairman of the Economics Department of a major eastern university. He obtained and analyzed a myriad of the relevant documents. At first he expressed concern and doubt as to the merits of the case but finally came to an opinion in Kodak's favor.

Kodak was represented by one of the major New York law firms. The senior trial attorney in charge of the litigation had an outstanding reputation. The other attorneys assigned to the case included a senior partner who had enjoyed a long and fine career at the bar and a senior associate who was also an experienced attorney.

Pretrial discovery was elaborate and intense. Kodak was directed to produce all interim reports, but the initial written communication from the expert to counsel expressing doubt on the merits was not produced on the ground that it was not an interim report. At another point, the expert returned to the law firm the great bulk of the documents he had inspected. When asked about these documents, the senior partner, who was responsible for this part of the case, falsely asserted that the returned materials had been destroyed. He ignored the whispered reminder of his senior associate that the documents were in fact still available. As a consequence, these documents were not then produced for discovery either.

The trial was before a jury and lasted six months. Kodak's expert was a final witness. He appeared evasive on cross-examination, arousing the suspicions of Berkey counsel, and finally leading to disclosure of the existence of the interim report and its production. At about the same late stage in the trial, the lie with regard to the destruction of documents was similarly disclosed, and they were produced.

The trial judge was shocked at the conduct. He said that the initial letter was an interim report. He told counsel that the credibility of the expert had been destroyed on the witness stand and initiated a criminal investigation into the conduct of the senior partner, who was ultimately convicted of contempt and imprisoned.

No one can be certain what led the jury to conclude as it did, but it returned a verdict against Kodak, which came to $113 million. For present purposes, it is appropriate to accept Kodak's contention that the jury was vitally influenced by the collateral evidence of obstruction and contempt and that this prejudiced jury consideration of the evidence on the merits.

Clearly the expert in *Berkey* had become an adversary scientist. He was an advocate in the most pejorative sense in which that term is used in the sporting or game approach to dispute resolution. He was personally evasive and hostile. He was a knowing participant and perhaps a prime mover in the obstructionist tactics of Kodak counsel. His conduct may even have persuaded the jury not only to discredit his affirmative testimony but to conclude the precise contrary.

It is more difficult to evaluate the effect of the expert's conduct on the judge, whose decision on the law was reversed on appeal. It seems reasonable to conclude, however, that his judgment on the legislative issues, which involved a balancing of public-interest factors, may also have been influenced by the collateral evidence of the expert's conduct.

Effects of Collateral Evidence

Berkey demonstrates the potentially tremendous adverse impact on the merits of collateral evidence of tactical impropriety by an expert witness as well as by a lawyer. Such impropriety could not occur at present levels unless all participants—clients, witnesses, and attorneys—approved or acquiesced. Confusion of roles is an important contributing factor to such approval.

Modern public-interest controversies can be tremendously complex. The typical nuclear-power controversy, for example, involves a host of scientific disciplines, such as nuclear physics, biochemistry, biology, and even icthyology and archaeology. Frequently there will be charges and countercharges regarding the motivations of huge organizations or of conspiratorial action, either of which can call for the analysis and evaluation of millions of documents and statements over many years; or the computer simulation of events that should never happen, such as the failure of a nuclear plant's emergency core-cooling system. No one can adequately understand all the merits, not even the skilled scientist.

How do judges and juries make decisions when they cannot understand the merits? They do so in much the same fashion that lay people generally make decisions about nonlegal complex issues. For example, a candidate for open-heart surgery might elicit the advice of an expert and then test his or her credibility by examining reputation, credentials, past successes and failures, and whether there are inconsistencies in what is said and done. If what is disclosed furnishes cause for doubt, the patient would likely reject the advice. In similar fashion, a jury might well discredit the testimony of the analytical chemist who claims to be presenting an impartial scientific evaluation of a compound if he or she appears evasive about the funding sources or is caught in a lie about the institution he or she attended.

Although there is not a great deal of available evidence, what little there is suggests that judges, juries, administrative tribunals, and arbiters frequently make important decisions in major complex public-interest cases on the basis of this kind of collateral evidence. Undoubtedly the best-known example is Ralph Nader's controversy with General Motors, in which GM's effort to uncover evidence personally damaging to Nader backfired. The result was that the Corvair automobile was removed from the market at a time when the statistics showed it to be by far the safest of all the compact cars. Apparently similarly damaging were Ford Motor Company's "pattern of delay and nondisclosure . . . through all its fuel tank litigation," which included Ford's citation "in at least five appellate court decisions for having obstructed discovery by giving false answers to interrogatories, and by hiding damaging documents"; Reserve Mining Company's conduct in its bitter and lengthy Lake Superior asbestos-like-fiber pollution case, concerning which the *New York Times* commented editorially about the trial judge's "exasperation at pettifogging and delay and . . . Reserve's outrageous tactics"; Firestone's legal tactics in its brand-tire dispute, which another publication described as involving "litigation, delay, contentious foot-dragging and appeal" and as posing the question, "What was Firestone trying to conceal? Why was [counsel] so concerned?"; and Mutual of Omaha Insurance Company's conduct, which led a trial judge to state that Mutual's defense against an insurance claim "could well have given the jury the indication of a deliberate cover-up."[3]

Remedies

Professor Keen's critical first question is, "Can most lawyers and most scientists really work together?" The IBM case, which took more than thirteen years to resolve, and a plethora of decade-long nuclear licensing and other environmentally oriented controversies, would suggest that the answer may be no. I hope that is not the case. We are in an advanced-science, high-technology society, in which law and science are inextricably intertwined. They cannot be permitted to function independently or in conflict with each other. Society must catch up with science.

First, we must put an end to this confusion of styles and roles. The scientist must remain a scientist, the judge a judge, and the lawyer a lawyer. I have seen little comment with regard either to the responsibility of the expert in *Berkey* or to the institutions of which he was a part, such as his university and his professional societies. Yet by his adversarial tactics, he negated his claim of adherence to the scientific method and his pretense to scientific impartiality. He also discredited his scientific institutions.

Individual experts should know their obligations, as should individual lawyers. But experts sometimes violate obligations, just as do lawyers, and their institutions should have responsibilities to prevent and police. Professional scientific societies should make clear in codes of ethics and elsewhere that the role of the scientist in an adversary proceeding is to present scientific data and opinion, not to engage in adversarial excesses.

Scientific societies must respect the independence of their members and not unreasonably fetter professional freedom. Limitations on adversarialism need not limit scientific freedom. One medical specialist testified frequently at nuclear-power licensing proceedings in extravagant adversarial fashion. His professional society finally determined that it had an obligation to society to prevent miscarriages of justice resulting from his extremes. It adopted a resolution expressing its scientific judgment with regard to his views and thereafter authorized teams of his peers to follow him wherever he testified, voluntarily and without compensation. As a kind of truth squad, each team read his condemnation into each record. When I heard this presentation in one case, it not only avoided the damage he might have done but generated enormous respect and credibility for science as an institution.

Second, we must eliminate the improper collateral evidence that characterizes so much of socioscientific dispute resolution. Adversarial extremes may be appropriate to traditional interparty disputes, but they have no place in socioscientific dispute resolution. They lead to results contrary to the public interest, as well as to that of the party employing them.

The rule of reason provides an alternative set of guidelines, which not only serves the interest of the party employing it but the public interest as well. This is not the place to discuss the details of legal tactics, but a statement of the rule of reason's specific procedural guidelines will be useful, with the caveat that there is far more to the approach than any brief summary can suggest.[4] Despite what some might conclude from their overall tenor, for example, the guidelines do not require the waiver of attorney-client privilege or trade-secret exemption, do not call for a party to bare its soul. They do not necessarily preclude cross-examination of a witness regarding collateral matters, including even alcoholism or sexual deviation. The rule of reason is an adversarial dispute-resolution philosophy, which is even more effective for the party employing it than the adversarial extremes it replaces. It eliminates inconsistencies resulting from tactical conduct, which can impeach on the merits. The rule-of-reason guidelines are:

1. Data will not be withheld because they may be negative or unhelpful.
2. Concealment will not be practiced for concealment's sake.
3. Delay will not be employed as a tactic to avoid an undesired result.
4. Unfair tactics designed to mislead will not be employed to win a struggle.
5. Borderline ethical disingenuousness will not be practiced.

6. Motivation of adversaries will not unnecessarily or lightly be impugned.
7. An opponent's personal habits and characteristics will not be questioned unless relevant.
8. Wherever possible, opportunity will be left for an opponent's orderly retreat.
9. Extremism may be countered forcefully and with emotionalism where justified but will not be fought or matched with extremism.
10. Dogmatism will be avoided.
11. Complex concepts will be simplified as much as possible so as to achieve maximum communication and lay understanding.
12. Effort will be made to identify and isolate subjective considerations involved in reaching a technical conclusion.
13. Relevant data will be disclosed when ready for analysis and peer review, even to an extremist opposition and without legal obligation.
14. Socially desirable professional disclosure will not be postponed for tactical advantage.
15. Hypothesis, uncertainty, and inadequate knowledge will be stated affirmatively, not conceded only reluctantly or under pressure.
16. Unjustified assumption and off-the-cuff comment will be avoided.
17. Interest in an outcome, relationship to a proponent, and bias, prejudice, and proclivity of any kind will be disclosed voluntarily and as a matter of course.
18. Research and investigation will be conducted appropriate to the problem involved. Although the precise extent of that effort will vary with the nature of the issues, it will be consistent with stated overall responsibility to solution of the problem.[5]
19. Integrity will always be given first priority.

Third, we need to change the ways in which scientists and lawyers work together. A *Science* magazine article, "Product Liability and the Technical Expert," explores how scientists and lawyers interact and points the way toward improvement.[6] We need far more of this kind of work.

Fourth, we need the help of scientific institutions in finding interim scientific truth. I am not an advocate of the proposed science court, but surely that proposal deserves public discussion, analysis, and testing. The scientific consensus-finding conference offers another approach, which I believe would be productive.

Undoubtedly there are many other ways in which scientists and scientific institutions might improve the role of science in adversarial dispute resolution. The public needs standards, benchmarks, risk indexes, certifications, and other procedures to aid in evaluating new scientific information and in measuring developments against known experience. We need the help of science to separate out value and quality-of-life opinion from scientific data and conclusion. We need communication aids to understanding.

Fifth, the private sector has a responsibility, and an opportunity, to move forward. There have been some significant advances, such as in the Chemical Industry Institute of Toxicology, the Council for Chemical Research, and the dispute-resolution program being sponsored by Exxon and Monsanto. These are only beginnings.

Finally, we need to develop more-effective rules and guidelines for institutional conduct in socioscientific disputes. Such controversies almost always involve governments, large corporations, and large law firms. The institutions concerned should have responsibilities to society. In the *Berkey* case context, for example, those responsibilities might be the following:

1. The law firm would have a responsibility to its clients and to society to ensure that the actions of its personnel comply with law, with legal ethics, and with client mandates and interests. If it failed to take reasonable steps to perform that responsibility, it would be held responsible to the client for the consequences.
2. The corporation would have a responsibility to see that what is done on its behalf complies with law, with its stated ethics, and with its own instructions. If it failed to take reasonable steps to carry out this obligation, it would be held responsible for actions taken on its behalf, despite the fact that they were performed by licensed and independent professionals.
3. All other institutions involved directly or indirectly, including the expert's university and professional societies and the judiciary, would have responsibilities to ensure that what they and their members and participants do serves rather than disserves society.

Notes

1. Edward Groth III, "Role of Scientific Expert Examined," *Harvard Law Record* 62 (1976):3.

2. Berkey Photo, Inc. v. Eastman Kodak, Inc., 603 F.2d 263 (2nd Cir. 1979), *cert. denied*, 444 U.S. 1093 (1980).

3. References for the quotations in this paragraph and more-detailed discussion of the subject, appear in Milton R. Wessel, *Science and Conscience* (New York: Columbia University Press, 1980), pp. 49-52.

4. That is the subject of Milton R. Wessel, *The Rule of Reason* (Reading, Mass.: Addison-Wesley, 1976). For a discussion of the rule-of-

reason approach in business, science, and society generally, see Wessel, *Science and Conscience*.

5. Wessel, *Rule of Reason*, pp. 23-24.

6. Henry R. Piehler et al., "Product Liability and the Technical Expert," *Science* 186 (1974):1089-1093.

Part IV
Learnings: A Summary

11 Toward Better Resolution of Regulatory Issues Involving Science and Technology

J.D. Nyhart and
Milton M. Carrow

An underlying premise throughout this book has been that the difficulties in resolving regulatory issues involving science and technology set those issues apart from others in both the regulatory and judicial systems in the United States. This premise is examined further in this chapter. The five case studies of institutional mechanisms for dealing with such issues, discussed in part II, and the more-general framework concerning the future of the regulatory and judicial systems, considered in part I, provide the context. The conclusion from this examination is that there is a need for better mechanisms for introducing science and technology into both the regulatory and judicial systems. This final chapter focuses on such need. A model of the components that we believe are basic in any effort to accomplish this task is also offered.

Science as a Special Case

The discussions in this book indicate that most of the authors agree that issues of science and technology in the law constitute a special subset of problems. Grobstein anticipates the point in chapter 6: "Now that science and technology have thoroughly permeated our society, regulation necessarily has a high scientific and technological content" (p. 115), and in the discussion he caught the sense of it again:

> I would suggest that there is [some specialness in science and technology in relation to regulatory issues]. And it is not, by any means, a unique kind of specialness; nor is it necessarily one that will persist indefinitely. And I would suggest that at the present time, given the rapidity with which scientific and technological knowledge has been growing, thereby in part swamping some other aspects of our culture—and, I think, in particular, our capability to make social decisions, with reasonable competency as to what will follow such decisions—that, at this time, science and technology do pose special problems for decision making, policymaking, and regulatory policymaking. [tr. p. 169]

255

Both Mashaw and Green questioned this premise, Mashaw saying, "It is not clear whether there is anything distinctive about the issues involving science and technology, as distinguished from other collective decision-making problems in which one is importantly concerned with some sort of bureaucratic structure for decision making." (p. 13) Green asked whether there is "any justification for expecting, or wanting, better decisions in that particular narrow area [involving science and technology] than we do in other regulatory areas, the legislative process and the judicial process." (tr. pp. 164-165)

We believe, however, that the specialness exists and that it may be described by four circumstances, which, when combined, characterize scientific and technical issues in regulatory disputes.[1] The first circumstance is that science involves a special set of persons, scientists and engineers, who are brought into the legal framework, with their own processes, culture, and high status. Harrison says that in order for a regulation to succeed, "it has to be credible to the scientific and technological community. Otherwise you are going to encounter all kinds of delaying action." (tr. p. 165) Other complications are also present. Most lawyers and judges do not know science and technology. Working communications are difficult. Words like *truth, fact*, and *probability* hold different meanings for each culture.

Another aspect is that science issues in regulatory disputes almost always involve scientific uncertainty, uncertainty that differs from the traditional fact determinations with which lawyers are familiar. Judges, lawyers, and policymakers are generally not the best resolvers of these kinds of uncertainties; scientists are.

When resolution of uncertainties is attempted, the values of the scientist are called into play. If the answer is unknown, the direction in which one tilts is often influenced by underlying beliefs, backgrounds, and commitments. The scientist's values may not be clearly visible, or they may be fused with the technical issues involved. Harrison and Grobstein, both scientists, recognize the problems associated with the role of value judgments or bias in scientific determinations. (pp. 177, 119)

The second circumstance is that scientific uncertainties, with attendant underlying value considerations, become elements of legal and policymaking processes, which are quite different in nature from those of science, since these legal and policymaking institutions are designed to decide issues and resolve uncertainties. Resolution is further complicated by the fact that regulatory issues involving science and technology are a particular subset of the science-policy process, as well as the regulatory process. The science-policy process, as Grobstein points out, is itself a new piece of the science framework. (p. 129) Further, two characteristics arise in the regulatory and policymaking processes, which Green suggests distinguish the resolution of regulatory disputes involving science and technology from other science-policy issues. First, since science policy is being made in the regulatory mode, the decision by the regulator must be made within the confines of a statute that is the source of the regulator's authority and power. When the facts are in hand, the decision maker's basic inquiry must be what the law requires on the basis of those facts. Second, in the regulatory mode, private interests have enforceable rights to have certain kinds of decisions made and to have decisions made through specified procedures. [p. 135]

A further consequence is that values of regulators, policymakers, and judges—those most closely identified with the legal and policymaking processes—may be caught up in the issue resolution. These may include legal issues—questions of equity, distribution of economic benefit, fairness, who bears the burdens of proof and of risk associated with the underlying uncertainties—and scientific issues as well.

The third circumstance is derivative. The roles or functions assumed by the different players often become confused or overlapped. Which uncertainties are being resolved by whom, with whose values underpinning, remains unclear.

Finally, the fourth distinguishing circumstance is that the impact of the decisions taken in the legal process is in these cases frequently of such broad significance—concerning national or international environmental maintenance, health, control of resources, safety of large classes of persons—that those affected demand to participate or be represented in some way in the decision process or otherwise to enforce the kind of rights to which Green referred. Ashford captured the essence of this when he observed that the attention science and technology in regulation has received derives "from the fact that the courts have been very good to the environmental movement in the last few years. . . . [and] it is big bucks that are involved." (tr. pp. 170-171)

Mechanisms for Infusing Science into the Regulatory Process

There are many existing means by which scientific and technical knowledge enters into the regulatory process. In rule making, they include expert testimony offered by the interested parties who are to be regulated or who will otherwise be affected. Counterparts in adjudicatory proceedings are the experts brought by the parties in the adjudication. Present in all aspects of the regulatory process is the expertise within the agency itself. Although depth of staff expertise varies from agency to agency, it is a major source of scientific and technical capability.

In part II of this book, several important institutions designed for getting science and technology into the regulatory process were examined. Two, the National Academy of Science (NAS) committee system and the use of advisory committees, can be considered general models. Two others are specific case studies: the Occupational Safety and Health Administration's (OSHA) generic carcinogen policy, an example of rule making in which scientific uncertainties were of critical importance, and the federal Food and Drug Administration's (FDA) public board of inquiry mechanism, the first of its kind. The fifth study dealt with the National Institutes of Health (NIH) consensus panels. It is the only one that is not directly a part of the regulatory process or used to channel scientific and technical knowledge directly into regulatory decision making.

These five case studies (chapters 5 through 9) illustrate a basic perception in this book: that the processes of science in regulatory matters must ultimately be placed in a legal procedural framework. The first, the effort by OSHA to develop a generic carcinogen policy, illustrates the extent to which scientific issues may be left without credible resolution in a wholly law-oriented process. Richard Merrill pointed out that "OSHA's proceeding never purported to be an exercise in scientific decision making." (p. 105) The next, the NAS committee system, shows the paradigm of a collective science-consensus effort. Here, legal process does not intrude directly into scientific process, though committee reports are often aimed from the outset at producing policy recommendations, and their scientific conclusions are given high value by regulators, who generally originate the request for the studies. NAS reports frequently enter the legal process. The NIH consensus panel case illustrates a new effort by the medical-science establishment to evaluate data bearing on medical issues, in order to reach a consensus, and to disseminate it in useful ways. As currently conceived, the consensus-panel concept is not meant to provide direct scientific input into the resolution of regulatory issues. It does, however, present a mechanism from the world of science designed to collect, review, evaluate, gain consensus, and propagate scientific knowledge, while simultaneously dealing with the problem of acceptance of that knowledge. The fourth study, OSHA's and the Environmental Protection Agency's (EPA) advisory committees, examines institutions created to meet several goals. Advisory committees provide sources of scientific input, sources of both scientific and political advice, and representation from a broad range of affected groups. In this respect the advisory committees, as Ashford suggests, are a multipurposed breed. (p. 166) The final study, the FDA's public board of inquiry aspartame case, returns again to a mechanism designed to resolve scientific uncertainty within an essentially legal process, this time an adjudicatory one. This experimental institution raises once more the problem of trying to effect a credible scientific process enveloped in a legal one. In significant respects, each of these mechanisms appears flawed. They are reviewed in the following sections.

OSHA's Generic Carcinogen Policy Formulation:
Lawyers Making Policy Concerning Science

The study in chapter 5 of OSHA's generic carcinogen policy (GCP) proceeding illustrates the manner in which lawyers and administrators make
policy about complex and uncertain science issues without serious collaboration with scientists. It is a legal proceeding intended to manage a set of
scientific issues. McGarity discusses four likely goals OSHA had or could
have had in mind for its generic policymaking: increasing agency efficiency,
reducing pressure to increase the number of health standards (by making
more standards), forging a consistent interagency carcinogen policy, and
forging a consistent interagency carcinogen policy in a public forum. Examining each goal separately, McGarity rates the process a mixture of success
and failure. (pp. 73, 76, 77 and 79) Merrill stated that the exercise "has not
been successful . . . in efficient gathering of facts that will ultimately
underlie individual regulatory decisions." (p. 105)

As to the science involved, the process did not resolve, and in fact was
not intended to resolve, issues of scientific uncertainty. Nor did it try to get
the best feasible science into the regulatory process. It may be, as McGarity
points out, that "[a]ccording to Anson Keller, the primary architect of the
GCP, the immediate aim of the GCP was to refocus attention in individual
hearings from the recurring scientific questions to the important nongeneric
questions of economic feasibility," presumably by handling the science at
the generic level once and for all. (p. 73) For whatever reason, it is clear that
the process "never purported to be an exercise in scientific decision
making" and that "the agency knew what policy it wanted to implement
when it issued its proposal." (Merrill, pp. 105; 106)

The relevant policies concerning science were developed by the ad hoc
committee report to the surgeon general entitled *Evaluation of Chemical
Carcinogens.* This report contained the so-called Saffiotti principles. Some
of these principles were reviewed and criticized by scientists in the Subcommittee on Environmental Carcinogenesis of the National Cancer Advisory
Board in November 1975. Although McGarity refers to the "apparent rejection of the Saffiotti principles" by the subcommittee, its report of June
1976 "did not depart any significant degree from the Saffiotti draft." (p.
59) Apparently this was the last formalized examination by scientists of relevant scientific issues prior to the OSHA GCP hearing process, which began
in the fall of 1976 and ended with the issuance by OSHA of its final GCP in
January 1980.

If in its critics' eyes, the policy determination failed to meet the agency's
own stated goals, it also failed as an exercise of science. Haun speaks of the
"absence of science as such and the overwhelming presence of scientists. . . .

This is a case history of the preeminence of the opinion of scientists over the objective analysis of data that can be called science.'' (p. 109) To him, the GCP process was ''a mechanism by which a group of scientists was formed and took the opportunity to put their combined opinions on the record''; it was in fact ''a lawyer's dream—a source of expert testimony that was predictable and resistant to cross-examination.'' (p. 109) His criticism of such policymaking processes as being nonscience is echoed in Merrill's comment that the GCP rule making was not an exercise in scientific decision making.

This case suggests that if the process is in the traditional adjudicatory or rule-making modes, the input of science will follow the time-honored, adversarial-based pattern of party-dominated testimony (with agency staff as one party), with one or more party's testimony being challenged or discounted, with no effort among the scientists associated with different parties to establish any consensus as to what are the best-available science views. McGarity discusses three paradigms OSHA had before it for resolving the uncertainties of scientific causality concerning potential carcinogens: the presumption-rebuttal approach, the weight-of-the-evidence approach, and the leave-the-issues-to-the-scientists approach. As he points out, the last, which would probably most nearly have assured full input by scientists, has not found favor. (p. 80) The other two are deeply rooted in the legal process and are essentially adversarial in nature. They are likely to leave the lawyers, who know best how to manipulate the legal processes, in control of the input of science. Use of either of these two approaches for resolving the technical and scientific issues is thus likely to maintain the basic adversarial character of the process through which scientific input is made.

There is also the question of the relative roles of policymakers and scientists when the policy issue is surrounded by scientific uncertainty. McGarity's model tilts toward ensuring policy formulation by nonscientists. In his analysis of generic rule making, he favors reliance on nonscientific policymakers when it comes to different kinds of science-policy questions— that is, those that superficially appear to be questions of scientific fact but that ''actually require the application of regulatory policy.'' (p. 67) An example is the so-called transscientific question, one that science cannot answer—for example, when an experiment would be impossibly impractical.

In cases where there are varying scientific interpretations of the same data, and therefore scientific judgment is called upon, McGarity argues that ''policy considerations must fill the factual gap left by the scientific dispute.'' He believes that problem resolution should not be in the hands of scientists but in the hands of the policymakers because the agency must apply ''its own policy judgments to the factual uncertainties.'' (p. 69)

Finally, in the case of scientific uncertainty caused by conflicting inferences, that is, where the scientists agree on a single interpretation of the existing data but disagree on the proper inferences to be drawn, McGarity would sometimes place the scientist in no higher level of authority than others on the assumption that lay persons often are competent to evaluate the underlying assumptions by applying common sense. He would thus turn to the nonscientific policymaker in such cases. Others such as Mashaw and Grobstein assert a different role for scientists in these areas of uncertainty.

National Academy of Sciences: Evolving
Policy Roles for Scientists

The committee system of the NAS is the traditional institutional process of science to examine issues in its realm. Differing from experimental work of science (see chapter 4), this institutional process epitomizes the scientists' collective process to define and evaluate what is known about any particular scientific issue.

Grobstein describes the NAS process's major objective as being "to assemble and evaluate scientific and technical data and to relate these to specific practical concerns." (p. 122) He divides the scientific contribution to policymaking and decision making, whether in regulation or other areas, into three parts: the substantive, which deals with the "assembly and interpretation of relevant scientifically valid information"; the transitional, a phase or function that "proceeds beyond the strictly substantive but is not truly decisional"; and the decision process itself, which arises "in the complex context of the social arena with conflicting values and interests playing their roles in a structured political framework." (p. 122) Several points in his analysis bear particularly on our discussion here of the problem of getting better science into the regulatory processes.

First, work in the substantive area, where the aim is to contribute to policymaking and decision making, is clearly different from that in the traditional scientific method. "Policy studies . . . differ from 'normal' science." (p. 123) Most importantly, the assembly of data and their evaluation are different. "To a research scientist data are the grist for new questions and hypotheses, to be answered or tested by seeking still more data." (p. 123) In policy studies,

> the questions are derived not from scientific data but from presented practical needs or problems. The task is to find and interpret whatever scientific data may be relevant, even though the data may not have been obtained for the purpose. Moreover, practical needs or problems usually do not fit into a single field of investigation or into one scientific discipline. [Ibid.]

Grobstein examines several resulting problems: mismatch of presented questions and immediately available data bases, the need to deal with uncertainty, the problems of relating the work of the expert groups with the policy context within which their efforts will be judged and used, problems of actual or conceivable bias, and problems of making the scientific product easily understood in terms of the needs of the target audience. (pp. 123-127) This enumeration of the problems of scientists doing science in the public-policy context is sufficient to require attention to the processes by which scientists develop data for regulatory policymaking. He assigns the substantive role to competent scientists and says the decision process itself "is not a matter of science and is not, therefore, the business of scientists qua scientists." (p. 122)

In Grobstein's second, or transitional, phase "there is uncertainty and controversy, among scientists and nonscientists alike . . . whether it exists and, if so, what role scientists can and should play." (Ibid) Thus, the issue of a functional role for the scientists in policymaking is once more raised. Describing the transitional as a "difficult area that needs to be addressed more decisively in relating science to policymaking," (p. 123) Grobstein identifies several functions appropriate for scientists:

> It is my impression that the legitimate scope of these activities necessarily goes beyond the single assembly and interpretation of existing data, the first and essential scientific contribution to policymaking. Beyond this, scientific expertise is necessary to recognize the need for new data accumulation to anticipate emerging issues, to point to possible or probable implications of new courses of action or changes of circumstance, to interpret for various audiences the scientific and technical content of political issues, and to provide access to decision makers, to the best and latest technical information. This is the content of the transitional component. It is the province of policy-centered and decision-oriented science, bridging into the decision-making process but stopping short of the decision itself. [p. 129]

Having asserted this role for scientists, he then establishes three essential criteria for its successful operation: "Such science in the policy mode must remain free of advocacy but also must be free of the constraints that limit its effectiveness in substantively enriching decisional arenas, with equal access to all contending parties." (p. 129) Thus, Grobstein sets out a role for scientists in the process that may be different from that which McGarity sees. We will examine whether this disparity is real or illusory and whether, if the latter is true, conceptual problems can be bridged in designing new processes.

This examination of the NAS committee model suggests that a new model may be useful to supplement existing institutions serving to infuse science into the regulatory system. In this connection, Green refers to the report of a special NAS committee, which made an internal review of the procedures and practices of academy committees engaged in studies involving risk assessment. He indicates that the report focused on several points, "the inconsistencies among committees as to basic approach; the narrowness of disciplines represented; the fact that the effort to achieve consensus operates to obscure important differences; and a failure to discuss uncertainty adequately." (p. 138) Grobstein also recognized this need. In responding to Mashaw's idea that questions asked of scientists should be framed so that they can give appropriate answers, Grobstein said:

> I agree with that. But I would suggest, also, that we may need a new apparatus for the assembly of the kinds of facts—and not only for the assembly but for the production of—the kinds of facts for the kinds of questions that come down the pike; and that there will have to be an interplay between those two in order to make the bureaucratic-rationality model more effective. But, at the same time, we will have to recognize the micropolitical accommodation aspect of proceeding, and, therefore, values will have to be built into the goals and purposes of the bureaucratic rationality model, more effectively than they have been in the past. [tr. p. 66]

In summary, Grobstein indicates the difficulties of the substantive job of the scientists and the necessity to provide processes by which they can accomplish the tasks inherent in the input of science to policy formulation. He sees a positive role for scientists as the process approaches policy decision making. As to mechanisms, he suggests the need for developing new ones.

NIH Consensus Panels: Aiding the Acceptance
of Medical Technologies

The consensus-development program of NIH (chapter 7) deals with a problem that is akin to but different from that generally addressed in this book. It concerns the need for a consensus concerning specific health technologies. Lowe says that sometimes health technologies are used "despite the lack of reliable information about their benefits and risks," or they have continued to exist after it has been "found to be ineffective or even harmful." Or, "validated innovations are published, [but] lags often occur between publication . . . and clinical awareness and application. (p. 139) These situations can result in a "bottlenecking of knowledge, inappropriate transfer of research results, and uneven access to advances in medical knowledge and technology." (p. 145)

In 1976, the President's Biomedical Research Panel, created by Congress to examine this problem, "observed that a major impediment to effective transfer of biomedical research to the clinical practice of medicine was the often-conflicting, confusing, or unsubstantiated interpretations of biomedical and clinical research." (p. 145) NIH's consensus-development program is an attempt to "reproduce in microcosm . . . the process of knowledge evaluation, transfer, and transformation that ordinarily occurs within the context of the entire biomedical system and its contingent systems.'' (p. 146)

Several aspects of this process are interesting when considering the improvement of mechanisms for getting better science into the regulatory process. First, it is a model developed by the scientific community to reach consensus on contentious issues of biomedical knowledge typically ''around which a brisk controversy revolves, application of research results that involve a major revision in very widely used procedures, or review of a procedure that shows high potential for possibly inappropriate application.'' (Lowe, p. 146) The process obviously differs from that of data collection and evaluation necessary for full resolution of many of the scientific and technical issues in regulatory processes we have examined—for example, in the GCP or FDA aspartame case studies (chapters 5 and 9). The NIH consensus panel does not bind anyone, whereas regulatory decisions normally do. However, the consensus-panel provides a model of a process by scientists for resolving controversial issues in a setting that is not adversarial.

Also, the nature of several of the scientific functions performed is very similar to those of the NAS committee system. The NIH consensus process is a means for collecting, evaluating, and validating the current state of knowledge regarding complex issues. It falls short of the scientific development of new knowledge described in chapter 4 by Haun.

The problems of potential bias and underrepresentation of a sufficiently broad range of scientific backgrounds and viewpoints persists even in a carefully constructed process such as the consensus-panel concept, at least in the minds of noninvolved observers. In the consensus-panel process, one of the institutes of NIH selects a particular technology for examination and identifies critical questions concerning its scientific validity. A chair for a public consensus conference is selected and a scientific program is formulated to answer the questions that are posed. Expert speakers are recruited, and a consensus panel is formed. The panel consists of scientists, clinical specialists, journalists, interested nonmedical professionals, and representatives of consumer and special-interest health groups. Most often panels contain one or more epidemiologists or biometricians. (Lowe, p. 147) In a carefully structured process, a consensus statement answering the questions is produced, then presented at a public hearing and subsequently disseminated to the medical community.

Whether this process provides for sufficiently broad representation is not clear. Mazur, for example, questioned whether the experts on the panel had already made up their minds. (Tr. p. B 66) Also, there was a question about how dissenting views are handled.

EPA and OSHA: Multipurpose Advisory Committees

Advisory committees are another mechanism for accomplishing goals related to the use of science and technology in the regulatory process.

Ashford's study of OSHA and EPA committees (chapter 8) recognizes three categories: permanent advisory committees created by statute to advise agencies on science, technology, or general policy issues; quasi-permanent committees to aid agencies in general technical matters or policy issues; or ad hoc advisory committees to deal with a specific scientific or technical issue.

Advisory committees can fulfill, in varying degrees, the goals of accuracy of statement and representative or consensual participation by a broad constituency. Ashford recognizes the multiple and sometimes conflicting purposes of advisory committees: bringing needed scientific or technical expertise to the agency decision-making process; providing a mechanism for reaching consensus on difficult scientific or technical issues; providing a mechanism for policy guidance when the factual resolution of scientific or technical issues is not possible in the traditional scientific sense; and providing a means of expanding the participation of interested parties in the regulatory decision-making process.

The first two functions Ashford identifies—bringing scientific and technological expertise to bear and reaching a consensus on difficult scientific and technical issues—are analogous to Grobstein's substantive, component of science's contribution to policy and decision making. Ashford associates these two purposes with fact finding. (p. 167) He associates the last two—policy guidance and expanded participation—with the process of arriving at decisions. This is similar to Grobstein's transitional component and McGarity's class of science-policy questions, which cannot be answered by science alone. Thus Ashford joins other authors in distinguishing among different functions. "As the circuit-court reviews of the OSHA cases state, issues on the frontiers of scientific knowledge are not factual determinations in the usual sense. They are social-policy decisions, legislative rather than judicial in character." (p. 167) This appears to be a perspective in legal terminology that is very close to that of Grobstein's perspective from science. As to the decision-making process, Ashford raises again the idea of balance of interests among the scientific experts.

> [If] scientific or technological issues are not resolvable in the technical sense, proper representation of interested (affected) as well as knowledgeable parties on the advisory committee would appear to be necessary to ensure a fair process. The distinction between fact finding and fair process begins to blur where scientific judgment is subject to prejudices and bias, or where difficult judgment calls . . . vary widely and there exist divergent, but not clearly incorrect, points of view. [p. 167]

In Ashford's view, it is the resolution of the policy issues, not scientific, that controversy occurs: "Most controversy occurs regarding policy issues, and not scientific questions, even where the science is uncertain. . . . In science and technology uncertainty is not a problem. It is not a problem in terms of what goes on in these committees." (tr.p. 269) This viewpoint argues for development of mechanisms allowing the scientists to make full input on the consensus-gathering functions while more deliberately monitoring the nature of their input when policy decision making is approached.

The last function in Ashford's model of advisory committees—providing an opportunity for participation—seeks to avoid adversary interactions. Advisory committees "have become generally a major forum for discussing and clarifying controversial issues before unnecessary adversary interactions occur." (tr.p. 268-269) In fact, because advisory groups tend to operate over a period of time, those representing various interests may tend to achieve accommodation or consensus. In Ashford's view, in the case of the EPA and OSHA advisory committees,

> they have matured; management and labor don't squabble with each other any more; public interest and industry have found a way to communicate. I find a very refreshing education . . . has occurred. . . .
>
> . . . I would submit that the maturation process is at a point where we have a great deal to gain by the use of advisory committees, in offsetting arguments, and clarifying, and in being fair. . . .
>
> The management people, who have been enlightened, the labor people who have been enlightened. . . . We can't live in a risk-free society; nor can corporations remain unregulated—those two poles are no longer argued. [tr.pp. 270-271]

Thus one of the contributions advisory committees make, perhaps because frequently they are bodies that operate over time, is to serve a consensus-building function, even in policy areas. Adversarialism is avoided.

The FDA's Public Board of Inquiry: An Attempt to Integrate Scientific Decision Making into the Legal Process

The importance of the institutional setting in building a workable collaboration between scientists and lawyers surfaces again in the final case. The FDA's public board of inquiry (PBOI) on aspartame provides an experience of a regulatory adversarial institution where there is an attempt to insert a new, basically scientific, process. The PBOI is "a consensual proceeding in which the parties waive their rights to an ordinary evidentiary hearing. (p. 182) In 1974, the FDA issued a regulation permitting the use of aspartame. Two parties, a Washington attorney and a Washington University (St. Louis) professor who had done research on the amino acids in aspartame, filed objections and asked for a hearing. They agreed to a PBOI process instead of an evidentiary hearing. Thus a group of scientists convened to answer scientific questions substituted for an administrative law judge. The board was established in 1979, held a hearing in January 1980, and in October 1980 found sufficient doubt as to the safety of aspartame so as to prohibit it from use. Subsequently all parties appealed to the FDA commissioner, and in July 1981 he reversed the board and approved the use of aspartame.

The PBOI format ostensibly provided the scientists with ample scope. Yet it failed, in large part because it did not keep the scientists within their appropriate role and did not fold the scientific process and fold it into the legal one. Brannigan says that it did not meet several essential criteria to significantly improve adjudicatory decision making. (p. 202) The outcome, Buc asserts, was to create "an utter mess." (p. 205)

This case study illustrates to an extraordinary degree the difficulties of introducing new mechanisms to get better science into familar legal institutions. Perhaps more than the other cases, the PBOI experience suggests the components of an improved process. The first component relates to Mazur's observation that although the PBOI was tagged as a science court, "it emphatically is not one, because it treats legal and policy issues which are emphatically excluded as a function of the science court." (tr.p. 95)

The PBOI was also criticized for not having the required expertise among its panelists; specifically a toxicologist (pp. 207, 209), and for possible bias among its members. (pp. 185-189) In more-practical ways, the PBOI failed because the process did not settle the dispute. Appeals were taken by all parties. Perhaps this is inevitable because this process was not intended to determine the outcome of the legal aspects of the case. Nevertheless, if all parties perceived that the best available science had informed the decision, an important source of dispute might have been withdrawn.

Perhaps most important are the breakdowns Brannigan describes at the interface between science and the law:

A lawyer's attempt to require the scientist to disclose all data in his files relevant to the proceeding, including, apparently, the literature references, as might be done in a pretrial discovery procedure. (p. 192)

The fact that the PBOI witnesses were not under oath (p. 194) and that the slides used at the argument were not made part of any record. (p. 194)

The fact that after the hearing, two of the PBOI panel visited the laboratory of one of the parties and conducted observations of relevant histological material. (p. 194)

The unclear status of the decision of the PBOI when it reached the agency head. (p. 197)

The absence of a clearly defined record of the PBOI hearing. (p. 199)

The fact that in making his decision on aspartame, the FDA commissioner apparently considered material additional to that considered by the PBOI. (p. 201)

In each of these instances, something was done or not done that might fall beneath customary or statutory legal standards of process. In several instances the actors were scientists, proceeding in accord with acceptable standards of scientific practice. Yet there was a mismatch between their activities and the expectations of the law. The problem is that the scientists' activities ultimately were subject to the standards of the legal process.

**Changing Frameworks for Science
in Regulatory Decisions**

The five case studies of special institutions for resolving regulatory issues involving science and technology have disclosed flaws in each of the processes examined. Most can be remedied. The learning from the studies and other analyses in this book can form a basis for designing less-flawed institutional mechanisms. The design of such improved institutions is the subject matter of the final section of this chapter. Before turning to that matter, it may be worthwhile to review briefly several relevant trends in the broad framework of regulation. They are the integrating of accommodatory forces into the regulatory sector, the mitigating of the adversarial character of regulatory processes, the evolving of the new links between science-policy institutions and the law, and the strengthening of the courts' ability to cope with science and technology.

*Integrating Accommodatory Forces into the
Regulatory Sector*

In chapter 2, Mashaw identifies an accommodation-oriented model of regulatory decision making characterized by informal structures and relationships among parties, by a cognitive style emphasizing the ordering of values and the making of distributive judgments as to who gets how much of what. The goal is to produce a harmonious accommodation of the interests that surround an issue or a decision. Consent is the legitimating factor. (p. 15)

Tendencies of this kind are found in several of the mechanisms studied in this book. Examples are the idea that the OSHA GCP rule-making process should be a "shoot out" in which all interested parties can be heard (p. 79); the transitional phase role for science in the policy mode as conceived by Grobstein (p. 129); the consensus-development program of NIH (chapter 7); the requirements for balance and representation in various advisory committees (p. 168); and the design of the PBOI to bring scientists and their methods into the adjudicatory process. (p. 181)

Mashaw identifies a more-formal approach in another model, the bureaucratic rationality model, which is more familiar to lawyers. It is essentially in the Weberian tradition of the exercise of power on the basis of knowledge. The assumption is that values have been determined, and the goal is to implement regulatory programs built around them. He sees the two models as being in conflict, creating continuing tensions in the regulatory sector. He asserts the difficulty of simultaneously realizing the two models in the agency, finding that their features are not only quite distinct but in some cases the opposite of each other. He says, moreover, that "neither model in its ideal form can be implemented." (p. 17)

A recurring theme at the conference was that in today's regulatory arena, reconciliation and integration of these two models is in fact taking place. Mashaw recognizes this; he sees the specific proposals in various chapters of this book, as well as other, familiar specific decision processes as some "mediation or working out of our inconsistent desire to realize both of these models simultaneously."

> We are engaged in an attempt to work out the ways in which we are prepared to live with compromises between rationality and politics that current regulatory systems represent. And whether we are discussing advisory committees, science courts, citizen-review panels, or restructuring the insides of agencies, in most cases the attempt is to put these models together in ways both that better accommodate our impossible dream of having both models simultaneously and that deal with the well-recognized failures of each. [p. 21]

There are significant links between the steady evolution of accommodatory forces and the beneficial growth of processes for obtaining better science in the regulatory sector. They are found in those instances that distinguish issues of science and technology from other issues in the law. These issues attract the interest and participation of a wide range of interested parties. Accommodatory processes arguably are more conducive to this need than the more-hierarchical structure of Mashaw's bureaucratic rationality model. More significantly, the concern for determining value, so common in issues of uncertain science, is integral to accommodatory characteristics, in contrast to those of the other model, where values are assumed already known.

The likely direction is for the accommodatory forces to be integrated into the more-formal hierarchical structure. Mashaw writes, "One lesson to be drawn from this discussion is that the B/R model is always potentially workable. It merely requires a political resolution of the relevant value questions." (p. 19) Grobstein, in discussion, added:

"We do not choose between them—and the last part of [Mashaw's chapter] made that clear—but, rather, we have to face the fact that neither model . . . works as an alternative option as to how we should do things, but rather these two things are constantly interpenetrating, as we fumble with the problems and attempt to adjust our thinking, to realities we have to confront.

And I would suggest that the first [bureaucratic rationality] model . . . is, in a sense, a kind of envelope within which the second [the micropolitical accommodation] model . . . must go on constantly adjusting to what are the inadequacies of the preliminary definitions that encircle the problems as given under the bureaucratic rationality model. [tr.p. 65]

Mitigating the Adversarial Character of Regulatory Processes

It is likely that there will be continued pressure to modify the adversarial system or at least to create workable alternatives to it. In March 1982, Chief Justice Warren Burger wrote that the high cost of the U.S. adversarial, litigation-oriented legal system is increasingly too expensive, time-consuming, stressful, and frustrating.[2] The chief justice's call for more emphasis on alternative means for resolving disputes may well herald long-term changes in the courts. The argument is equally persuasive that many characteristics of the adversary system do not adequately meet the needs for resolving scientific and technical controversy when making regulatory policy decisions.

Problems of science and technology in an adversary system traditionally have been dealt with as a special problem in the law of evidence. American court systems typically have relied on scientific and technical-expert testimony brought into court by the parties. The ability of the judge to handle questions of science and technology beyond the perspectives brought by those parties is limited by the absence of an inquisitorial perspective. The extent to which a trial or an appellate judge may go outside of the material brought into the court or found in the record has traditionally been narrow.[3]

The adversary system, whether in regulatory adjudicatory proceedings, judicial appeals, or in common-law cases with a technical aspect (such as nuisance or product-liability cases) makes it very easy for the scientist to become what Wessel calls the adversary scientist and for the science itself to become adversarial. In recalling the *Berkey Photo* case, where the expert witness, a well-known economist, became an advocate of the party that employed him, Wessel points to the serious extremes to which adversary science can go, discrediting the role of science in the legal process generally. On the other hand, in cross-examination, some lawyers treat scientists and engineers in a manner that tends to discredit the legal process in the eyes of the scientific community. When these circumstances are considered together, the prospect for getting the best science into the legal process seems dim.

It is not only in formal adjudicatory processes that the adversarial nature lessens the prospects for good science to enter. Merrill points out, agency lawyers coached the scientists in the rule-making hearings to establish OSHA's GCP "in advance of the rule-making hearing . . . much as an antitrust lawyer would in an antitrust trial." (p. 106) The traditional formal rule-making process tended, if anything, toward judicialization "rather than in the direction of more-informal attempts to invite the participation of scientists and facilitate resolution of scientific issues." (Ibid.) Haun described the hearing process as a lawyer's dream: "These people [the scientists on one side] could come in, they're almost totally resistant to adverse cross-examination because they simply say, 'it's not my opinion; it's the opinion of this august body, of which I was a part'." (tr. pp. A62-A63)

The trend toward modifying adversarialism in the regulatory processes is taking the form of alternatives to the command and control practices of the past decades. Early negotiation, marketing mechanisms, double team, and single text negotiation are all steps in this direction. In one sense, these are aspects of the integration of accommodatory forces into the regulatory processes.

Evolving New Links between Science-Policy Institutions and the Law

Another contextual change involves the increasing presence of science in legal and policy decisions, a presence accompanied by growing roles for science institutions in related decision-making processes. Compare, for example, Haun's description of the classic scientific method of empirical research with Grobstein's excerpt describing the transitional phase of science policy making. As the latter concept is filled out substantively, new roles for scientists are sure to evolve. Thus, as new science-policy institutions develop, there should be opportunities for collaboration between lawyers and scientists and their respective institutions aimed at improving the quality and usefulness of science in legal processes. The note by Harrison (p. 179) that scientists of the American Chemical Society and other professional societies may begin to review EPA test standards on an annual basis may provide one illustration. She also identified new roles played by other institutions. (p. 178) Ashford's accounts of the scientific inputs of advisory committees in chapter 8 provide further illustrations.

Strengthening the Courts' Ability to Cope with Science and Technology

Finally, challenges to regulatory action may end up in the courts, with interested parties relying on rights of action already on the statute books. Further, Congress may direct the courts to take on greater scruting of agency action, including matters of technical substance. (p. 41) With any combination of these outcomes, science and technology issues are going to be in the federal courts for a long time to come, and it seems likely that their special burden on the judicial system will continue.

Ross makes clear his belief that the federal courts of appeal with which regulatory lawyers are most familiar, can gain sophistication in dealing with the substance of scientific and technical reality. They have broadened the categories used to distinguish how they handle various scientific issues, emphasizing that questions of policy may require a separate approach from those given questions of fact, conclusions of laws, or procedural review. And they have learned to recognize different degrees of scientific certainty underlying the issues before them. He believes that judges can continue to improve these skills, just as do lawyers practicing before them. (p. 31)

Breyer joins Ross in urging that, ideally, the courts ought to be out of the business of dealing with the substance of agency decisions. Yet both Ross and Breyer conclude that given the alternatives, the courts must be involved in the substance, that is, in the science and technology aspects, so far as necessary to give agency rules "a hard look." (pp. 27, 37, 45) Having considered the arguments on both sides of the Bazelon-Leventhal dialogue, they, with some reservation, tilt toward the Leventhal view that appellate courts to some extent have to be involved in this substance.

Adding to the burden on the courts, the prospective movement toward Mashaw's micropolitical accommodation model's characteristics of value orientation and accommodation will simultaneously tend to increase the importance of procedural fairness while at the same time introduce additional sources of scientific and technical contention. Similarly, the introduction of more science and technology institutions into the policymaking processes will both complicate the voices of science and technology coming to the courts and at the same time provide opportunities for getting better science into the decision making.

These observations of the judicial role in dealing with science and technology suggest the desirability of easing their burden on the courts. This goal implies that attention must be given to improving the institutions that bring their product into the legal system. If new mechanisms can be created that improve the quality of science before the courts, the judges may spend less time on the substance. This goal also implies that the products of science are well received by the legal system. The accommodation and use of science ultimately is subject to the law's concern for fairness or due process.

A Model of Law and Science Collaboration in Resolving Regulatory Disputes Involving Science and Technology

The lessons of the five case studies suggest a need for better models of processes for getting the best feasible science into legal and policy decision making. We have seen that today's mechanisms are flawed, as perhaps tomorrow's will be also. We use the experience of these mechanisms to set out several elements of processes that we believe form the necessary, yet minimal, components for improving methods of getting good science into the regulatory process. Actual mechanisms will, of course, vary with the particular agency or adjudicatory system, including the judicial process.

The generic model has six components, which were identified briefly in chapter 1: the distinguishing and allocating of function, the framing of issues, the providing of free scope for scientific work, the ultimate fitting of that work into the legal process, the building of understanding and trust between scientists and lawyers, and the providing of access to a fair proportion of scientific abilities, thereby assuring acceptance of the process by all interests.

It may be useful to recall some of the main features that distinguish the science-in-the-law issues from other legal problems. The coupled problems of uncertainty and values cause the most trouble. Typically, substantive scientific issues involve uncertainty. How to handle the uncertainty, who should bear the responsibility for making decisions, and the differences in the concepts of uncertainty between science and law cultures are all important. Another set of questions concerning the role of scientists and lawyers, including decision makers, involves values, which may or may not be on the surface. The six elements of the new model seek to deal with these twin problems.

Distinction and Allocation of Functions

Functions of lawyers, scientists, and decision makers should be clearly identified and related to their respective capabilities and authority. Who is in charge of particular functions needs to be established in a collaborative rather than a competitive manner. Value judgments should be related to the functions and be explicit. Ideally, the decision maker should be capable of evaluating the scientific, legal, and policy issues.

The functions that must be performed in resolving regulatory disputes involving science and technology, some of which have been identified in other chapters, will vary greatly with the nature and circumstances of each case. They include:

1. Assembly and interpretation of relevant information. This task Grobstein calls "substantive" and is akin to the first two of Ashford's four purposes served by advisory committees. Harrison states that any given regulation, to have credibility with the scientific community, must not be inconsistent with the current state of scientific knowledge.

2. Development of new scientific data in anticipation of, or in response to, emerging issues. Recognizing the need for such data is part of what Grobstein calls the "transitional stage of science policy." Presumably, developing the data would proceed along the lines of the traditional scientific process of empirical research described by Haun. (p. 47)

3. Identification of possible or probable implications of new courses of action and changes of circumstance.

4. Interpretation for various audiences of the scientific and technical content of political issues. In connection with this and the preceding function, Ashford identifies the provision of scientific guidance on policy issues when the science is unknowable. (p. 166)

5. Provision of access by decision makers to the best and latest technical information. Ashford refers to the bringing of needed scientific or technical expertise to the "agency decision-making process." (p. 166) Harrison speaks of "informed scientific judgment." (p. 177)

6. Intermediation or translation between judges and scientists when that is appropriate. Keen sees a need for an information broker between the scientist and the judge to solve the fundamental problem of barriers to mutual understanding. (p. 214)

7. Policy formulation, including the working out of alternatives and deciding on them.

8. Implementation of the policy decisions. The fundamental premise of Mashaw's bureaucratic rationality model is that the policy decision is already made; the direction of the regulatory program is already laid out, waiting to be implemented. It is by no means the first on this list.

9. Communicating with the public regarding the scientific aspects of policy decisions so as to gain their widest acceptance. Harrison calls attention to the importance of regulations' having credibility with the public. (p. 175) In doing so, there is a need, Ross says, for better separation of "those bases for public action which rest on scientific fact (or on an assertive view of scientific fact) [from those] that rest on something else." (tr. p. 167)

The desirability of separating fact from value, whenever possible, underlies this functional component of the model. Making a clear demarcation of the tasks to be performed by scientists, lawyers, judges, and decision makers improves the likelihood of separating fact from value. Some doubt that this separation can be made. They believe that values, even in experimental science, are an integral part of the activity. Wessel spoke of the "distinctions drawn between data and policy, science and value, etc., all predicated upon the assumption that there is some distinction between the 'science' or some body of things that scientists do and the other category of values, quality of life, policy—what lawyers do and the public does." (tr. p. 159) He agreed that conceptually there is such a distinction. "But in my experience as essentially a trial lawyer, I have never seen that distinction made with any practical significance. . . . Every time I cross-examine a scientist, what we've gotten down to . . . has been his or her injection of a value, a quality of life conclusion, in what he pretended or purported, probably innocently, to be a scientific statement." (Ibid.)

Referring to the suggestion that "there is no way in which one can sort out science and value," Grobstein said:

> It is, I believe, correct philosophically, or histologically, that we had some problems in separating fact and value.
>
> It seems to me that in the context in which we are talking here, [of] the practical problems of regulation, they are separable—both in concept, and also in individual behavior. It is possible to behave in a way that at least minimizes the value assumptions that bias these issues, and to focus pretty largely on scientific fact. [tr. pp. 169-170]

Harrison pointed out that scientists distinguish among three categories: "knowledge, and value considerations . . . [and] one in between . . . and that is informed opinion." (tr. p. 73) Informed opinion, or judgment, enables scientists with long experience in a field to "anticipate pretty well" where valid experiments would come out. This capacity

> is not at all on the same basis as knowledge.
>
> And then the other thing we have to pull separate from that are the value considerations. And, of course, the real problem then becomes, which way are you pivoting on this informed opinion? Are you driven entirely from the knowledge side, or are the value judgments also creeping in? . . . It's very, very difficult to know what's going on. [tr. pp. 74-75]

Harrison, referring to the work of the American Chemical Society (ACS), writes:

> Although it may be difficult to distinguish between informed scientific judgment and value judgments relating personal commitments to the

enhancement of the quality of life and the quality of the environment, it has become increasingly clear that ACS must continue to endeavor to make this distinction and to articulate the necessity to make the distinction. [p. 177]

The same can probably be said of the scientific community generally. Even when such separation is not wholly achievable, a clear distinction among functions makes more likely than otherwise an appreciation as to whose values are being involved in what issues.

There is ample additional support for demarcation of function. Despite the apparent doubt about the possibility of achievement, Wessel refers pointedly to the "all-too-common feature of socioscientific litigation and its battle of experts," the "adversary scientist," the "remodeling of the judge into a legislator," the "lawyer into a lobbyist," and to the fact that the "courts, administrative tribunals, and other dispute-resolution mechanisms have been called on to deal with risk-benefit controversies . . . which are essentially legislative or political controversies, not judicial disputes in which relatively fixed rules are applied to facts." (p. 245) He later suggests that "we must put an end to this confusion of styles and roles. The scientist must remain a scientist, the judge a judge, and the lawyer a lawyer." (p. 248) He also asserted that one of the critical problems is first to "go as far as we conceivably can in separating science and nonscience things, and then, as to the remainder, make . . . clear that 'this is value, and I, as a scientist, don't pretend [having] a greater degree of certainty, or assurance, or expertise, than anybody else has.' " (tr. p. 160)

In the FDA PBOI study, having defined his knowledge and option models (p. xxx), Brannigan states that both scientists and lawyers (or policymakers) operated in the format of both models. "We have to think clearly when we are doing what! The difference between these two facets of thought . . . permeates all of our discussions and it requires some clarity." (tr. p. 158)

The ease with which the complex series of functions can be confused is illustrated by the OSHA GCP case. It shows that the functions actually performed in a process may not be what they seem to be on the surface. Merrill points out that the GCP rule-making process was not the place where the scientific issues were in fact resolved.

Thus, not only should functions be identified, but it is necessary to set realistic expectations about when and where scientific exploration, discussion, and resolution are going to take place. McGarity backed up this point, saying that anyone who reads the final OSHA carcinogen policy could not, in his view, "come away with the conclusion that OSHA has been finding science, has been determining science. Over and over again, it's 'for policy reasons we're doing this. We're looking at it, we're resolving it, this way and that way.' " (tr. p. 49)

The confusion may also arise from the linguistic form and content of statutes and regulations. Mashaw referred to the possible "confusion between fact-finding and policy choice, such that, at least at the level of the general public, one has the illusion . . . that scientific questions that as a matter of scientific method have not yet been resolved, are indeed resolved— that the principal tentativeness of scientific inquiry is lost, because of the institutional weight of the governmental pronouncement, couched in language that purports to be about facts, rather than about policy." (tr. pp. 138-139)

Allocation of Functions—The Human Component: If it is correct that factual determination should be separated when possible from value judgments and that achievement of this goal is aided by separation of the various functional roles, the question then arises as to who should be in charge. Our model postulates two norms: that the allocation be made collaboratively rather than competitively and that it recognizes the lawyers', scientists', and decision makers' respective capabilities and authority.

In chapter 10, Keen suggests that both norms are affected by the nature of the parties' cognitive styles. He focuses on differences in modes of thinking of judges, lawyers, managers, scientists, and engineers. In examining preliminary data from the results of a standard cognitive-style test that he and others have administered to judges and other professional groups, Keen observes that (1) There are marked specializations in modes of thinking among specialized professions; (2) Those differences have been shown to relate to key aspects of personal and interpersonal behavior, communication and decision making; (3) There are some data that suggest that state judges are very different in style from scientists (p. 214). Later, in discussing cognitive differences between scientists and lawyers (as distinguished as a class from judges), he further asserts: that (1) Most lawyers are closer in style to the scientists than are most judges; (2) The gap between the scientists and judges is so substantial that it amounts to two separate cultures; (3) The legal profession as a whole is more decisive and structured in its thinking than most creative scientists (and than the helping professions in medicine and psychology); (4) The legal profession may at the same time be intolerant of and impede the academic researchers' less decisive, more adaptive mode of work and, hence, of expertise. (p. 235)

Keen's studies are at a very preliminary stage and in the conference discussion there were cautionary statements about drawing conclusions. Mazur pointed out that "each profession has certain procedural standards which can sometimes be mistaken, or compounded, with cognitive styles" and that "within any of these professions, there is a vast range of cognitive styles, and probably that within-profession range is much greater than any between-profession averages, to the extent that they indeed exist." (tr. p. 243) Keen also recognized the early stage of the conclusions, saying "larger

samples of cognitive-style measures of lawyers are needed before firm conclusions can be reliably drawn" and that "there are as yet no systematic
studies of judges and lawyers in this context." (pp. 235, 214)

Whatever the state of social science's development of knowledge about
cognitive differences among scientists and lawyers, there appeared in the
conference to be considerable intuitive recognition of their significance.
Breyer, citing major difficulty arising from "the fact that many technical
agency decisions involve lawyers and scientists working together," said that
they are governed by different canons of good performance [and] thus, "an
agency might reach results that would look irrational to a judge but are rational from the scientist's perspective." He cites as an example the necessity
of the lawyers', judges', or policy makers' taking "all relevant factors into
account, even if only superficially, when making a decision," in contrast to
the training of the scientist to "hold other things equal and to go into one
issue thoroughly. . . . Therefore scientists are more likely to characterize the
evidence . . . and they will leave the policy conclusion to the policymaker."
As a result, the "agency and the judge may find it particularly difficult to
decide what reasonably follows from the scientist's conclusion." (pp. xxx-
xxx)

Allocation—The Nature of the Functions: Among different functions identified, there is probably consensus at each end of the spectrum. Few would
disagree with Grobstein's assertion that in the substantive area of science, it
is the scientists whose authority, competence, and capability must prevail.
At the other end, there is little disagreement with the idea that once the
scientific issues are laid out, the policymakers prevail. It is in the middle
where ambiguity and confusion are likely to arise.

This middle area involves the issues of uncertainty and concerns about
values crowding out objectivity. The problems apply to both regulatory and
judicial branches. As to regulatory agencies, one approach, outlined by
McGarity, is to tilt toward allocating responsibility to the policymakers
when so-called science-policy questions are at issue. These questions at first
"appear to be questions of scientific fact, but . . . require the application of
regulatory policy." McGarity argues that agencies "must carefully identify
such questions and resolve them in accordance with result-oriented policies,
the content of which must derive primarily from the agency's statute." (p.
67) To McGarity, the alternative of deferring to scientists is "in my judgment impermissably delegating . . . policymaking functions to a group of
unaccountable experts." (Ibid.) His rationale is that "[s]ince policy
judgments must fill the factual voids, the scientists to whom such decisions
are delegated will simply apply their own result-oriented policy preferences,
which may or may not have a statutory basis." (Ibid.)

An effort to apply these concepts was OSHA's reliance in developing its GCP on the presumption-rebuttal approach over the leave-it-to-the-scientists approach earlier favored by the White House Office of Science and Technology. The latter approach meant that valuations and risk assessments of certain classes should be performed by scientists on a case-by-case basis and not by policymakers, whose role would be limited to weighing assessed risks against benefits.

The presumption-rebuttal approach leaves it to the policymakers. However, it would be subject to several limitations. It may not be clear whether a question is a factual one or a policy one; that is, a factual basis may be asserted by one party and yet denied by another. Whether one sees facts or policy may depend upon the particular view as to what is to be gained by the outcome of that categorization. The statute itself may not provide a policy, or value, or factual predicate to guide the policymakers, leaving the regulations dependent upon their own political values. This could result in undervaluing scientific perspectives or failing to take them into account at all. Harrison writes:

> To formulate an effective regulation, the agency must look to the scientific community to supplement its own literature search and assessment of that literature; to the technological community for information concerning current practices, planned technological changes, and an assessment of future capabilities; and to the public to learn what is acceptable to those who seek the protection of regulations. (p. 176)

The benefit of science's perspectives on the issues of uncertainty—to recognize the need for new data, to point to implications of new courses of action, to interpret the scientific and technical content of political issues, as Grobstein describes the transitional phase—seems too valuable to risk losing.

In this connection, Breyer described his experience on the NAS-NRC saccharin panel saying that he "ended up . . . rather wishing that there were a way the scientists on the panel would make the judgment rather than the administrators." (tr. p. 106) He recognized that neither the scientists nor the administrators knew what the standard should be nor, in fact, did Congress. In view of such general ignorance, Breyer said:

> If I am going to give it to my children or myself . . . they [the scientists] know more about it than I do. . . . They didn't like that idea, that they would make that decision. They wanted to say, "No, that's somebody else's decision."

> But if it's judgmental in the first place, why isn't it better to have them do it; and we can at least have them go and say, "I think it should be banned," or "I think it shouldn't be banned." [tr. p. 107]

Responding to comments by the scientists who said they did not want that responsibility, Breyer continued, "I know they don't [and] so the result is, have a lawyer do it, on the basis of stuff he doesn't understand. . . . At least I'd like to have [the scientists] make a judgment on the ultimate question." (tr. pp. 107-108).

Scientists may be ambivalent when their roles come close to the policy-decision end of the spectrum. In discussing the work of scientists in the areas of fact, values, and informed judgment, Harrison commented, "when you get over into the mores of society, as scientists—or as individuals—we are part of the public, and, in that sense, are a part of that evaluation—but not because we are scientists." (tr. p. 127) Referring to her comment, Grobstein cautioned that probably "more controversy has occurred in relation not only to policy issues, but even within the body of science, between people who believe they are providing informed judgment, and these informed judgments are not in concordance—and that leads to [the] kind of controversy that confuses the issue." (tr. pp. 112-113) His opinion, perhaps a further reflection of ambivalence, was that scientists would then say that "unless knowledge is firm enough to be regarded . . . as established fact . . . they didn't think their view should be injected into the public controversy." From their own viewpoint, the scientists were "no better informed than the man in the street, since they did not have the facts that they could rely on." (tr. p. 113)

Finally, there is another concern that limits any leave-it-to-the-policymakers approach, which it may also account for scientists' wariness of their role, namely, where it appears that scientific issues have been decided when, in fact, they have not. In that respect scientists hope that neutrality will be maintained as to the further path of scientific inquiry and determination of the future science agenda in the area, Haun observed that the "worst part of the quasi-science to be found in testimony on this issue is the almost reverent attention laypersons, particularly lawyers, will pay to the wildest possible speculation when cloaked in authority." (p. 111) Something far less than the best science is developed and propagated as science.

In summary, the most-difficult issues of allocation of functions concern those tasks and responsibilities lying between areas of clear science work and clear policy decision making and implementation. Leaving them either entirely to the scientists or to the policymakers suffices. Collaboration among scientists, lawyers, and policymakers is necessary, based on allocation of responsibilities explicitly made, and depending upon the capabilities of each and the needs of the individual case. The scientists' responsibility should stop short of actual decision making but should include providing advice to the policymakers up to that point. Scientists and lawyers should work in tandem and in collaboration.

In the appellate courts we find increasing sophistication about scientific uncertainty, including recognition of different kinds of uncertainties. These are discussed by Ross (pp. 33-36) who points out that in recent years much of the examination of the need to separate functions has been in discussions between Judges David Bazelon and the late Harold Leventhal. Although the role of U.S. judges in separating fact from value has long been a basic jurisprudential issue, there now is more willingness to trust the judiciary to make many value judgments.

Breyer points out that there are good reasons for distinguishing functions at the judicial level. Courts are effective at being fair—that is, at producing a decision "where the parties directly concerned agree that it had been decided honestly, that they had an opportunity to present their arguments and evidence, . . . fair in terms that the people directly involved feel that they have had a fair and impartial decision." (tr. pp. 123-124) He contrasted this with their ability to be accurate, so that they act in "correspondence with the true facts in the world . . . particularly with a legislative, or rule type, matter [one] that really does what you think it will do in terms of the world." (tr. p. 124) A question such as "is it good or bad for the country if [we] ban saccharin" is a question where fairness is not important, but accuracy is. (tr. p. 110) A judge can be fair in terms of process, but there is "horrendous distance between the appellate court judge and . . . [the] facts in the world." Canons of practice "bind [the judge] to the record [and] that's why I would say, if it's a question of fairness, we're the group you want. If it's a question of accuracy, forget it—I mean, in terms of the facts of the world." (tr. p. 111)

Concerning cognitive styles, Keen has clearly indicated the problems science/policy issues cause for judges and scientists. (pp. 214, 236) Ashford suggested that judges work from paradigms that lead them to ask very different kinds of questions from those asked by scientists or social scientists. "Scientists tend to look for truth. They tend to look for the most likely event." (tr. p. 108) Scientists and economists, he said, are trained to look for the correct answer, the simple answer, the model, the defendant answer. In response, judges see whether that was done correctly. (tr. p. 109) He pointed out that in certain cases, judges also ask whether the decision in the agency was basically "within the bounds of not [being] clearly incorrect" and that this differed from the scientists' way of looking for a consensus of scientific opinion, for the greatest probability of the correct result. (tr. p. 110)

Grobstein agreed with Ashford that the role of both the scientist and the economist were circumscribed by the need to attempt to simplify to the point of gaining knowledge. He contrasted this kind of knowledge with "in the round" knowledge that takes into account all considerations, saying that "we assume that the function of the judge comes closer to that kind of 'in the round' capability to make judgments, than that of the scientist or the economist." (tr. p. 112)

Framing the Question

Questions addressed to the scientists and technologists should be framed so that they can respond in a way consistent with their functions. In particular, value-laden questions should be minimized.

The allocation of the various functions or roles to the scientists, lawyers, or decision makers or policymakers can both govern and be governed by the form and substance of the questions put to them. This is particularly true of questions to the scientists. The FDA's public board of inquiry case study provides a good illustration of the importance of framing the question carefully. As Brannigan points out, three questions were put to the panel in final form: whether the ingestion of aspartame either alone or together with other substances poses a risk; whether it causes cancer; and, based on the answers to these questions, whether aspartame should be allowed for use in foods or should be withdrawn. (tr. pp. A5-A6) The third question, the should question, caused trouble for the scientists.

Staying away from the should questions is not enough. Mashaw points out another problem. To ask the question in a form that demands a yes or no answer is also to frame it in the wrong way from a scientific perspective because scientists deal so frequently in terms of probability. If the policy question is, what is the probability that X causes cancer, for example, then scientists can "begin to respond more cheerfully. They can come forward with some estimates of the probability that X causes cancer." Mashaw asserts that "[h]owever penetrating the inquiry, . . . there are ways to structure questions such that scientific people can give an answer that is responsive and is not irresponsible from a scientific perspective." (p. 18) Mostly that means restructuring the question in a way that restates factual inquiries into probabilistic terms.

Two further problems arise. The first, also raised by Mashaw, involves instances where the statute tells an agency what to do about facts but not about probability estimates. "In order to do that, the agency must make a value choice concerning risks. (p. 18) Here again the value issue is raised, but as McGarity points out, it is appropriate that the agency has the task of making the policy decision—that is, the value decision.

The second problem is raised by Haun. He agreed with Mashaw that if the general question, "Does X cause cancer?" is asked, a proper or rigorous scientific answer would typically be: " 'According to so and so's tests, when he subjected X strain of mice to a dosage of this amount, for this period of time, there was or was not statistical evidence that there was cancer in those mice.' " (tr. pp. 62-63) Haun pointed to the obvious difficulty: the move from science to opinion. In the process of trying to qualify an answer, as the scientist desires, there is a push for a yes or no opinion. Once into opinion, the difficulty starts anew because the different parties in the adversarial system, or even in an honest scientific controversy, will challenge the qualifications of the opposition scientists and offer the competing opinions of their own scientists. As Haun says, a party will say, " 'I have the equally qualified Dr. Smith over here, and he read the same data, and he came to a different conclusion.' " (tr. p. 63)

Haun said that the "administrative agency must always drive toward that 'yes' or 'no' kind of answer, particularly in [Mashaw's] bureaucratic model, [in] which . . . the implementation is to seek facts that fit into the model and to reject facts that don't." (tr. p. 63). Mashaw would apparently agree. In discussion, he refers to the kind of question in which the scientist is asked to "certify that this gap in our knowledge is not a gap." He says that the professional scientist, then, "is in a terribly awkward situation in which the question being put seems to be a fact question, but he or she knows that it is not, and that it is indeed a policy question. And what he would really like to say is 'Here is a set of facts; what would you like them to mean?' and not, 'What do they mean?' " (tr. p. 64)

Building Effective Communication, Understanding, and Trust

Communication among the scientists and technologists, lawyers and decision makers requires a specific effort to establish trust and understanding across discipline lines. This requirement may involve translation of the scientific and technological information into the legal and policy framework in which the decision maker must operate. A lawyer or a scientist may undertake this translation function.

This component of the model underlies the others. Efforts to clarify responsibility for clearly demarcated functions, to formulate the issues in answerable form, to match responsibility with capability, to evolve processes enabling scientists best to perform their scientific tasks while simultaneously meeting the expectation of legal processes—all will require communications between scientists and lawyers of a higher quality than now exist. That is the learning coursing through these chapters and the conference discussion. The conclusion appears self-evident. Yet good communications, understanding, and trust are about the most-difficult objectives to achieve in complex societal relationships.

In the earlier chapters in this book, the scientists most clearly issued the call for improved communication. In order for a regulation to be effective,

Harrison writes, it must have credibility. And in order for it to merit credibility, there must be "effective communication among those who regulate, those who are served by the regulation, and those who bear the burden of regulation." She also suggests what the substance of such communications will have to contain if credibility with those sectors is to be attained. (pp. 175-176)

In the NAS study Grobstein argues that society "cannot afford to have public policy made without assured lines of deliberate communication with expert technical resources." (p. 133) Referring to interaction between the federal government and the NAS complex, he says that it is "in some significant cases on a catch-as-catch-can basis, without guarantee that the two parties understand each other as to objectives and their feasibility." (p. 133) In a sense, the federal government and the NAS can be regarded as stand-ins for law and science.

In a summation passage, Keen writes that "there is an obvious potential barrier to mutual understanding between lawyers and scientists, especially since the rules for debate and determination of valid fact and opinion are more comfortable for the judge than for the scientific expert." (p. 235) The need for better communications is implicit in his basic working hypothesis: that there are marked differences between judges and scientists in perceptions of fact and evidence, and between lawyers and judges on the one hand and many professionals in the social sciences on the other. These differences in cognitive style make mutual understanding and even mutual respect difficult. More importantly, the scientist's or psychologist's mode of explanation may be significantly impeded, from each viewpoint, by many aspects of the legal process. (p. 214)

The establishment of trust, as well as understanding, is concomitant with the kind of communications sought in this component of the model. Declarations of lack of trust did not surface explicitly in conference discussions. Yet implicitly, it ran throughout. It is difficult without further research to know fully what these exchanges imply for collaboration between lawyers and scientists, but they suggest that there is often apprehension and anxiety inherent in the prospect of working across the disciplinary cultural borders and that these are given expression through a sense of competition, a lack of understanding, and an absence of trust. It seems clear that until the distancing, mistrust, and misunderstanding apparent in such exchanges are overcome by better communication, the collaboration called for in the remaining components of the model will remain unfulfilled.

In the OSHA GCP study, several anecdotal illustrations arose, beginning with Merrill's characterization of the GCP process as "emphatically, from the beginning, a lawyer's process." (tr. p. 52) McGarity referred to the OSHA administrator's "express adoption in his heptachlor chlordane suspension notice of a 'basis for evaluating the carcinogenicity of pesticides' which generated concern among some agency scientists that agency lawyers had articulated an agency cancer policy without sufficient scientific help." (p. 58) Again, there is reference made to lawyers' attempting to secure EPA agency "recognition of the seventeen cancer principles by filing a motion for official notice of the seventeen principles in the pending hearing involving the pesticide mirex," (p. 59) thus trying to give concepts the status of fact through legal rather than scientific processes.

McGarity also notes a meeting, which he describes as one skirmish in a larger battle between lawyers

> in the Office of General Counsel and scientists and managers in the Office of Pesticides Programs over whether the agency's cancer policy was to be based on the testimony of outside experts in adjudicatory hearings or on the initiative of in-house scientists. The battle ultimately ended with the "protest" resignations of three agency lawyers and the establishment of an in-house 'Carcinogen Assessment Group.' [note 33]

Another instance involved an agency hearing in which a lawyer was cross-examining a scientist in which the latter blew up, cursing the lawyer and saying, " 'I wish they'd throw all of you out the window.' " The lawyer recounting the incident said, "and, of course, we used that right on up to the Supreme Court to show that this man obviously had an axe to grind, was biased, and really was deserving of no credibility. It was a wonderful thing for us that he did that. But . . . that really doesn't solve anything. So that's an aside." (tr. pp. 148-149)

In the FDA PBOI discussion, a nonlawyer commented that it "is fairly typical for somebody who is closely associated with an administrative agency, part of whose functions may be separated from it, to resist the separation." In response, the question of turfing surfaced most clearly. A former FDA lawyer said, "It's a question of lawyers' turf versus other people's turf—and there, I think my views are clear." (tr. p. 81) A passage in Buc's comment gives a sense of the distancing that appears likely to have been present in the aspartame process: "In essence, the commissioner told the PBOI to make its judgment and then the agency would take it when it came back up." (p. 205)

Scientists as well as lawyers are sensitive to these issues of who is in charge. Commenting on the NAS's saccharin committee's examination of the costs and benefits of regulating saccharin, Grobstein commented: "The statutory basis for current regulation was analyzed and found to be excessively elaborate, legalistic rather than scientific in concept, and rigid in implementation. It was proposed that Congress should reconsider the basic statute and make changes to yield wider regulatory options for FDA, while assuring it heightened availability of scientific advice." (p. 133)

Competition, mistrust, and misunderstanding between the two cultures is also evident in practical experiences. The rejection of the leave-it-to-the-scientists approach in the OSHA GCP case study is one illustration. Another is the issue of expert personnel to serve on the FDA PBOI. Here each side presented a list of scientists to the FDA commissioner, who made the final selection. One person who was chosen had coauthored articles with a consultant to one of the parties. The articles did not concern aspartame. In fact, the proposed panelist had never worked on aspartame. The question of conflict was raised. Brannigan said, "In a legal context, in my opinion, that level of interaction would have raised the suspicion, or appearance, of conflict, sufficient to trigger the usual legal remedies of refusal; but, in fact, in this case, among scientists, it was felt that, judged by scientific standards of conflict of interest, there was no conflict at all." (tr. p. A8) And in commenting on the whole issue of conflict of interest, Peck said, "If the conflict-of-interest definition is not modified, few, if any, qualified toxocologists could be appointed to a board of inquiry. In the future the definitions of conflict of interest and bias should be examined very carefully and narrowed to mean scientific experimentation with the chemical under discussion or close association with disagreeing parties." (p. 209) Clearly the two cultures have differences of view as to what constitutes conflict of interest.

Another point arose over what Brannigan terms the authenticity issue. He pointed out that

> this is a typical evidentiary, policing type of issue, that is resolved in administrative and judicial proceedings all the time; and there's no reason to believe that the scientists on the board would be any better at discovering, or understanding, the implications of whether or not the data [were] authentic.

> So what happened was that a board had been set up, and evidence (which should have been sanitized) to be presented to the board, was not sanitized, in any sort of adversarial process, and so the board has done its entire work on evidence which a later hearing might find to be so defective that it was a waste of the board's time. [tr. p. A14]

Here again is an instance in which the issue is particularly a lawyer's issue, the lawyer's culture or standards being expressed about the way the scientists went about their work. Two points are worth noting. It must always be remembered that the work of scientists normally will have to be folded into a legal process; however, as part of the same process, the scientists have to be free to do their own work in a manner they see fit.

What can be done to improve the communications process? Keen's arguments lead him in several directions. First, he sees the lawyer as a necessary translator or information broker between the scientist and judge.

> If there is a fundamental problem of mutual understanding between many judges and most scientists, some brokerage role is essential. Judges cannot be expected to alter their effective fact-dominated, structured mode of evaluation. . . . The scientists may not be able to change their mode of explanation; even if they try, they are not likely to be clear or convincing. A formal translator is essential, one who understands both the legal and scientific mind without being an expert in both fields. [p. 214]

Keen sees the lawyer as the translator and information broker between the scientist and the judge. It would seem, though, that some scientists would also be able to assume this role.

Next, he suggests that those in the judicial process "need to recognize that a key issue in assessing scientific explanations is to focus not on conclusions but on assumptions." Further, those in the legal procession need to learn that "accepting uncertainty is the issue for science." (pp. 214, 215) Finally, he sees the need for processes in the law allowing scientists to make their explanations in their own terms.

That improved communications will also result from clearly articulated functions and from questions carefully crafted to their addressees' capabilities should be clear. This need for improved communications applies to formal documentation, as well as informal working communications. Merrill expressed the view that "there is a tendency among people in the scientific community . . . to mistranslate, to misassess the operational importance of decision making that seems . . . necessarily to have resolved the question, when, in fact, the agency is only saying, 'when in doubt, this is where we come out, as a matter of judgment or . . . of policy.' " (tr. p. 151) But he went on to say that "the location problem is not only in the scientific community, and [it] may be exacerbated when an agency tries to address things at this level of generality (exhibited by OSHA's generic cancer policy statement)." (Ibid.) He then referred to a statement in the OSHA document that a crucial conclusion regarding benign tumors in animal tests "was well supported by the *scientific* . . . evidence presented at the hearing. (tr. p. 152) Merrill continued:

> Now, I suggest to you that that is a statement that is susceptible to interpretation as a resolution, for the moment, of a scientific debate. OSHA, I am sure, would tell us that it was intended to be an articulation of the policy that the agency would, in the absence of resolution of that debate, pursue. But that language is equally susceptible of two interpretations; and I'll bet one could find five hundred other examples of it in [the document]. [tr. p. 152]

Thus, he sees an integration of what appears to be a scientific conclusion and an agency policy position in the absence of scientific resolution. At the level of generality inherent in regulatory policy writing, such an integration adds to communication difficulties. Matters may be further complicated if, as Merrill suggests, that is a tendency in writing a regulatory document to have an eye on its reception by the judges. "You're always writing with more conviction than you probably really feel . . . because it's advocacy." (tr. p. 153) Again, functions are confused, and communications are weakened as a result.

In summary, cognitive-style differences, confusion of roles, and past experience all appear to contribute to a state of inadequate communications between lawyers and scientists, which gives rise to feelings of competition, distancing, misunderstanding, and mistrust. These in turn engender further confusion of roles and poor communication. In order to achieve a true collaboration between science and law, these feelings must give way to perceptions that those engaged in the two enterprises can work together. Mechanisms must be developed to facilitate this objective. Special efforts must be made to achieve workable communications in each instance of regulatory collaboration among scientists and lawyers.

Room to Breathe for Scientists

Scientists and technologists should have room to breathe in carrying out their agreed functions, that is, scientific or technical data should be gathered, developed, evaluated, and presented in a form and manner acceptable to the presenter and his or her peers.

Keen introduced the phrase "room to breathe." (p. 214) It is a concept that seems to capture the need for science, done by scientists, in modes acceptable to science, as a routine component of better regulatory processes. He writes that scientists need to be able "to make their explanations in their own terms and at their own pace. . . . The legal rules of procedure do not allow the scientist thirty minutes to think." He finds judges are "often irritated by the seeming inability of psychologists to make any coherent explanation," while expert witnesses from the social sciences "generally complain that the process is one of interrogation in which they cannot complete a thought." (p. 214) Cognitive-style differences, he believes, lie at the heart of these problems; new processes can help solve them.

Difficulty of achieving this arises from familiar dilemmas. First, while it is important to get the best feasible science into regulatory decision making, "doing" the science may require periods of time that are impermissibly long from the regulatory viewpoint.

Second, it is not clear that the science work must be done as an integral component of the legal process. Harrison, for example, points out that there are many ways for science to feed into policymaking. Among the institutions she mentions are the Interagency Testing Committee, a permanent committee established under the Toxic Substances Control Act, comprised of representatives from eight government agencies; the Toxic Substances Strategy Committee, with representatives from a wide range of entities within the executive branch; the Organization for Economic Cooperation and Development's program in the protection of health and the environment from adverse effects of chemicals; and various scoping workshops and public meetings. (p. 178) In some instances, the provision of scientific input will be separated in time and institutional mechanism from policy formulation or legal procedure. Each agency or adjudicative proceeding would expectedly evolve its own form of process.

A preliminary idea of sufficient room to breathe for scientists can be suggested from the conference proceedings for the purposes of the model. There should be, or should have been, a scientific examination of the issues involving science and technology that was participated in or provided clear opportunity for participation by scientists from the full range of interests involved in the legal process, including secondary parties who would be accorded standing if the matter came to litigation. The scientific process should be designed and carried out by scientists in a manner acceptable to the broader science community and in its implementation be unfettered by lawyers or considerations of legal process other than those basic considerations necessary to ensure the full use of the work in the ultimate legal process. Its purpose, minimally, should be the collection, review, and evaluation of the current state of scientific thinking pertaining to the scientific issues involved in the regulatory decision making (Grobstein's first or substantive component), and the bringing to bear of scientific expertise in identifying new data requirements concerning emerging issues, implications of new courses of action, and the science content of political issues, as well as making available the best and latest technical information to the decision makers (his second or transitional component). Whether new scientific research in its traditional meaning was also included (see chapter 4) would depend upon the needs of the individual case and the availability of requisite time and money. Finally, the science process envisioned here would have to meet the minimum legal procedural process requirements so as to gain eventual acceptance in that process.

Neither the FDA aspartame PBOI nor OSHA's GCP rule making, the two case studies having origins in legal procedures, meet these minimal criteria for this fourth component of the collaborative model. The PBOI comes the closer of the two. Brannigan describes its scientific nature:

> The transcript of the hearing indicates that it was a model scientific debate. There were virtually no lawyers in the room, and certainly they played no significant part at all after Turner's attempt to get the other evidence in—they played no further part in the hearing. And for substantial periods of time, the record does not indicate that there were any lawyers for the parties in the room. It just continued as a presentation, examination, scientific argument, of relatively high order. [tr. p. A16]

Yet, in the eyes of Peck, a scientist, it was an unacceptable process because it did not include a toxicologist. (p. 209) And it is not clear that several aspects of its process would have passed scrutiny if fully challenged as to procedural adequacy in the courts.

The OSHA GCP rule making failed the above criteria in that it was not a process of science. It was, to be sure, a proceeding open to all potential participants in which everybody had "a shot at being heard on the central issues." (Merrill, p. 107) But it was not a shootout of science. "[I]t would be essentialy accurate, although possibly unfair, to say that OSHA's proceeding never purported to be an exercise in scientific decision making. From the beginning, it was an exercise in regulatory policy formulation." (p. 105) "Any departures from the standard model [of traditional quasi-formal rule making] tended in the direction of judicialization rather than in the direction of more-informal attempts to invite the participation of scientists and facilitate resolution of scientific issues." (p. 106) Nor is it at all clear from chapter 5 that any connected shootout of science—an effective consensus gathering and evaluating of known science—had been held and fed into the GCP rule making.

Several further comments seem useful in defining the goal of providing scientists full room to breathe within a legal context. It should be clear that the range of problems (Grobstein, pp. 123-127) to be expected in this kind of scientific endeavor should be dealt with in a manner satisfactory to the scientific community at large.

Next, there may be difficulty in sorting out which specific issues are really for the scientists and which are for the lawyers. This comment is not intended to beg the question of allocation of function. The issue of authenticity in the PBOI case study provides an example.

An additional concern is to make sure that the criterion "acceptable to the broader scientific community" does not shut out what might be termed the disputed scientific minority. Olney and Turner (p. 181) and those scientists supporting the Saffiotti principles (p. 57) might fall into this category. So might have Galileo.

Finally, the provision of full room to breathe at the appropriate point in the process ought not to be taken as bringing closure for all time on the related scientific uncertainties. This concern, of course, underlies a basic criticism of generic rule making. (See p. 68) If working well, this component of the whole collaborative problem-solving model would generate agenda for future needed research rather than cutting off inquiry.

Folding the Scientific into the Legal Process

Since the scientific data, their evaluation, and presentation will likely be used in a legal process involving legal rights and powers, care must be taken to ensure that the scientific input can be satisfactorily folded into the legal process. Specifically, due-process and fairness standards appropriate to the nature of the legal process must be met; multiple interests affected, public and private, should have an opportunity to be heard and their views considered; and a record must adequately reflect the scientific and legal processes at work.

In the resolution of regulatory issues involving science and technology, the work of science will end up in a legal process. In a related context, Grobstein points out that regulation "stems from a need to integrate part processes into an effective whole." (p. 115) That whole, in the instances with which this book is concerned, is most frequently defined by a legal framework. In a sense, the interaction of science with that process can be analogized to the creation of a play within a play, where the integrity of both must be respected if the whole is to be successful.

Frequently it is considerations of due process that establish the integrity of the legal side. The concept of due process embodies much of the law's concern for fairness. Requirements pertaining to representation, opportunity to be heard, impartial adjudication, a record, and reasoned decision are important. In chapter 1, we pointed out that the courts in the past decade have approved a wide range of due-process models based upon the nature of the issues and the context in which they arise. The FDA PBOI, OSHA GCP, and NAS case studies provide useful illustrations of issues arising from the need to ensure that the science done by scientists will meet basic legal requirements.

The several ways in which process in the PBOI on aspartame appear to have fallen short of criteria of accepted practice from the legal viewpoint are summarized cogently by Buc:

> The questions about whether their own views are evidence, their viewing of the slides, not putting anybody under oath, not having a record, not even citing one single source in the record in their opinion—is a source of rather considerable aggravation to the lawyers who are then going to have to make something out of it, that certainly will be reviewed by a court, since there are parties apparently willing to sue on either side. . . .
>
> Similarly, many of the other matters for which the board had such disdain, such as regular legal procedure, will have to be dealt with on appeal to the commissioner. . . .
>
> Finally, and probably most important, somebody has to do the mating of the scientific judgment to the statute. (p. 205)

A somewhat similar failure to attend to legal requirements is noted by McGarity in the OSHA GCP study. In promulgating its emergency temporary standards for fourteen potential carcinogens, OSHA failed to place in the record one key committee report on which it had heavily relied. The resulting appellate-court decision remanded twelve temporary standards to the agency and vacated the other two. (p. 57) The attempt by lawyers in EPA to establish the seventeen cancer principles of that committee's report as fact by having them legally declared as such through the device of official notice (p. 59) shows also that legal processes offer a potential means for forcing or distorting the work of science. In this regard, it resembled the attempt by lawyers in the PBOI case to impose a form of discovery practice on that science process. (p. 192) In a different vein, McGarity's description of the formulation of EPA's weight-of-the-evidence approach to the problem of assessing potential carcinogens and OSHA's later development of its presumption-rebuttal approach (pp. 60-62) illustrate the critical but difficult task of transferring scientific processes into legal ones.

Grobstein points out that policymaking requires the consideration of experts. It, along with issues strictly legal in origin, is also part of the fold-in problem. As in the case of legal process, part of the problem may spring from the fact

> that many expert groups confronted by policy-generated issues are unfamiliar with the policy context within which their effort will be judged and used. The natural habitat of many of the experts is in secluded laboratories, generally academic but also industrial, far from Washington. Their expert status derives from assiduous avoidance of the very habits of thought and ways of life that characterize governmental policymaking. (p. 125)

He also reminds us that the needs or expectations of Congress may have to be taken into consideration and so become a part of the fold-in question. In the saccharin case, Congress's need for answers in a very short time frame and at two different levels of detail and scope affected both the organization and result of the NAS committee's work. (p. 132)

These examples point to the consideration that must be given to the manner in which the work of science is carried out and then transferred into the related legal work. One way of alleviating the problems might be to include routinely an early review by scientists and lawyers of the prospective criteria that the law will employ in assessing the adequacy of the scientific data from a legal-process viewpoint. Such a review, ideally before the scientific work gets underway, would entail an effort by lawyers to guide their collaborators from science, acting as translators perhaps of some essentials of due process and legal formality. Examination of the instances where lack of regard for the eventual procedural expectations of the law lessened the usefulness of earlier scientific work suggests that such an effort would be rewarding.

Ensuring Acceptance of the Process

There should be a sufficiently equitable distribution of the scientific and technological expertise among the parties in interest so that they will accord both credibility and acceptance to the process by which the scientific work is done.

This component of the model is qualitatively different from its predecessors in that it focuses primarily on differences among the several parties with interests at stake in resolving the regulatory disputes. The earlier components were directed primarily at differences between law and science (and their practitioners). Throughout there has been an emphasis on collaboration.

The concern here is gaining acceptance for the scientific input among the various parties at interest in the legal process. The need arises from the likely multiple-party nature of legal issues involving science and the common demand by those directly and indirectly affected to participate in the process. These were described at the outset as distinguishing characteristics of law-science issues. This concern recognizes that there is sense of vital self-interest among the parties that is probably less collaborative and more adversarial in nature and that this self-interest will spill over into the task of getting the best feasible science into the legal process. There is a need to ensure a sufficiently equitable distribution of scientific capability among the different parties so that a basic sense of fairness of scientific process exists among all parties. There will, then, exist among the parties an elemental perspective that science or scientists can be one-sided no matter how collaborative and nonadversarial an effort is made. In this sense, some equitable proportioning of scientific resources may be analogous to ensuring procedural fairness in law, in part by providing broad rights of standing and of the right to be heard.

The issue of fairness in distribution of scientific resources surfaces indirectly in Ashford's discussion of balance among members of advisory committees (p. 168); Harrison's reference to the possible review by the American Chemical Society and other professional societies of EPA test standards before they go into the Federal Register (p. 179); Lowe's discussion of the composition of the consensus conference (p. 147); Thompson's discussion of different perspectives toward risk and power (p. 155); Brannigan's perceptions of the issues of bias and conflict in the FDA PBOI case (p. 188); and Grobstein's discussion of the credibility of the work of the NAS committee system (p. 126).

The issue arose more explicitly during conference discussion. Ashford observed that "the scientific and academic community largely is accessed by one-sided questions; that is, industry has an access to academic and technical people . . . [who are] more consonant with industry's view, than with the public interest view." (tr. p. 171)

Ultimately the problem is often expressed as an economic one. Ross commented that "principal tensions come from the inequality of resources to try the case. . . . Some people are better able to contemplate the cost, expense, and delay of trying the case than others. . . . A large utility or a very large company with considerable resources has more bargaining leverage in settlement process than others might have." (tr. pp. 66-68) Buc had a somewhat different view, saying of the assumption that well-off economic interests will be the parties most willing to try a case, that "we're going to have to start thinking about . . . the fact that public interest groups—the law . . . environmental . . . and consumerist groups—are among those for whom litigation is, in some respects, at least, apparently a free good; and they're the ones who very often are least willing to settle anything." (tr. p. 72)

The context in which this exchange took place—consideration of the relationship between Mashaw's bureaucratic rationality and micropolitical accommodation models—is pertinent. Ross apparently saw the structured, hierarchical formality found in much of the legal system as a barrier to equality of access to the the law's dispute-resolution mechanism. To Buc, it must have seemed that it was the theoretically economically less well-off interests who used the formality of the law to hold on to the controversy. They resisted the accommodatory forces that would tend toward settlement. The difference in perspective sharply etches the tendency of different parties at interest to use the institutions in place to their own ends. By building in the aim of ensuring some balance of scientific input available to the different parties, an important source of potential inequity in the institutional mechanisms is diminished and acceptance of the process and outcome should be increased as a result.

Conclusion: Practical Applications of the Model

The several elements of the collaborative decision-making model described in this chapter have been designed to improve the ways in which regulatory issues involving science and technology are resolved. In order to realize their potential, however, they need to be experimented with, molded, improved on, or discarded as experience suggests.

Several specific steps may lead to the development of ongoing guides for particular proceedings. The suggestions presented here take the form of a set of documents for each proceeding, which are based on the main elements of the model, set forth the process to be followed and identify the persons who are the actors in it. They are proposed primarily as a method of approach rather than a detailed checklist. Such a list could eventually be built out of successful experiences.

As to functions: An identification of functions—legal, scientific and decisional; statements covering who has responsibility for each of them; the method by which differences are to be worked out, with specificity as to where collaborative approaches are or are not useful and with a specific acknowledgment of the areas where agreement is not feasible; and a statement about the anticipated problems arising from perceived differences between the science and law aspects.

As to issues: An agreement among all parties on the questions to be presented to the scientists. It may be desirable, in this context, to do the same for other issues.

As to providing scientists room to breathe: A statement by the scientists about the manner in which they will answer the questions put to them— whether they will be concerned only with scientific fact, respond to questions regarding their informed judgment, and/or recommend policy.

As to folding the scientific data into the legal process: A statement joined into by lawyers and scientists from all parties setting forth the procedures to be followed to meet due-process requirements, the manner in which the scientific input is to be introduced, and how it is to be translated for the nonscientists.

As to communication: An understanding regarding acceptable means of communication among the lawyers and the scientists.

As to equity in scientific resources: A statement setting forth the interests and persons affected by the proceedings and who have a stake in their outcome, together with an agreed means for having them adequately represented.

Documents of these kinds may be developed and used in a variety of ways. They may be incorporated as part of the regulatory process. They may simply be used by parties independently. They may be made available by outside entities that specialize in this kind of activity. In sum, they could provide the important elements that meet critical needs in resolving regulatory issues involving science and technology.

Notes

1. For an earlier characterization of such disputes, see Nyhart and Heaton, Jr., "Proceedings of the Task Force on Disputes Involving Science and Technology, July 23-24, 1981," in *Dispute Management: A Manual of Innovative Corporate Strategies for the Avoidance and Resolution of Legal Disputes* (New York: Center for Public Resources, 1980), supplement 7.

2. Burger, *Isn't There a Better Way?* 68 Amer. Bar Assn. J. 275 (1982).

3. See Nyhart, Meldman, and Gilbert, "The Use of Scientific and Technical Evidence in Formal Judical Proceedings, in *Science, Technology and Judicial Decision Making: An Exploratory Discussion* (Washington, D.C.: National Science Foundation, 1981).

Index

About the Contributors

Nicholas A. Ashford received the Ph.D. in physical chemistry and the J.D. from the University of Chicago and is the assistant director of the Center for Policy Alternatives at the Massachusetts Institute of Technology. His specialty is the interface between technology and law, on which he focuses his extensive publications and his work as associate professor of technology and policy in the MIT School of Engineering. He also serves on the EPA Science Advisory Board and the National Advisory Committee on Occupational Safety and Health.

Vincent Brannigan, a specialist in administrative law, is an assistant professor in the Department of Textiles and Consumer Economics, University of Maryland. His research, publications, and practice as an attorney center on federal and state consumer-product-safety regulation and municipal and state building and fire codes.

Stephen G. Breyer is a judge on the bench of the U.S. Court of Appeals for the First Circuit. He was professor of law at Harvard University, specializing in antitrust and administrative law and economic regulation. His publications cover a wide range of substantive areas of government regulation. His most recent work focuses on the reform of regulation.

Nancy L. Buc is a partner with the Washington, D.C., law firm of Weil, Gotshal and Manges. Ms. Buc has served as chief counsel to the Food and Drug Administration, as assistant director of the Bureau of Consumer Protection, and as an attorney with the Federal Trade Commission, including a period as attorney-adviser to the chairman.

Harold P. Green is a partner in the law firm of Fried, Frank, Harris, Shriver and Kampelman and professor emeritus of law at the George Washington University National Law Center. His extensive list of publications centers on issues in public policy for science and technology, particularly risk-benefit assessment, with emphasis on the legal and regulatory issues in nuclear energy and biotechnology.

Clifford Grobstein is a professor of biological science and public policy at the University of California at San Diego. His work has centered on growth and development, the effects of the expansion of biomedical technology on the human environment, and other topics simultaneously affecting biology, medicine, and social policy. He has served on many advisory committees, including the National Institutes of Health, the National Science Foundation, and the President's Science Advisory Council.

Anna J. Harrison is currently professor emeritus of chemistry at Mount Holyoke College. She is an internationally known chemist and a prominent leader among those concerned with the growth and development of the science. Ms. Harrison has published widely in scientific journals and received many research and academic appointments. She is past president of the American Chemical Society, has previously served on the National Science Board, and is president-elect of the American Association for the Advancement of Science.

J. William Haun is the vice-president of engineering policy at General Mills, Inc. He has served as an instructor of chemical engineering at the University of Texas and as a research group leader at Monsanto Company and was formerly chairman of the Environmental Quality Committee at the National Association of Manufacturers. Mr. Haun is a member of the U.S. Chamber of Commerce Committee on Environment, the National Task Force on Technology and Society, the board of directors of the World Environment Center, and of the U.S.A./Business and Industry Advisory Committee to the Organization for Economic Cooperation and Development.

Peter G.W. Keen is chairman of the board of Micro Mainframe, Inc. Dr. Keen's research and consulting focus on decision support systems, implementation, and strategic planning for information and telecommunications systems in multinational organizations. Most recently an associate professor of management science at the Sloan School of Management, Massachusetts Institute of Technology, he has also held faculty positions at Harvard University, Stanford University and the Wharton School of Finance and Commerce.

Charles Upton Lowe is the acting associate director for medical applications of research of the National Institutes of Health. He has a long and distinguished career involving intensive research, publication, and teaching on different aspects of pediatrics, human development, and nutrition. Dr. Lowe has served on a variety of private and government advisory and research groups that focus on human development and health.

Thomas O. McGarity is professor of law at the University of Texas School of Law. Earlier he served for three years with the Environmental Protection Agency. His publications focus on environmental law and other legal issues surrounding federal efforts to regulate health and safety in various administrative agencies.

Jerry L. Mashaw is a professor of law at Yale Law School and specializes in administrative and regulatory law. He is president of the Administrative

Law Section of the American Association of Law Schools. His recent publications center upon the improvement of various administrative and regulatory processes, including those that affect social-security hearings, auto-safety regulation, disability claims, and policy-oriented empirical research.

Richard A. Merrill is dean and professor of law at the University of Virginia. From 1975 through 1977, he served as general counsel of the U.S. Food and Drug Administration. His numerous publications concerning regulatory law focus principally on the regulation of foods, drugs, and environmental health hazards. Mr. Merrill is an elected member of the Institute of Medicine of the National Academy of Sciences and of the NAS Board on Toxicology, and he is also a consultant to the Administrative Conference of the United States.

Harold M. Peck is a toxicologist who recently retired from the Merck Sharp and Dohme Research Laboratories where he was vice-president for safety assessment. His publications concern toxicologic methodology and the evaluation of the results of such studies. Dr. Peck has served on toxicology committees for the World Health Organization, National Research Council, Environmental Protection Agency, Food and Drug Administration, National Institutes of Health, and U.S. Department of Transportation, and is continuing some of these activities. He is a past president of the Society of Toxicology.

William Warfield Ross is a senior partner in the Washington, D.C., law firm of Wald, Harkrader and Ross, specializing in antitrust and regulated-industry matters. He previously served in the Executive Office of the President, the Department of Justice, and as an assistant solicitor for the Federal Power Commission. He has been active in administrative law reform and was chairman of the American Bar Association Administrative Law Section (1978-1979).

Kenneth M. Thompson received the Ph.D. in political science from the University of Wisconsin and a law degree from Antioch University School of Law. Formerly an associate professor of political science at the University of Southern California, he is currently a senior public-policy analyst at the Joint Center for Political Studies in Washington, D.C., where he concentrates his research in the field of public participation and policy formation. His publications appear in legal, political-science, and policy-study periodicals.

Milton R. Wessel is counsel to the New York and Washington, D.C., law firm of Parker Chapin Flattau and Kimpl, and general counsel to the Association of Data Processing Service Organizations, the Chemical Industry Institute of Toxicology, and the Council for Chemical Research. He has published widely on computers and the law, socioscientific dispute resolution, and the ethical issues confronting attorneys when dealing with public safety and health litigation.

About the Editors

J.D. Nyhart is professor of management at the Sloan School of Management and the Department of Ocean Engineering at the Massachusetts Institute of Technology. His current research and writing focus on the use of scientific and technical material in formal judicial and administrative proceedings, as well as the development of economic and regulatory models appropriate for deep ocean mining and oil-spill control.

Milton M. Carrow is the president of the National Center for Administrative Justice. He has been in private practice in New York City and has had appointments to the law schools of Georgetown University, George Washington University, and New York University. He has been active in the reform of administrative procedures and has been chairman of the American Bar Association Section of Administrative Law. His scholarly publications center on studies of various regulatory and administrative processes.